The Literature of Cinema

THE LITERATURE OF CINEMA presents
a comprehensive selection from the multitude
of writings about cinema, rediscovering materials on its origins, history, theoretical principles and techniques, aesthetics, economics,
and effects on societies and individuals. Included are works of inherent, lasting merit
and others of primarily historical significance.
These provide essential resources for serious
study and critical enjoyment of the "magic
shadows" that became one of the decisive cultural forces of modern times.

Our Movie Made Children

Henry James Forman

ARNO PRESS & THE NEW YORK TIMES

New York • 1970

Reprint Edition 1970 by Arno Press Inc.
Library of Congress Catalog Card Number: 74-124028
ISBN 0-405-01646-8
ISBN for complete set: 0-405-01600-X
Manufactured in the United States of America

OUR MOVIE MADE CHILDREN

THE MACMILLAN COMPANY
NEW YORK · BOSTON · CHICAGO · DALLAS
ATLANTA · SAN FRANCISCO

MACMILLAN & CO., LIMITED
LONDON · BOMBAY · CALCUTTA
MELBOURNE

THE MACMILLAN COMPANY
OF CANADA, LIMITED
TORONTO

OUR MOVIE MADE CHILDREN

By

HENRY JAMES FORMAN

With an Introduction by

Dr. W. W. CHARTERS

Professor of Education and Director of Educational
Research in Ohio State University, Chairman
of the Committee on Educational Research
of the Payne Fund

New York

THE MACMILLAN COMPANY

1935

Set up and printed.

Published May, 1933

Reprinted July, 1933

Reprinted October, 1933

Reprinted November, 1933

Reprinted March, 1934

Reprinted May, 1934

Reprinted November, 1934

Reprinted August, 1935

PRINTED IN THE UNITED STATES OF AMERICA
BY THE POLYGRAPHIC COMPANY OF AMERICA, N.Y.

CONTENTS

INTRODUCTION | PAGE vii

CHAPTER

I THE SCOPE OF MOTION PICTURES 1

II WHO GOES TO THE MOVIES? 12

III WHAT DO THEY SEE? 28

IV HOW MUCH DO THEY REMEMBER? 54

V MOVIES AND SLEEP 69

VI OTHER PHYSICAL EFFECTS 90

VII HORROR AND FRIGHT PICTURES 105

VIII "UNMARKED SLATES" 121

IX MOVIES AND CONDUCT 141

X MOLDED BY THE MOVIES 158

XI THE PATH TO DELINQUENCY 179

XII MOVIE-MADE CRIMINALS 196

XIII SEX-DELINQUENCY AND CRIME 214

XIV DETERRENT AND CORRECTIONAL 233

XV MOVIES IN A CROWDED SECTION 251

XVI SUMMARY AND CONCLUSION 273

INDEX 285

MOTION PICTURES AND YOUTH: An Introduction, by W. W. Charters, combined with GETTING IDEAS FROM THE MOVIES, by P. W. Holaday and George D. Stoddard

THE CONTENT OF MOTION PICTURES and CHILDREN'S ATTENDANCE AT MOTION PICTURES, by Edgar Dale

THE EMOTIONAL RESPONSES OF CHILDREN TO THE MOTION PICTURE SITUATION, by W. S. Dysinger and Christian A. Ruckmick, còmbined with MOTION PICTURES AND STANDARDS OF MORALITY, by Charles C. Peters

MOTION PICTURES AND THE SOCIAL ATTITUDES OF CHILDREN, by Ruth C. Peterson and L. L. Thurstone, combined with RELATIONSHIP OF MOTION PICTURES TO THE CHARACTER AND ATTITUDES OF CHILDREN, by Mark A. May and Frank Shuttleworth

CHILDREN'S SLEEP, by Samuel Renshaw, Vernon A. Miller, and Dorothy Marquis

MOVIES AND CONDUCT, by Herbert Blumer

MOVIES, DELINQUENCY, AND CRIME, by Herbert Blumer and Philip M. Hauser

BOYS, MOVIES, AND CITY STREETS, by Paul G Cressey and Frederick M. Thrasher

HOW TO APPRECIATE MOTION PICTURES, by Edgar Dale

INTRODUCTION

THE basic material which Mr. Forman has used in preparing this volume is found in the studies which are listed by title on the opposite page.

These investigations, made during 1929 to 1933 at the request of the Motion Picture Research Council, were supported by the Payne Fund, an organization interested in the radio, motion pictures and reading in relation to children and youth.

The investigators, whose names appear as authors of the studies, organized a program of research and delegated to members of the group the responsibility for studying one or more problems in the field in which they were competent. These studies were carried on independently. The investigators were not expected to pool their findings as a group and make a pronouncement about the movies. They rather conducted twelve independent investigations to furnish data for those who wished to use them. As chairman of the group I was requested to write a summary of the studies in a monograph of the series.

To Mr. Forman was entrusted the task of preparing a popular summary, and I was charged with the responsibility of attesting the accuracy of the scientific findings as set forth in his book. I have examined Mr. Forman's manuscript. He shows a thorough grasp of the facts in

vii

the complicated materials presented in the nearly three
thousand pages which constitute the report of the twelve
studies. His interpretation of the studies, however, his
selection of illustrative material, his literary style, his
dramatic and emphatic presentation are of necessity entirely his own.

Disregarding those differences in details of interpretation and individuality of style which are inevitable, I
agree with the author in the fundamental position that
the motion picture is powerful to an unexpected degree
in affecting the information, attitudes, emotional experiences and conduct patterns of children; that the
content of current commercial motion pictures constitutes a valid basis for apprehension about their influence upon children; and that the commercial movies
present a critical and complicated situation in which the
whole-hearted and sincere coöperation of the producers
with parents and public is essential to discover how to
use motion pictures to the best advantage of children.

W. W. CHARTERS,

Chairman of the Committee
on Educational Research of
The Payne Fund

May 6, 1933

OUR MOVIE MADE CHILDREN

CHAPTER I

THE SCOPE OF MOTION PICTURES

WHO, in these searching times, would not desire to have an answer to the question, Are the movies good or bad for my child? harmful or helpful?

In a general way most of us are aware that the motion picture is a boon to mankind, second in importance—if second it is—only to the art of printing. So vast and far-reaching are its possibilities for the instruction and entertainment of humanity that did it not already exist we should, if we possessed enough imagination, pray for its invention. The all-pervasive and permeating quality it has demonstrated in the space of a single generation is surely in itself a proof of the pressing human need it represents. The attainment of many of the larger possibilities of mankind must inevitably be helped by its agency, and though we are, in moods of depression, all too prone to see no farther than a pauper's grave with limitless wealth lying all about us, many people already perceive the great possibilities for good' in the motion picture and are not a little concerned lest it should be exploited in a contrary direction.

"For the purpose of making and influencing public opinion and thought," declares Dr. John J. Tigert, former United States Commissioner of Education, now president of the University of Florida, "the motion picture in its present stage is the most powerful influence now known, and as its use increases and its field of operation develops, its power to influence the public will increase."

A good motion picture, briefly, with its peculiar and inherent capacity to circulate throughout the globe, to penetrate into the smallest town and even into rural areas, represents a social force which may be described as nothing short of a godsend.

In "A Generation of Motion Pictures" the Motion Picture Research Council lists, as representative of hundreds, possibly thousands, of commendable motion pictures that have been made, a few sample specimens as satisfying even exacting social standards: Ben Hur, The Big Parade, The Covered Wagon, The Vanishing American, The Pony Express, Abraham Lincoln, The Ten Commandments, The Hunchback of Notre Dame, Chang, The King of Kings. More recently we have had such examples as Sorrell and Son, Arrowsmith, Cavalcade, and doubtless many others. Impossible to quarrel with productions of this character. Pictures of that order, be they American or foreign—and they are mostly American—should be a source of pride to the industry as they are a boon to audiences.

Insofar as concerns the movie in education, its history has scarcely begun. Though educational films have been made and are being made, the domain of the textbook is still largely unimpaired, but its monopoly is disputed. As this is being written, Dean Holmes, of the Harvard School of Education, announces the discovery that where talking motion pictures supplement the textbook in class, knowledge of students increases from 20 to 40 per cent. For the visual aid, the semblance of living actuality presented on the screen, is almost incalculably powerful. Children, as will appear in this volume, have been found to retain an average of seventy per cent of what an intelligent adult would carry away from a dramatic film. This visually attained knowledge carries with it a curious expansive quality, so that in many cases, after a lapse of months, the children actually remember more than they remembered directly after seeing the picture. Obviously, in these conditions, the film must emerge as one of the most potent of all educational instruments.

With facts and implications like these it can surprise no one that the wealth of motion pictures poured out annually from the studios, shown to an audience conservatively estimated in 1930 at 77,000,000 weekly in the United States alone, should produce effects upon the conduct, behavior patterns, morals and even upon the health notably of the younger spectators, that is, those still in their formative years. As Messrs. Malcolm M. Willey and Stuart A. Rice put it in "Recent Social Trends," the last great survey issued by a Hoover Commission, in 1933:

"Although the motion picture is primarily an agency for amusement, it is no less important as an influence in shaping attitudes and social values. The fact that it is enjoyed as entertainment may even enhance its importance in this respect. Any discussion of this topic must start with a realization that for the vast audience the pictures and 'filmland' have tremendous vitality. Pictures and actors are regarded with a seriousness that is likely to escape the casual observer who employs formal criteria and judgment. Editors of popular motion picture maga-

zines are deluged with letters from motion picture patrons, unburdening themselves of an infinite variety of
feelings and attitudes, deeply personal, which focus
around the lives and activities of those inhabiting the
screen world. One editor receives over 80,000 such letters
a year. These are filled with self-revelations which indicate, sometimes deliberately, more often unconsciously,
the influence of the screen upon manners, dress, codes
and matters of romance. They disclose the degree to
which ego stereotypes may be moulded by the stars of
the screen." In other words, here is evidence of the influence of motion pictures and their impersonations upon
the character, conduct and behaviour of vast numbers of
our nation and especially upon the more malleable and
younger people.

2

This discovery of Messrs. Willey and Rice, new as it
appears, is no news to the Motion Picture Research
Council. Some years ago this body, of which the director
is Mr. W. H. Short and the present head Dr. A. Lawrence Lowell, former President of Harvard University,
realized the vast influence of the motion picture "in
shaping attitudes and social values," and succeeded in interesting the Payne Fund, a foundation devoted to the
welfare of youth, in financing a nation-wide research into
the degrees of influence and effect of films upon children
and youth. A group of social scientists—psychologists,
sociologists, and educators, representative of their fields
in various universities of the country—under the general
direction of Dr. W. W. Charters, dividing the immense
amount of labor inherent in so large an enterprise, be-

gan that body of research—stretching over a four-year period from 1929 to 1933—which yielded an accumulation of findings that with their graphs, tables and techniques will fill several volumes. As those monographs when published will demonstrate, this is the most complete research upon the influence and effects of the motion picture thus far attempted. Though laying no claim to being exhaustive, the research nevertheless represents the fullest fund of scientific knowledge relating to the movies thus far assembled in a single framework.

So much of the general notion concerning the movies consisted in surmise or guess work that the need for carefully collected data, scientifically collated, unbiased and free from prejudice, became virtually imperative. Who, for instance, has not heard the assumption that movies stimulate to crime, to sexual misconduct, to imitation of crime technique, of patterns of loose living, of reprehensible or vulgar conduct, and so on? Upon the one hand we know that some excellent pictures have been and are still being made, and that pictures in general supply entertainment and knowledge to audiences not hitherto reached by dramatic presentation. Yet, upon the other, we have men of the standing of Dr. Nicholas Murray Butler asserting that "daily broadcasting of the passions and caprices and adventures of men and women in plays and on the screen, interpreted by ill-equipped authors and directors, cannot but be destructive of ideals that have proved to be wholesome and worthy of preservation." Or, as a man of the grasp of Professor Ernest W. Burgess of the University of Chicago concludes categorically: "It is quite evident that the boy comes into contact with influences in the motion pictures . . . that are in conflict with the standard of the home, the school and the church."

If those men are right then clearly their statements should be susceptible of substantiation. If, however, they are wrong, then that too ought to be provable. A number of the social scientists concerned with the Payne Fund survey and notably Professor Blumer of the University of Chicago and Professor Thrasher of New York University expended considerable time and effort in careful research along these lines and most of their material and findings forms a basis for the treatment of the subject in the pages of the present volume.

Crime and conduct, however, though of tremendous importance are not the only domains indisputably subject to movie influence. Many educators and laymen alike, without the support of comprehensive data, have had a conviction that the motion picture with its immense range and vast reach falls little short of being a supplementary educational system of our nation. Indeed, some laymen have gone so far as to believe that the motion picture vies in importance with the national school system. And when we recall, as has been pointed out, that children carry away and retain on the average 70 per cent as much as adults and sometimes fully as much as adults, from any given motion picture there is assuredly some ground for such assumptions. That very fact, however, the immense retention of motion picture knowledge, is in itself a part of the many illuminating data discovered by the Payne Fund research. Dr. George D. Stoddard, head of the Iowa State Child Welfare Research Station, and Dr. P. W. Holaday of the University of Iowa, were the first to establish definitely the figures of memory and retention of motion picture content on the part of the young, thus giving a large body of facts to visual education advocates, as well as satisfying the general reader's demand for knowledge upon this point.

Do pictures have a propaganda value? We know that they have been used as propaganda, but the question is, can they change the mental attitudes of children and young people? If they can do that they are the powerful educational influence many of us have believed them to be. And if influence they are, then quite naturally they must work for good as well as for evil, depending upon their contents and use. Drs. Mark A. May and Frank K. Shuttleworth, of Yale, have worked along this line of inquiry and Dr. L. L. Thurstone and Miss Ruth Peterson, of the University of Chicago, in signally successful experiments, have secured some very definite and clear-cut results upon this point.

But what of physical influences—of emotional disturbance and effects? Dramatic pictures are powerful emotional factors to any of us, even to mature adults. That is one reason why many of us go to see them. Is there any way of measuring such emotional effects? Do they have specific influences upon the health and nervous systems of children? If so, what are those influences? Drs. Christian A. Ruckmick and Wendell Dysinger, psychologists of the University of Iowa, were charged with the task of obtaining measurements of emotional index or effect, with results of which the reader in the pages that follow, will have opportunity of judging for himself.

Similarly with sleep. Many scientists have studied the subject of sleep, but no one had actually investigated the effect of movie attendance upon the sleep of children. Does movie-going affect the sleep of children, or does it not? If the sleep of children is unaffected, neither enhanced nor impaired, by movie attendance, that is something we should like to know. *If*, however, their sleep is sufficiently affected by movie-going to influence not alone their school work and tempers, but their health, and even their growth, then the knowledge of that fact is even more necessary to parents and indeed to all of us. Dr. Samuel Renshaw, a psychologist of Ohio State University and his aides, in a comprehensive study, have brought forth some highly interesting and definite knowledge in this direction. They discovered that not only does movie-going affect the sleep of the majority of children, but they also sought to measure these effects and to describe some of the circumstances which modify them, one way or another.

Much of popular opinion that was based on surmise or untrained observation, in short, has been brought by a diversity of laboratory techniques into the domain of approximately accurate knowledge.

Do the films as a whole fall below or rise above the *mores* of the land? If they are as powerful in the impress they leave upon the minds of the spectator, and in especial the young spectator, as various investigators have shown, then this question of mores, or moral standards (a very imperfect definition of mores) must be patiently and searchingly examined. At least one of the Payne Fund studies, that of Dr. Charles C. Peters of Pennsylvania State College, has made a very important beginning in this field and some of his results indicate the reactions of widely varied groups of Americans to different aspects of the conventional standards of conduct and morals as presented in our motion pictures.

A recent report of a British Commission on "The Film in National Life" goes so far as to declare that "the constructive use of the cinema is a form of national planning" and adds: "For the prestige of a nation is already affected by the films which it exports, and will increasingly be judged thereby." The same report, frankly recognizing that the work of the Commission was done in ignorance of facts they would like to have known, admits that "a generation of film going children is learning to pick up points and impressions on the screen very quickly—how quickly and how permanently we do not know."

An effort, however, to gain as nearly as possible reliable knowledge upon facts as capital in importance as how much and how permanently children carry away "points" and knowledge of what they see on the screen, played an important part in the research undertaken by the Payne Fund group of investigators. The British Commission as well as our own nation must learn with keen interest from the study completed by Drs. Stoddard and Holaday, that not only do children retain on the average seventy per cent of what adults retain after seeing films but that no single category of scenes into which the contents of the film were subdivided by the investigators completely passes over the children's heads. The children, that is, they discovered, retain much more from a film than, prior to these experiments, any of us would have given them credit for.

The movies, in short, under whatever aspects studied, form an important, even a powerful factor in the lives of their audiences, notably in the lives of the younger members of the audiences. While perhaps not the sole factor, since life is highly complex, they figure with sufficient prominence to justify the comprehensive studies undertaken by the investigators and the numerous documents they produced.

The very content of the movies was elaborately studied, and by a painstaking analysis of 1500 feature pictures distributed over a considerable period of time, Dr. Edgar Dale arrived at some searching conclusions as to the fare, both good and bad, offered to the public by the tremendous output of the film studios. The categories and kinds of characters were examined, their goals and aims in life, the kinds of life they represent, their numbers and distribution, their acts and the consequences of those acts. The reader, in face of this material, can hardly fail to come to some conclusions, new or reenforced, as the case may be, touching both the merits and the limitations of our present-day screen.

And that those conclusions cannot but be of value appears in itself conclusive when we discover from Dr. Dale's carefully collected data that the vast movie audience consists of 77,000,000 people weekly in the United States alone, more than one-third of that number being children and adolescents and about 11,000,000 under fourteen years of age—in constant contact with the screen. Viewed in that light our already national interest in the screen must become even more acute than it now is, more alive, more searchingly particular. For no one factor of this magnitude in the nation's life can we afford to overlook and neglect, or to survey with indifference.

If, as the British Commission believes, "only the Bible and the Koran have an indisputably larger circulation than that of the latest film from Los Angeles," then all the more it behooves us to extend our knowledge relating to the contents and effects of motion pictures, so that they may tend to become positively and increasingly a beneficent influence in the lives of our children rather than the reverse.

A European proverb has it that from the same timber may be hewn either a cross or a shovel. It is the use we make of a great invention that determines its service to us. The motion pictures, though at times misused, have also at times shown by certain specimens and examples how immense can be their service for wholesome pleasure, entertainment, and even enlightenment, to their vast audiences. And since the motion picture has assuredly come to stay, the points upon which every one of us, whether as parent or as citizen, urgently desires information, are, What are the movies likely to do to my child? How are they likely to affect, if at all, the children and young people of our country, the parents and citizens of the future? What influences will they import into our homes, into the great majority of homes in our nation? Are they, in their present forms, an asset or a liability to the progress of our national development and consciousness?—some of these questions, it is hoped, will find answers in the chapters that follow.

CHAPTER II

WHO GOES TO THE MOVIES?

It had been popularly estimated that 115 million people in the United States attended the movies every week. Considering that a certain proportion of the Nation is physically or otherwise incapacitated from movie going, it means that virtually every mother's son and daughter in America, free to go, is a member of our vast unprecedented movie audience.

When has the globe ever known the like?

The millennial dreams of all the saints and sages could scarcely have aspired so high. Here is an instrument fashioned at last in universal terms. Send forth a great message, broadcast a vision of truth and beauty, if only you broadcast it by means of the so-called silver screen, literally all America will be your audience. Who could have imagined a population more nearly, more inclusively unified by a single agency?

The investigators in their efforts to gain as nearly as possible accurate knowledge and correct figures find the actual American movie audience to be some millions smaller than the rotund numbers of the popular estimate.

They approached their problem in this manner: The 1930 census shows the population of the United States to consist of 122,775,046 persons. Of that grand total, so considerable a number as nearly eleven and a half millions are under five years of age. Now, though some of these infants are doubtless being broken in to the movies by enthusiastic parents, their number is probably not large. The blind, the halt and the maimed, moreover, those imprisoned by infirmity, or actually held in our jails and penitentiaries, must number about five million, which is not an excessive estimate, especially since, as will appear, movies are shown in many prisons, and even in some hospitals. That leaves us about 106,000,000 able to attend the movies. The popular estimate tops this figure by about nine million, which would yield an average of over one attendance weekly for every hale and competent human being in the United States.

To the investigators this figure appeared far too high. Taking a county in Ohio with a population of over 360,000, they arrived, after careful survey, at the figure of three-quarters of an attendance each week per person. But even this they believe to be a top figure since that particular county contains the capital and the university city of Columbus. A student population, I believe, goes twice as often as non-student. With this .75 as an index, however, and always remembering the total of possible movie goers as 106,000,000, we arrive at an attendance of 79,500,000 persons a week. But even this must be high, since the producers have estimated that there are but eleven million seats in our motion picture theatres. The researchers, therefore, estimate, somewhat more conservatively, a weekly attendance of 77,000,000 persons— surely an impressive figure enough, which neither the legitimate drama nor any other form of entertainment or instruction ever dreamed of capturing.

This brief outline of their process is given mainly to show the care and the conservative judgments with which the investigators and their assistants in this imposing research approached their task. What they desired was to gauge as accurately as possible the number of children and adolescents in America exposed to motion picture influence. Not only that, but they were curious to discover how often the young people frequent the movies; whether boys or girls numerically predominate; who were their companions; their favorite days for attending, and even the hours spent in the movie palaces. All these facts, as the reader will quickly grasp, become of capital importance to every individual one of us no less than to the nation as a whole.

To describe the technique of the investigators in arriving at their results of motion picture attendance would take far too much space, and part of the reason for the existence of this book is the elimination of the technical. The reader, however, may safely accept the assurance that the methods used were the most thoroughgoing and complete as yet attempted in this field, as consultation of the original monographs will attest. Some of the devices employed to obtain facts were the stationing of trained observers at the doors of theatres with the ticket takers; the answering of simple questionnaires by children old enough to deal with them; weekly reports by the children, and reports by the parents and teachers based upon interviews with them.

Of so universal and far-reaching an interest did the

findings prove, one regrets that no more than the high spots can be shown here. For instance, in a sample community, which means your community and mine, any average community in America, even young children from *five to eight* years of age were found to attend the movies on an average twenty-two times a year. And since something over one-fifth of them declare that they do not go to the movies at all, the attendance of the remaining four-fifths of these very young children was considerably larger than twenty-two times a year.

Leave these five- to eight-year olds, however, and the figures jump rapidly. In a sampling of 35,491 boys and girls taken virtually at random between the ages of eight and nineteen, the number of movie patrons during a single week was found to be 35,155. A somewhat more detailed analysis showed that the average attendance for each girl in that large group was forty-six and for each boy fifty-seven times a year. In other words, we are probably the only population on earth whose children attend a movie a week—fifty-two movies a year!

Remember that these are averages. When we recall that there must of necessity be some children who do not attend at all, it follows that significant numbers must go to the movies more than once a week. Among the many thousands of children studied, Dr. Dale had occasion to glance at numerous aspects of the problem. In summarizing the data from 12,071 boys and 11,931 girls he found that by asking certain samples a direct question he secured these results:

"How many times did you go to the movies last week?" Of the boys twenty-nine per cent declared they had not been at all; forty-four per cent, once; eighteen per cent, twice; six per cent, three times, and three per cent, four or more times. Of the girls thirty-six per cent had abstained from going; forty-three per cent had been once that week; sixteen per cent, twice; four per cent, three times, and one per cent, four or more times. Briefly, regardless of the abstainers, one hundred "typical" boys had gone to the movies one hundred and ten times a week and one hundred "typical" girls ninety-one times, maintaining our national average of a movie a week for each child. "A movie a week" is with us a national slogan, almost a physical trait absorbed by the children with their mother's milk. Can we doubt that the influence of the motion pictures must of necessity bulk large in our national life, in the lives of our children, when it is practically universal?

The chief aim of this particular survey, however, was not so much the study of the complete motion picture audience, as the discovery of the percentage of children and adolescents in it. It happens that Columbus, Ohio, is not one of the richest cities in children under fifteen. While but a single city, yet among twenty-one cities in the state with a population of over 25,000, Columbus, with its figure of twenty-three and a fraction per cent in point of children under fifteen ranks only nineteenth. Many cities in the United States exceed Columbus in their under-fifteen population. Detroit, for instance, Pittsburgh, Cleveland, Baltimore, Philadelphia, Boston, New York, Chicago, all have greater percentages of this age group than Columbus. Out of eleven cities, only St. Louis with its figure of twenty-three per cent and Los Angeles with twenty-one per cent stand lower than Columbus in this particular age-group. In the entire country this age group, of children under fifteen, forms a little more than twenty-nine per cent. So that Columbus with its six per cent under the national average was certain to give conservative results. For this reason, among others, Columbus was chosen, and fifteen theatres including the most expensive, the medium-priced and the cheapest, were selected for a careful survey of the motion picture patrons that composed the audience.

From accurate figures of these fifteen houses, the total weekly attendance for the entire city could be estimated, and it was found to be 239,727. The minors in this audience, numbering 88,077; formed nearly thirty-seven per cent of the total audience. These figures, compared and checked by means of other data, gave the investigator the acceptable figure of thirty-seven per cent as the juvenile part of the American movie audience. And since, according to the last census, thirty-one and a half per cent of our American population is between the ages of five and twenty, with the group aged four and under contributing, we surmise, but a negligible number of of movie goers, we see that thirty-one and a half per cent of our country's population, the children and adolescents, constitute thirty-seven per cent of the total motion picture audience of the United States. Clearly they pull their weight in the boat, those youngsters.

To say that they contribute 5.2 per cent, as the house organ of the Motion Picture Producers and Distributors of America declares, or 8 per cent as Mr. Hays once stated, appears quite inadequate. Dr. Dale made his estimate very carefully and is firm in his position. Thirty-seven per cent is more than one-third of the audience and it means that virtually our total minor population is subject to movie influence.

And if such a term as "minor population" seems vague, it may be of interest to see of what actual age-groups this thirty-seven per cent of the American movie audience is made up. The figures show that in the area studied those under seven form but 2.8 per cent of the total. Children aged seven to thirteen form 11.8 per cent, or nearly twelve per cent of the audience. The next age-group from fourteen to twenty numbers 22.1 per cent.

Putting it in figures, it means that out of the total thirty-seven per cent, or 28,259,000 minors weekly attending our movies, 11,242,000 or nearly one-sixth of the entire movie audience are under the age of fourteen. And we must remember, always, that these are averages. Professor Thrasher, for example, in his survey of a congested area in New York City found, by clocking the audience as it entered the doors of theatres in the neighborhood, that fifty-three per cent of the entire attendance in that region was under twenty-one, and seventeen per cent under seven years of age!

2

Dr. Dale, however, explored a great deal more than mere frequency of attendance. He found answers to a variety of questions, all of which have a bearing upon the movie-going habits of our children, the children of the nation:

Is the attendance about the same on all nights and days, or, if not, which nights and days are loaded heaviest?

Do young children go as frequently to the movies in the evening as do older children?

Who accompanies these children on their pleasure jaunts to the movie theatres?

On what days do most parents accompany their children?

How long do the children stay in the picture theatres?

From a careful study of over 55,000 school children, ranging in age from kindergarten to the last year of high school in forty-four communities in Ohio came the answers, sufficiently representative to be reliable. He found that the most popular days for youthful movie-going are quite naturally Saturday, Sunday and Friday, in that order. The week-end, that is, carries the peak of juvenile attendance, comprising approximately three-fourths of all their movie-going. Only one-fourth of the visits are distributed over Wednesday, Monday and Tuesday, Thursday being the low-water mark of youthful interest in movies. Possibly this concentration of frequency in the three end days of the week may have some bearing on the plans of producers, should they ever desire to show special pictures for the young.

Then comes the question of hours. Do the young go to the movies chiefly in the evening or in the afternoon? Do any of them like to go in the morning? Even you and I, who keep scrupulous track of our children's habits, cannot always remember their ways and customs in these respects. So long as they are very young, they may still conform more or less to the rules we lay down for them. But once they have reached that transitional period called adolescence, our control of their wills either gradually or abruptly diminishes.

Possibly you would like your children to do their movie-going in the morning? Try and make them! Hardly any of them will go in the morning because it is simply not done. Only a little over two and a half per cent of all boys and girls were found to resort to morning attendance at the movies. By the time they are eight or nine years old they already indicate objection to that unfashionable hour. Bonds of custom!

Very well, you say. The morning, after all, is no time for anybody, child or grown-up, to spend within the walls of a theatre. The word matinée may have meant morning once upon a time, but for us today it means an afternoon performance. That is, anyway, the natural time for children's amusement hours.

Well, up to ten or eleven, a child may remain amenable to good sense and conform to your solicitude and your plan of hygiene. From the ages of ten and eleven on, however, begins the march toward later hours. The investigators have plotted a set of curves which appear almost startling in the way they commence at these ages to drop down abruptly, indicating less and less afternoon attendance, and to rise upward to more and more evening attendance. In the single year between thirteen and fourteen for boys the curve of afternoon attendance moves down six per cent, and for girls eight per cent.

By the time the girls are nineteen only fourteen per cent of them attend in the afternoon, and only eleven per cent of the boys. About eighty-eight per cent of those young people, in short, insist upon forming part of the evening audience.

The morning, with its negligible attendance, is what

the children themselves would call a "wash-out." The afternoon is somewhat better with an average attendance of about thirty per cent from the boys, about thirty-three per cent from the girls, and an average for both of about thirty-one and a half per cent. But the imperiously fashionable evening hours top the list with about sixty-six per cent, or two-thirds of all juvenile movie-going. That is, they go when everyone else goes and see the pictures everyone else sees.

That these seemingly unimportant facts have a far-reaching effect upon the sleep and health of the children will be brought out in a subsequent chapter. Meanwhile, it will be of interest to glance at some additional peculiarities of youthful movie-going.

The companionship they have at the theatre is an important factor. The effect of motion picture experience upon the child, Dr. Dale is convinced, depends at least in part upon the circumstances which surround the going. Upon that fact virtually all the investigators responsible for this research agree. Later, when we come to scan the effect upon children's nerves of scenes of anguish and terror as presented in ill-selected pictures, we shall see that the presence of the protective influence of parents seated beside the children may play an important rôle in mitigating some of the harm resulting.

Of late years even fairy tales dealing with theft and killing, anguish and horror, have been questioned by some educators as tending to implant disturbing images in the young consciousness. And fairy tales, we know, are a very mild form of entertainment, usually enjoyed within the familiar walls of the home, far from the vividness of the screen. In the case of fairy tales, however, a parent or some other adult is virtually always present to remind that "it is only a story."

Similarly, when a child attends the movies with a parent, or some other older relative, there is a chance of reducing harmful effects by explaining that "real life isn't like that," or that "this can only happen in the movies," and so on. In some states the statute books, doubtless envisaging such contingencies, positively prescribe adult accompaniment for children under certain ages. Later when we see to what manner of sequels attendance alone on the part of children in such theatres of the metropolitan congested area as are known as "dumps" may lead, cheap places where, as the Thrasher-Cressey survey at New York University found, the management has little control over the amatory as well as the rowdy instincts and conduct of the audience, it will become distressingly apparent why children should not enter such places at all. But even aside from that and granting that the "dump" is peculiar to congested areas, we shall realize more and more acutely that no child should go to a movie unaccompanied by an adult, unless the picture is carefully selected in advance.

We are, however, a busy people. For many necessities we simply cannot spare the time. The pressure upon the lives and time of parents is admittedly severe. Yet some day a wise man will write a book enumerating the many things we have no time for, and we shall be appalled to learn that the things we lack time for are the essence of life.

We discover, for instance, that when our boys are

eight years old about forty-four per cent of them are accompanied to the movies by both their parents, their fathers, or, more likely, indeed more than twice as often, by their mothers. By the time boys are fifteen, the percentage accompanied by parents is seven per cent! We have no time. With the girls the figures are slightly higher; the eight-year olds begin with a 56.83 per cent accompaniment of mothers; at nine the percentage drops to 40.75 per cent. At the eighteen-year age level, parental accompaniment has fallen to 8.66 per cent.

Who, then, are the children's companions in their motion picture experience?

Our boys, it would appear, at least a goodly proportion of them, like to go alone. Even at the age of nine nearly twenty per cent declare themselves as unaccompanied at the movies. By the time they are fifteen over twenty-eight per cent of these citizens of the world prefer the companionship of their adolescent dreams to any other when experiencing the thrills of the movies. And at eighteen, when the long, long thoughts of youth hold the theatre of their minds, nearly thirty-two per cent of them visit the temple of our modern muses alone. The average for all age-groups is well over twenty-five per cent—which appears to this writer both touching and significant. For those are the years when both good pictures and bad, undoubtedly make their most incisive impressions. One would very much desire to give them the best.

The girls, for their part, go alone more seldom. At the age of ten appears, oddly, their greatest show of independence with a ten per cent solitary attendance. The figure drops, from then on, with a slight bulge again, to nine per cent, at fourteen, until, at eighteen, only a little over two per cent attend alone!

How, then, are those companioned who are not alone? The findings in this respect are very revealing. At as early an age as thirteen upwards of seventy per cent of the girls go to the movies either with brothers and sisters, "someone else," or with their own friends; and more than sixty-two per cent of all boys are similarly companioned. By the time the girls are seventeen forty-seven per cent of them have for companions their "own friends." Their "own friends" may be either girls or boys. Whichever they are, they are clearly not grown members of the family. In short, whoever companions the young at the movies, obviously, it is not the adults, and our completely untrammeled dating time of boys and girls has the free play in the high-school years for which our country is noted.

How much time do the young people actually spend at the movies? The average performance, including feature picture, comedy and news reel, is about two hours. The research reveals, however, that about twenty-four per cent of the boys and twenty-one per cent of the girls stay to see either the main picture or the comedy twice. With both sexes the comedy emerges as slightly more popular than either the news-reel or feature picture. This means that an appreciable proportion of the children spend considerably more time in the theatre than the duration of a performance. Two hours at a time within the walls of the average movie theatre one would think to be sufficient. But not for them. As they grow older, however, they are less and less likely to stay for a second showing. By the time they are seventeen only a negligible percentage of them stay for more than the one showing. So that it is the younger children, more likely the unaccompanied, who are most apt to deprive themselves that much more of the outer air, within the none too salubrious atmosphere of the average theatre. It is Mary and Johnny, aged somewhere between seven and thirteen, but recently initiated into the independence and thrill of going alone to the movies, whom we may see electrified, excited, scarcely able to hold their seats. With large and eager eyes through the murk of the often stuffy theatre, watching the unfoldment on the screen of the ubiquitous themes —love, sex and crime.

3

If, then, movie attendance is a widespread activity of children and young people in all parts of the country, it is certain that it colors their behavior patterns. Not only that, but as we shall presently learn it affects in various degrees their sleep, their conduct, and, in a variety of ways, even their morals. A number of other investigators have uncovered a wealth of telling facts to leave no doubt as to the truth of this statement.

Dr. Dale, however, has concentrated his attention first of all upon the accumulation of as nearly as possible accurate figures of attendance. But being an educator of wide experience, he cannot refrain from making certain suggestions in the light of this startling discovery that, conservatively calculated, thirty-seven per cent of the American movie audience is composed of minors between five and twenty years of age. He wishes neither to advocate the destruction of the movies nor to counsel their being boycotted. In common with other thoughtful observers, he accepts the motion picture as an institution that has come to stay. But he does earnestly desire to safeguard American youth.

Many children, he concludes, are quite simply unable to interpret properly the events which they see on the screen. "Literally hundreds of times," he finds, "one notes there a portrayal of character and of conduct which gives totally erroneous notions of the situation or event as it actually occurs in real life. A mature adult who has a wide range of experience, can at once discount in some degree what he has seen on the screen." That the immature child or adolescent is just as certainly unable to discount what he sees is obviously and equally true. The child, with the apparent sanction of all adulthood about him, can only accept.

There are those, of course, who will immediately bring up the question of over-solicitude and excessive supervision of children, contrary to progressive methods of education and training. But the educator here concerned is convinced that it is not a desire for inculcating independence that has brought about the present grave situation. Rather is it thoughtlessness, based often upon the lack of adequate knowledge.

Parents, he believes, ought to familiarize themselves thoroughly with what is shown on the screen:

"They ought to formulate in their own minds the deficiencies of such pictures, and make every attempt to see that motion pictures which do not have such deficiencies are made available to all children. Next, they should see, in the degree that they cannot correct the situation, that antidotes be supplied the child, if they still find it desirable for him to attend, knowing the harmful effects that may accrue."

What some of the effects may be for both good and ill, forms a large part of the contents of the present volume. But first it will be of use to glance at the content of our motion picture output and to see what it offers to its weekly audience of 77,000,000, of whom over 28,000,000 are children and adolescents.

CHAPTER III

WHAT DO THEY SEE?

"Let's go to the movies."

"All right, let's. What shall we see?"

"I don't know, but there's a new show at the Palace and the poster is a honey."

Jack, schoolmate and friend of your daughter Joan, has come on pleasure bent. They are not exactly sure what they are going to see at the movies, because titles are so numerous as to be confusing. But Jack has seen what he calls a honey of a poster, which is almost certain to be a highly colored lithograph of a man embracing and kissing a girl. As to what the movie is about, neither of the children has any clear notion, but the chances are seventy-five in a hundred that it will deal with love, sex or crime.

Both Jack and Joan are lovely children, for are they not yours and your neighbors? You want them to enjoy themselves, and doubtless they will enjoy themselves, but there may be just a faint uneasiness in your mind. Those movies! You cannot help wondering whether they are wholly good or wholly profitable for the young people. Of course, you yourself go to the movies, but then you are a mature adult and understand that much of the stuff is just so much hokum. It is different with the children, so eager and so naïve, so inexperienced in life.

Many movies, we know, are based upon stage plays. It never occurs to us to let our children see every play presented, but somehow it seems different with the screen. These movies must fill their heads with all sorts of queer ideas.

Right. They do. And so that you and I, and all of us, may clarify our minds of precisely that vagueness as to what the run of movies contain and deal with, certain investigators went to considerable pains to analyze, classify and sort out the contents of the vast and ceaseless output of Hollywood. It was no easy job. Dr. Edgar Dale undertook this task of sorting out, classifying and analyzing some 1500 movies and their contents. Without going into the details of laboratory technique, it will suffice to say that he took 500 pictures, output of each of the years 1920, 1925, and 1930. This included all the feature pictures produced by the leading companies in those years and, as we can readily see, gave him large samples to work with. With the utmost care he first of all classified them under headings running something like this: crime, sex, love, mystery, war, history, children, travel and geography, animals, comedy and social problems. Considerable diversity in these headings, as we see. What he found was that out of 500 pictures in 1920, eighty-two per cent dealt with the three major themes of crime, sex and love; in 1925, seventy-nine per cent were preoccupied with these themes, and in 1930, seventy-two per cent. In that year, however, mystery and war pictures, which often included crime, or, at all events, violence, rose from small figures to nine per cent, which goes to swell the above totals. In other words, somewhere between seventy-five and eighty per cent of all pictures dealt with love, sex, crime or mystery films.

That, in any case, should clear our minds as to what Jack and Joan are likely to see at the pictures. The chances are three out of four that every time they go to the movies they will see some story unfolding a plot dealing with the three major preoccupations—love, sex or crime. This probably explains why foreigners viewing this particular mirror of American life, so frequently conclude that we must be a highly erotic and criminal nation.

Let us for one moment think what all this means in terms of children. Granting, as we have found, that a child attends at least one picture program a week, or fifty-two a year, it means that at least thirty-nine of the feature pictures he sees will have for their themes crime, sex and love—the inescapable themes. But what is their effect upon young boys and girls? Imagine a visitor from another planet arriving for a survey of our manner of life, and finding that this is what we allow them, apparently without any effective objection on our part, to feast their eyes and minds upon week in, week out, through the years. Could he conclude otherwise than that we have fallen into a way of exaggerating those themes out of all proportion?

The classification "love" includes romantic love stories. Many of these are beautiful; some of them, clearly, are not meant for children; others, however, are quite harmless, even charming. In 1920, Dr. Dale finds, about forty-five per cent of all pictures could be classified under love. By 1925 this class of pictures had fallen to thirty-three per cent; by 1930 it was only thirty per cent. Primarily this shift was made from what is called straight love pictures to comedies, crime and sex pictures. As to children's pictures, those, that is, especially designed for children or in which children are the central characters, there were only four in 1925, and only one out of 500 in 1930. If children go to the movies they must see the regular run-of the-mill output of love, sex and crime.

2

Now, before delving deeper into the analysis of content of motion pictures as a whole, that is the total average, it is only fair to recall that virtually every one of us has at one time or another enjoyed some motion pictures and that we have come home, after witnessing a remarkable movie, filled with the idea of its particular stirring qualities, its beauty and the importance of the entire art and craft of the pictures.

Certain films already mentioned in Chapter I, and others in the same category, doubtless still linger in our minds as unforgettable. The writer, for one, will probably never wholly lose the impression left upon him by such a picture as "The Covered Wagon." That portrayal of the American pioneer upon his westward march, at once veracious, tender and simple, endeared itself to even sophisticated audiences, not only in America, but throughout the world. Its very crudities were precious, for in fact the human race is not averse to crudities, if only they are not objectionable and are based on truth. Children and adults alike saw in "The Covered Wagon" a great and stirring motion picture and gave it an allegiance of attention and patronage probably hitherto unprecedented.

Virtually the same may be said of the film of "Ben Hur." That vast canvas depicting phases of life in Judea and the Roman Empire in the time of Jesus, filled in with a careful selection of detail that made the historical past of two thousand years ago as vivid as yesterday morning, engraved upon the minds of spectators another unforgettable series of events, rich and colorful and beautiful. What other form of art could bring to so many so thrilling and precious an experience in their lives? Those who have seen it still speak of it, and it is films of this calibre that have convinced most of us of the vast possibilities and scope inherent in the art of the motion picture. "The Ten Commandments," "The Hunchback of Notre Dame," "Chang," "Grass,"— even people who discerned imperfections in them here and there were generously eager to overlook them, to give the producers all credit for the painstaking care with which they had been made, realizing as they did, that these and similarly satisfactory films justified the existence of the art and rightly created for it, in an incredibly brief space of time, a world-wide audience.

Quite recently there have been produced such pictures as "Arrowsmith," "Cavalcade," "Maedchen in Uniform," examples of the film-art that satisfy both as to their artistic level and their breadth of view, the harmless, indeed uplifting quality of their content. And even certain pictures of less artistic merit, as attested by evidence of the investigators to be cited later, have at times the effect of stirring spectators, and especially young spectators, to compassion, to repentance, to resolutions to help others and to enter upon new forms of life.

The educational influence of motion pictures, a theme to be often touched upon in this book, derives some illustration from experiences of young people who saw "Ben Hur" and were moved to religious emotion; saw "Beau Geste" and vowed to preserve a warmer brotherly affection, or saw such simple themes as "The Old Nest" and "Over the Hill" and were moved to a greater tenderness toward their parents. As many as seventy per cent of a large sample of grade school children declared that pictures have at some time made them want to do "good things," and even delinquent girls testified that at times movies have made them "want to be real good."

Consider, also, a variety of pictures with which the theatre cannot compete at all—the various animal pictures, like "Bring 'em Back Alive." The educational value of such films is not only great, but by any other medium unapproachable. In the picture "Grass" showing an Asiatic nomadic tribe, trekking in search of pasture for its cattle Dr. Stefansson, the explorer, pointed out to the writer that the tribe never seems to rest but is always marching. That is doubtless true. But how otherwise than upon the screen could this phase of human life be portrayed in all its vividness?

Briefly, and this is not conveyed as a piece of news, some pictures are excellent—not only legitimate but highly desirable from even the strictest angles of social vision. They can be a beneficent as well as a pleasurable factor in life. Were that not the case, the present writer's faith in human nature is sufficiently firm to believe that the entire industry would have been either abolished or revolutionized some time ago. That it has not been so revolutionized, that it has been encouraged to grow to its present vast proportions, testifies both to the appreciation of the good in it upon the part of the public and to the need of it as a source of universal entertainment. Unfortunately, however, the total content of the movie leaves much to be desired. So influential is it on the whole, both in desirable and undesirable directions, that the survey was undertaken to present to the public without prejudice some needed facts and knowledge.

3

We shall therefore glance a little more closely at the content of the average motion picture. Bearing in mind that in, say, 1930 there were among 500 pictures 137 dealing with crime and, in addition, 43 dealing with mystery and war, we arrive at the conclusion that thirty-six per cent of all the pictures were loaded with scenes of either crime or violence. Now, let us face the problem squarely. Do we mean to imply that crime is never to figure on the screen at all? Dr. Dale quotes Mr. Will Hays, as saying:

"The proper treatment of crime as a social fact or as a dramatic motive is the inalienable right of a free press, of free speech and of an unshackled stage or screen."

With this opinion there is no quarrel whatever. The key to the situation, however, lies in his second word—"proper." That crime is a social fact in this country, and in virtually all countries, there is no doubt. That it is emphasized on the screen out of all proportion to its place in the national life is equally clear of doubt, indeed, glaringly obvious. Were crime to receive similar emphasis in the life of any one of us as individuals, we should properly expect to be either in jail or in an insane asylum. Dr. Dale puts it conservatively when he says that this preoccupation with crime "robs the screen of pictures of beauty, idealism and imaginative charm." A screen on which nearly 400 out of 500 pictures are occupied with love, sex and crime is barren of so much else that would serve as inspiration and enlightenment in life, that the very inquiry upon which this volume is based is a sign of the uneasiness felt by all of us. Practically it is a sign of the alarm we feel that our children should be exposed to a screen product of which between forty and fifty per cent is occupied with crime and sex.

No one can intelligently defend the complete exclusion of the fundamental and adequate treatment of crime from the screen. But to give crime and sex so large a representation in the motion picture is surely to threaten the morals and characters of our children and youth. Now, as has already been foreshadowed and as we shall presently see in greater detail, pictures leave some impress upon the mind of every individual. If we believe that good pictures have a beneficent effect, it is clearly useless to say that my child is proof against adverse influence, or that this crime picture will not count, or that that gangster picture or sex picture will make no impression upon any particular child or some especially favored boy or girl. In any such optimistic temporizing psychology is dead against us. As the late William James, in his book, *Psychology,* puts it:

"The drunken Rip Van Winkle, in Jefferson's play, excuses himself for every fresh dereliction by saying, 'I won't count this time!' Well! he may not count it, and a kind Heaven may not count it; but it is being counted none the less. Down among his nerve-cells and fibres the molecules are counting it, registering and storing it up to be used against him when the next temptation comes."

We certainly hope that the good influences count. Can anyone, then, conceivably imagine that the constant iteration of the crime theme in motion pictures, which during 1929 were attended weekly by 11,000,000 children of thirteen years of age or under, will in the slightest degree help the solution of the crime problem? Some producers, as we know, maintain that pictures of crime will lessen crime, and possibly for that reason produce so many pictures of crime. The film critic of *The Nation,* however, Alexander Bakshy, disagrees with them. Recently he wrote:

"Gangsters and racketeers play so prominent a part in the American life of today that it would be little short of a miracle if their exploits were ignored by the movies. Nor are they. In fact, the number of films dealing with the underworld and its criminal activities is altogether too great."

"Too great"—let us see. In 115 pictures taken at random from recent productions and analyzed by Dr. Dale, there are 59 in which murders and homicides are either attempted or committed. Seventy-one deaths by violence actually occur in fifty-four of the pictures. The hero, being a hero, is responsible for only twenty-one per cent of them; forty per cent fall to the villain's share, and the rest are variously distributed. The Bureau of Child Research of the University of Kansas not long ago presented a questionnaire to children between the ages of nine and thirteen, as to why, if for any reason, they dislike motion pictures. Following are brief summaries made by Dale of some of their answers, showing that even young children feel the excessive and inartistic overloading of pictures with crime:

Nine-year old boys: Killing—don't like to see people killed. Don't like to look at them.

Nine-year old girls: Danger and killing. Looks "offel." Not good for your mind. Scares me. I pity the people.

Ten-year old boys: Killing—makes you too excited. Makes me sad. Wild west not good.

Ten-year-old girls: Killing—hate to see people killed. Don't like it. Makes me feel it's true. Scary. Bloody ones make me sick. Show you how to kill. Sad.

Eleven-year-old boys: Killing makes you have bad habits. Don't like blood. Like to laugh.

Eleven-year-old girls: Shooting and killing bad. Makes me scared to go anywhere after night. Hard on the eyes and mind. Too tiresome. Too exciting. Hate to see people suffer. Not good for children.

Twelve-year-old boys: Killing reacts on the nervous system too much. Too sad.

Twelve-year-old girls: Shooting and killing makes me sick. It looks so awful to see people killed, and do not think it is right. Scares me. Not interested. Not good for children.

Thirteen-year-old boys: Too much killing—learn to do wrong things. Learn you to do stealing.

Killing and killing and more killing—that is the impression left upon these children. Their nerves ravaged and their nascent consciousness of the glorious new world into which they are being initiated marred and shocked by foolishly excessive violence. Of course, these are other people's children, but to other people our Jack and Joan are also other people's children. In his analysis of 115 pictures to determine the most frequent crime committed in them (he did not include bad art) Dr. Dale arrived at some fascinating figures. They are, as these Kansas children indicate, "bloody," "gory," "offel."

The heroes, those handsome and debonair heroes of the screen, are alone responsible for thirteen good sound murders; the villains and villainesses for thirty. Heroines who, according to the axioms of the trade, must not be robbed of sympathy, are still kept comparatively unstained, with only one murder to their credit in the lot. Altogether some fifty-four murders are committed, to say nothing of fifty-nine cases of mere assault and battery. Thirty-six hold-ups are portrayed and twenty-one kidnappings, numerous other crimes scattering. The score, on the whole, is remarkable; forty-three crimes are attempted, and 406 crimes are actually committed, a total of 449. All in 115 pictures! When we consider the universality of a picture, its permeation of the entire country, its penetration into the smallest towns and even hamlets, how otherwise can this scarlet procession of criminal acts or attempts be described than as a veritable school for crime—especially to certain types of boys and girls?

Immediately someone calls me to task in rebuttal. Is not the criminal portrayed as unattractive, and does he not therefore serve as a horrible example to the youth of the land? Frequently he is in effect so portrayed. But not always.

The hero of one picture (Jack Holt) is the leader of a band of outlaws who terrorize the whole region by their hold-ups and robberies. There is a price upon his head, but throughout the picture he is shown as a man of great physical courage, admired by his followers, fair and clever.

Another: The hero, (Lawrence Tibbett) leader of a robber band, is a handsome and colorful person. At the beginning of the picture he is seen as joyous, happy-go-lucky, disarmingly self-satisfied, and kind and thoughtful to his mother and younger sister. The death of his sister, however, arouses in him a flaming hatred of the aristocracy and a desire for vengeance. He possesses great physical courage, a beautiful singing voice, and his followers admire and respect him.

A third: The hero (Edmund Lowe) is a notorious gambler who is wanted by the police. He attempts a robbery on board the liner upon which he has taken passage. He is depicted as goodlooking, extremely well-dressed, pleasant, courteous, clever and courageous. His past is indicated as vivid and glamorous.

In some espionage stories on the screen, Victor Mc-Laglen, Gary Cooper and Marlene Dietrich are shown as gay, jaunty, adventure-loving and courageous.

From the memories of all of us this list could be continued indefinitely—a list of criminals so attractive that they tend to make crime alluring and criminality distinguished. The tendency to imitate conduct by attractive characters, Dr. Peters believes, is probably greater than if the characters were unattractive. In any case, regardless of what they may do, the conduct of attractive characters is certain to be imitated. That it is so imitated has been proven by investigators when they surveyed the effect of movies on conduct, delinquency and crime.

4

With the idea that screen criminals are alleged to present "horrible examples" to the young spectator, Dr. Dale asked this question of the movies: What are the consequences of the criminal's act to the criminal himself? A detailed analysis of forty pictures, in which no less than fifty-seven criminals committed sixty-two crimes, gave him the answer:

Three of the fifty-seven criminals were arrested and held; four were arrested but released; another four, after being arrested, escaped; seven were arrested and their punishment was implied. In one group of five, three were arrested, one gave himself up, another's arrest was allowed to be inferred and all were legally punished. Twenty-four criminals were punished by what may be described as extra-legal methods—by their own henchmen, other gangsters and in a variety of ways with which the law had nothing to do. In seventeen cases the punishment was primarily accidental, and fifteen criminals went wholly unpunished. Some of the unpunished crimes were, murder by the hero, as in "Rogue Song"; kidnapping by the hero, as in "Devil May Care"; kidnapping by the villain, as in "Sea Legs"; stealing by the hero, as in "Along Came Youth"; embezzlement by the hero, as the "Six-cylinder Love"; embezzlement by the heroine, as in "Miracle Woman", and house-breaking by the hero in the same picture.

The immediate answer is that the movies are, after all, a make-believe world, two-dimensional, in which the characters are not real, mere shadows on the screen. Evidence, however, will presently appear that to many young people and particularly to the younger children the world of the movies is not less real than life itself; the emotions and responses of the young to the fevered life of the screen are much the same as to those in actual life. Consider, if only one-fifth of the criminals in motion pictures are shown as receiving legal punishment and many going scot-free, is there any doubt but that such facts are infallibly registered within the youthful minds? "Surely," pleads Dr. Dale, "children and youth need assistance in interpreting such motion pictures. Many parents believe that they should not be seen at all."

For not only is this amazing and morbid preoccupation with criminals untrue to life, but the screen criminals themselves are untrue to life. They appear, as Dr. Dale points out, ready-made, with no future and almost no past. Minerva-like, they spring from the head of Jupiter, full-grown and more than fully armed. In the forty pictures analyzed in more minute detail, it was only rarely that he found the slightest indication that criminal patterns of behavior developed as a product of a long process of interaction between the individual and the successive social situations in which he lives. A feature picture seldom takes more than an hour and a quarter to show. This brevity of unfoldment makes it difficult if not impossible to portray a comprehensive development of character, with the social and psychological factors bearing upon it and making it what it is.

Here of course the novel has a great advantage. European pictures, however, are frequently better than ours in this respect. Charlie Chaplin's pictures were often superior upon this point of character development.

The failure to portray the continuity of experience which produces the criminal is one of the worst features of crime pictures and goes far toward nullifying their claim, often made, of being an aid in the cure of crime. Their realism is a pseudo-realism, such as the showing of blood spurting from a wound, gun battles with the police, or the gallows upon which the criminal is to swing. The true causes of crime, such as insecurity and unemployment, disorganized homes or a chaotic social environment are almost never shown. Where they are shown, they are usually inadequate. In the film, "Scarface," for instance, the conclusion reached by the picture is that the individual citizens must see that more laws are passed and that they are obeyed, and that gangsters who are not citizens must be deported. And in this fashion the crime problem will be solved. After the examination of the plots of many crime pictures, this appears to be a fair specimen of movie criminology.

It is not, however, in the matter of crime alone that motion pictures depart from reality by exaggerated presentation and superficial solution. The range of reality to which they confine themselves is so narrow that they succeed in producing a distortion of life, its occupations and preoccupations.

"We are going to write, subject to our own limitations, about the whole of human life," is the way H. G. Wells outlines the scope of the novel. Yet, notwithstanding the almost fabulous opportunities of the motion pictures for the widest possible scope and the highest ideals, they concentrate upon a narrow range of themes, mostly trivial, on a regrettable dwelling upon crime and a preoccupation with sex that has aroused the complaint of all except possibly the least intelligent sections of the public.

Nor is that the only type of distortion. Thirty-three per cent of the heroes, for instance, and forty-four per cent of the heroines, fifty-four per cent of the villains and sixty-three per cent of the villainesses in 115 pictures—all these prominent protagonists, are either wealthy or ultra-wealthy. Of leading characters who are poor the run is only between five and fifteen per cent. The largest single class of occupations for heroes on the screen, in Dr. Dale's analysis, is "professional." The largest classification for all characters combined, including women, is "no occupation." Ninety characters in 115 pictures, the second largest group, may be labeled as "commercial." Well, commerce is, or was, one of the dominant occupations. The next two groups, however, with eighty characters in each, come under the headings of "occupation unknown" and "illegal occupation," including such trades as gangster, bootlegger, smuggler, thief, bandit, blackmailer and prostitute. The next largest grouping, "theatrical," with seventy-six representatives, may be excused on the ground that the majority of scenarists live in Hollywood. Servants and "high society" characters follow next numerically in this curiously arranged world of moviedom. All of these groupings together account for some six hundred and forty characters out of a total of eight hundred and eighty-three. The remaining quarter of this crazily assorted population is scattered among many callings, notable in that common labor is not included in them at all. A few agricultural laborers exist only because there are western ranches in the pictures. Were the population of the United States, the population of the globe itself, so arranged and distributed, there would be no farming, no manufacturing, almost no industry; no vital statistics (excepting murders), almost no science, no economic problems and no economics. Such a world would speedily starve to death.

The movie world is built upon Oslerian lines. Apparently, almost every human being over forty in screenland has been chloroformed. Most of us admittedly like to see young people on stage and screen, but when sixty-seven per cent of all the characters are between the ages of nineteen and forty, the favored age being from twenty-three to twenty-six, it becomes obvious how remote all this is from life. Of those over forty, only a mere twenty-six per cent is left, and nearly half of the majority does not exceed the age of thirty.

Yet, though perilously treading on the verge of extinction in that world, where few toil and none spin, these movie characters play their rôles preponderantly in full accoutrements of formal dress. In seventy-three per cent of the films formal attire figures tremendously, and sixty-eight per cent of the men and women are doomed sooner or later to appear in it in the course of the picture. The silk hat, relic of Victorianism, is still prominent in the wardrobe of this strange people and the morning coat looms large. As to the dinner coat, it appears more essential than underclothes, so ubiquitous is it. Even a gang leader in his office cannot do without it. The very manikin in one picture plies his trade in full dress, and the tailor who employs him to extol his confections is similarly modish. And yet so many of these characters lack occupation that in a real world they might well be a concern to the police as having no visible means of support. They nearly all smoke, of course, to the number of eighty-seven and a half per cent. That one fact, one would think, is strictly true to life. As to drinking, of the 115 pictures sixty-six per cent show it and forty-three per cent exhibit intoxication. Seventy-eight per cent of all pictures contain liquor situations.

No medium has ever been blessed with a greater freedom from limitation in its choice of scenes and settings than are the movies. Yet with the entire world as their range, the interior of a bedroom figures in forty-nine of the 115 pictures, or forty-three per cent of the total, the largest single heading under a classification of "settings." The living-room and the office come next in point of frequency of settings used, but the bedroom triumphs over all.

As one sums up the people of the screen, always remembering that fine pictures have included many splendid characters, exhibiting fine manners and beautiful clothes, the total impression that survives, after reading the Dale analysis, is of a tawdry population, often absurdly over-dressed, often shady in character, much given to crime and sex, with little desire or need, apparently, of supporting themselves on this difficult planet. A people whom, for the most part, we should not want to know or live amongst. Poor be-glamoured, unprepared adolescents, however, may be moved to imitate them.

Despite the ceaseless preoccupation with love, marriage suffers from a sort of pernicious anæmia on the screen. Curiously enough the marriage ceremony itself which is the consummation of many plots and is supposedly popular with women, is seldom seen in the movies. Whereas, the United States census declares over sixty per cent of the males and females of the population to be married, in the movies only fifteen per cent of males and twenty-one per cent of females have submitted to matrimony.

The goals in life of these baseless, rootless people of the screen are often as tawdry as they are themselves. Of "social" goals, the highest goals of mankind, the numbers are very small. Out of a total of 883 "goals" they run like this: performance of duty, 26; welfare of country, 15; apprehension of criminal, 8; solution of crime, 8; welfare of school, 7; scientific achievement, 4; to see justice done, 3; supremacy of state, 2; welfare of mankind, 2; philanthropy, 1. Of the sixteen "goals" figuring most frequently· in the 115 pictures listed by Dr. Dale, I will give you the first ten in their order of frequency: 1, winning another's love; 2, marriage for love; 3, professional success; 4, happiness of loved one; 5, revenge; 6, happiness of friend; 7, crime for gain; 8, performance of duty; 9, illicit love; 10, protection of friend. This takes up 492 goals of a total of 883. A survey of these most frequent goals brings to our attention the fact that only one of them—performance of duty—and that one holding eighth place—can be interpreted as a social goal. Six of the remaining nine goals are strictly individual, and the other three, while involving the welfare of another person beside the character most concerned, still lie within the realm of the purely personal.

Other headings are such as publicity, social prestige, getting one's own way, desire for power, and desire for an easy life—all of which carry their own commentary.

Winning another's love, marriage for love—these are the two highest goals, so to speak, of the inhabitants of moviedom. Admirable as they are in themselves, they may very easily create a surfeit. Not without bearing upon this point is a quotation from Mr. Elmer Rice's satire upon the world of the movies entitled "A Voyage to Purilia":

"I spoke of love, and well I might, for love is perhaps the key to the whole Purilian world. Not such love as we know on earth: one dynamic element in our complex lives, with manifold biological, psychic and esthetic implication; but love as the be-all and end-all of life, love as the sole substance and meaning of life, love as a thing in itself, love universal and all-permeating, without any implication whatever. Such is love in Purilia; and an overpowering thing it is. And the reader must understand that the broad plains and the mountain-ranges, the quiet hillsides and the pebbled beaches, the many-towered cities and the straggling towns, and the hordes of animate creatures who inhabit them, are but the paraphernalia of this eternal, cosmic love."

Dr. Dale could not help commenting upon the fact that less than nine per cent of the total goals are social in nature, and that even among these are some probably inimical to the best interests of society. "It is apparent," he points out, "that children will rarely secure from the films goals of the types that have animated men like Jenner, Lister, Pasteur, Jesus, Socrates, Grenfell; Edison, Noguchi and Lincoln; and women like Jane Addams, Frances Willard, Madame Curie, Clara Barton and Florence Nightingale."

"It is apparent," he proceeds, "that were we to include motivations of the type which actuate these characters, it would mean that we would have to introduce social ideas into more pictures." Yet so necessary is this type of picture that if private initiative does not produce it, a subsidy of public funds should be forthcoming. The United States Department of Agriculture releases each year thousands upon thousands of feet of motion picture film in order to increase agricultural production. "If," he asks, "it is worth while for the government to subsidize an effort to make two blades of grass grow where one grew before, is it not equally worth while to make two social purposes grow where one grew before?" Possibly Dr. Dale has realized, like many of us, that our civilization is a pyramid standing upon its apex instead of on its base; that grass, which few people want to increase, is encouraged; that character, which all of us imperiously need, is not only not encouraged by certain vital but uncared for factors in our national life, but is in the way of being undermined by them.

"Perhaps one of the greatest lessons youth needs to learn," observes Dr. Dale, returning to the subject of marriage, "is that marriage should be thoughtfully entered into. Is it not possible, then, for the creative scenario writer and director to give us a picture now and again of the more fundamental meanings involved in the circumstances surrounding the beginning of marriage?" He cites the casualness, even cynicism, with which a profligate girl treats the subject of marriage in the early scenes of a picture entitled "Letty Lynton." "Ten minutes ahead is as far as I ever look," declares the girl to a young man with whom she has begun a flirtation.

5

While the charge is frequently brought against so-called "movie reformers" that they foam at the mouth at the mere mention of the word sex, it may be stated with positiveness that even less than the social critic is the professional motion picture critic a reformer. In a manner, he lives by motion pictures virtually as does the actor, director or producer. It would seem perfectly fair, therefore, to quote some words from one of those professional critics, Mr. Welford Beaton, editor of the *Hollywood Spectator*. For a recent book of Mr. Beaton's Mr. Cecil B. DeMille himself wrote an introduction. Mr. Beaton records how during a convalescence he was obliged to live on a diet of milk, and then, one day the revulsion came and he has been unable since to drink a drop of milk or to see anyone else drinking it. He adds:

"The other day I was watching with keen appreciation of its many artistic qualities 'The Easiest Way,' Constance Bennett's latest starring vehicle produced by Metro. For the second time in my life there was an exact moment when the point of revulsion was reached. I had had enough sex. I want no more of it in my screen entertainment. . . .

"The makers of our screen entertainment may continue to earn dividends by selling the immorality of women, but no longer can they sell it to me. I serve notice that every sex picture that I review from now on is going to be estimated for what it is—a filthy thing manufactured by business men."

In studying the fact to which Mr. Beaton objects, Dr. Dale found that in twenty-two pictures out of 115, illicit love appears as the "goal" of thirty-five of the leading characters, including the heroes and heroines. Is it surprising that, as will be brought out later in this volume, sex delinquency in many cases appears as desirable, nay, irresistible, to the young? A Hollywood writer on screen topics for the *Newspaper Enterprise Association* points out that with the vanishing of the old-fashioned screen vamp, oddly, the entire moral fabric of the motion picture has deteriorated. The vamp, he says, seems to have passed out of the picture to be replaced by the modern leading lady "with all the sweetness and charm of Marguerite Clark combined with the more or less loose morals [on the screen] of a Theda Bara." The good-bad girl is in high feather on the screen today. He calls a roll of screen heroines, which includes Greta Garbo, Marlene Dietrich, Joan Crawford, Constance Bennett, Jean Harlow, all of whom have replaced in their single persons both heroine and vamp of an earlier day.

"Throughout her entire career," he observes, "Garbo has at least touched on the shady side of life. I cannot recall a single film in which she portrayed what might be regarded as a good woman." And of Miss Shearer he adds:

"During some years on the screen Norma Shearer's

success was only mediocre until she came along as the reckless girl in 'Divorcée.' In every film since then— 'Strangers May Kiss,' 'A Free Soul,' 'Private Lives,' and now 'Strange Interlude'—she has been ravishing and revealing, almost a torchbearer for the double standard. And the fans have flocked into her camp. . . .

"And so it goes. Practically the same thing can be said of almost every one of our younger actresses who are getting along these days. Virtue may have been at a premium once—but apparently it slumped along with other leading stocks."

These are the quite recent musings and reflections of a movie critic. Thus, Dr. Dale's own conclusion, that the movie drama of the sex and marriage problems in contemporary life is "trite, banal, superficial and exaggerated," appears very mild, though equally damning. That good, even excellent pictures from time to time appear, there is no doubt. As this is being written critics unite in praising "Cavalcade." Yet of a vast part of the movie output, the conclusion is inescapable that loose, blatant and vulgar is the just description. How rarely now do we get such a film as "The Covered Wagon" or "Arrowsmith"! Vulgarity and double meanings have become essential not only to the so-called comedies, but to the humorous and comic scenes of virtually all present-day movies. The excuse is that adults can stand it and that so far as concerns children, these sallies merely pass over their heads. Very little, however, passes over their heads. Children absorb and learn with astonishing rapidity. Whole chapters might be written, books, indeed, upon the pervasive and insidious vulgarity of a large percentage of the movies which is vulgarizing the nation. Dr. Dale has collected a considerable number of specimen lines from a variety of motion pictures, the vulgarity of which hinges on double meanings tinged with obscenity. It is useless to quote them, for we have all encountered them in our own movie-going.

The answer probably will be that the screen is giving the population what it wants, reflecting the life outside the cinema theatre. But, as Dr. Dale puts it: "We ought to expect the cinema to show a better way of living than the average we find outside the cinema. There is so much that is commonplace in life outside the theatre, there are so many commonplace motives, so many commonplace activities, so much commonplace thinking, that it seems indeed unfortunate to have the motion picture merely reflect current life. [As we have seen, it is far from doing even that.] We need to see the screen portraying more of the type of social goals which ought to be characteristic of a decent civilization. We need more often to catch a glimpse of the immortality of great characters who have sacrificed opportunities for personal aggrandizement in order that the larger community might have a fuller measure of life."

Yes. Such ought to be, at least in a measure, the character of the movies. But what it really is we have seen. What are some of its worst effects we shall see presently. A farm-hand, almost a moron, known to the writer, when asked what he desired to see at the movies, replied, "Shootin' and kissin'." If that farm-hand's standard is the norm, the movies fulfil it generously. But, we may recall, two young people in whom we have an interest, Jack and Joan, had started off to the movies, and with a vague uneasiness we were wondering what they were likely to see. In view of the above brief analysis of general movie content, our uneasiness grows increasingly. For that they will see something they should not, something we wish they had not seen, the chances are fairly overwhelming.

There is just a bare possibility that they may see an "Abraham Lincoln," which may prove to be an inspiration to all that is finest in them. Or they may see a "Covered Wagon" which will thrill them with pride in the courage and fearlessness of their forefathers, in the irresistible conquest of obstacles. They may see a "Ben Hur" which will broaden their knowledge of the ancient past and stir their sympathies. They may even see a romance or a simple love story that will stir their young emotions harmlessly.

But the chances are more than even that they will encounter upon the screen an unsavory sex picture, a crime picture poorly and superficially contrived, or something bristling with vulgarity and innuendo, abounding in shoddy characters with tawdry goals in life, of questionable morals or occupations, or wholly immoral. And if that be true, and since children and young people retain a great deal of the impression left upon them by scenes and characters on the screen, it comes home to us irresistibly not only that we must more and more carefully select the pictures which our children are to attend, but with sharp insistence, too, we must demand better pictures on the screen. A demand sufficiently cogent, one supported by box-office evidence, that is, patronage of good pictures and neglect of the bad, is virtually certain to be heeded.

CHAPTER IV

HOW MUCH DO THEY REMEMBER?

ONE comforting thought remains to us. Jack and Joan will remember very little of what they see at the movies. Almost before they know it—they are so young and wholesome!—they will forget practically all of whatever picture they saw at the Palace last night. But will they? Let us see.

Over 28,000,000 of our young, we have found, see the pictures every week, and more than 11,000,000 of them are thirteen years of age or under. If all of them, from those aged five upward, forget virtually everything they see, then there is no problem and all is right in the best of all possible worlds. Mrs. Alice Miller Mitchell, a social investigator, who studied the movie attendance of more than 10,000 children in Chicago, declares that "the majority of children come in contact with the movies once or twice a week." "Any institution," she adds, "that touches the life of a child with this persistent regularity becomes of high importance to his welfare."

Yes, but only if he remembers all or a great part of what he sees. If practically all of it glides off his mind as water from the proverbial duck's back and vanishes clear out of his memory, then, obviously, it carries much less importance than that suggested by Mrs. Mitchell. Clearly, the thing to do was to find out the truth or

falsity of this assumption. Do they or do they not remember what they see? If they do remember, then the
movies do veritably assume that "high importance"
mentioned by Mrs. Mitchell; they assume, in fact, the
gravity of an educational system, and we must no longer
guess about them. We must know.

The task of finding out was assigned, as one element
in the four-year motion picture research of the Payne
Fund, to Dr. P. W. Holaday, working in the University
of Iowa, under direction of Dr. George D. Stoddard,
head of the Iowa Child Welfare Research Station, and
an authority widely known in his field.

How, the reader may ask, can one determine what a
child does or does not remember of a movie? We
hardly know how much we ourselves remember. True.
The business of the psychologist, however, is to find
out. And if there are no established means of finding
out, the first thing to do is to devise them. And this is
what Dr. Holaday proceeded to do. With elaborate care
and with the assistance of a staff of research workers he
went about preparing a series of tests. And to give
validity to the tests a large number of participants were
necessary. Actually some 3000 persons were used in
the experiments. Most of them were children, but a
certain number of adults were necessary for purposes
of comparison. Children, happily, are plentiful, and
by the coöperation of local exhibitors, the public and
private schools of Iowa, Ohio, and other states, parents
and teachers, of the faculties and graduate students of
the Universities, ample material was supplied.

The most difficult thing, often, to arrive at in life
is simplicity. The tests devised had to be so simple

that a second-grade child could, in his way, deal with them as naturally as an adult. Every picture used by the investigators was studied beforehand, viewed over and over, until familiarity made possible the careful selection of only the most natural items for attention. On technical points experts from different departments of the University were consulted. For the younger children questions and points were framed in the simplest possible language. Over and over, throughout the experiments, it was emphasized that participants were not expected to strain toward an exaggerated attention or an especial alertness, but that they were simply to look at a picture as does any other spectator in a theatre, with the purpose of seeing an enjoyable film. In these conditions more than 20,000 testings were made upon 3000 persons and including over 813,000 items of information. Upon these the findings were based. And it may as well be said right here that the amount they found a child carries away from the movies is astonishing.

2

What is knowledge? The answer to this question might lead us into fields of speculation as futile as those suggested by the famous query of Pontius Pilate. The question, what is correct knowledge, is a little simpler, more nearly negotiable and somewhat closer to our business and bosoms.

Suppose that you and I had never seen the inside of the gasoline engine operating a motor car. Now, if our knowledge of the subject were nil, and someone were to tell us that the gasoline inside the engine turns a wheel, we should very probably believe it. Once we have looked inside such an engine, however, and realized that the gasoline explosions within the cylinders depress a series of piston-heads, thereby turning a crank-shaft, our wrong knowledge would thereby be corrected and changed to right or correct knowledge.

One of the things that interested the investigators was to find out if our knowledge, and more especially our children's knowledge, was affected by the contents of the motion pictures exhibited. For instance, if you and your ten-year-old child see such a picture as, say, "Ben Hur," it is certain that the stock of knowledge you both may have possessed of life in Palestine under the Roman Empire will be considerably increased. Insofar as the facts and the details of that picture are presented accurately and correctly, you will get correct information. If, however, the producer has for any reason presented inaccuracies in a picture you see, it follows that you will obtain incorrect information and your stock of correct knowledge will be proportionately reduced. In other words, instead of knowing more facts correctly as a result of seeing the misinforming motion picture, you will come to know more things that "ain't so."

But it works both ways. When the data and facts of a picture are accurate and correct, your stock of general knowledge expands accordingly. From the spectators concerned in his experiments Dr. Holaday found, upon testing, that true pictures increased the extent of the knowledge of eight and nine-year olds by about twelve and a half per cent; thirty-one per cent in the case of fifth and sixth grade children, and about thirty-four per cent for those in the first two high-school years.

Take as an instance the picture "Sorrell and Son."

Leaving to one side the story and plot of the picture, which is generally a favorite, there are many details of custom, of architecture, furnishings, settings, geographical and historical particulars which, if correct, are in themselves educative. Well, after seeing this picture, the second and third grade children, upon being tested, showed changes from fifteen to twenty-seven per cent of correct answers three days later, during which time the film was the only known influence varying from that of previous experience. The fifth and sixth grade groups changed as much as from three to fifty-six per cent, the two first high-school years from thirteen to sixty-seven per cent, and adults from forty-one to seventy-three per cent. To establish whether this knowledge obtained from the screen would fade out and die away, all groups were tested again, without warning, a month later. The fifth and sixth-grade children and the high-school group showed that so far from having lost any of their knowledge, it had at times increased, due to a process of maturation recognized by the investigators.

But how much of incorrect information is scattered among us by the movies? That was the other facet of the problem the experimenters sought to examine. Thus, in a picture called "New Moon" they found "facts" like this:

A Russian second lieutenant, who is a peasant, marries a princess, whose uncle, that is, her father's brother, is only a count. Now, not only is the marriage of a peasant with a princess exceedingly unlikely, but according to the Russian system prevailing before the Bolshevist Revolution, all the sons of a prince were princes, so that the girl's uncle could not have been a count. By the very accident of birth he was a prince. The second lieutenant, moreover, is not only in charge of a full company of soldiers, but later he is in charge of an important frontier fortress. A telegram, in the same picture, is sent from the Caspian Sea to Petrograd, the response being received almost instantaneously, an impossible accomplishment at that distance and under similar conditions even in present-day America. That picture contains many other data as incorrect.

In "Fighting Caravans" a tank car of kerosene is shown as hauled by wagon-train across the prairies in 1861. Historically, interposes Dr. Holaday, kerosene became something more than a scientific curiosity only late in that decade with the advent of the kerosene lamp. It is, at all events, a certainty that no tank car went across the prairies in 1861. Now, in general, producers take considerable care in arriving at correct data and facts, and all the larger studios maintain "research" departments. Rapidity of production, however, as well as carelessness, often lead to misinformation. Perhaps, when they realize the tremendous teaching power of the movies, they will be led to insure the greatest possible accuracy in the pictures they produce.

What happens when misinformation, the property of certain motion pictures, is shown to an audience? Encyclopedic minds are scarce. When the above pictures were shown to the assembled audience of Dr. Holaday's and Dr. Stoddard's experiments, subsequent tests showed that their stock of correct information was materially reduced. They knew fewer things that were so and more things that weren't so. And if the reader happens to be interested in percentages, he may like to

know that the correct information of the participants
upon items shown incorrectly in the movies was reduced
by nearly eight per cent after absorption of these incorrect data of the films, and this in the case of children
as young as eight and nine years. Fifth and sixth grade
children, that is, eleven and twelve-year olds, lost nineteen per cent of their laboriously acquired knowledge,
and the high-school group thirty-four per cent. Adults
lost all of thirty-seven and a half per cent. In other
words, the more you know, the less you know after
witnessing a careless, ignorantly-written and badly-docu-
mented picture.

Now, though these percentages of loss of knowledge
apply only to the pictures used in this portion of the
experiment, still those pictures were selected as a cross
section of movies in general, and the figures may be
accepted, Drs. Holaday and Stoddard assure us, as approximately correct. The realism with which children
look at pictures as true to life, registers impressions on
their minds with especial incisiveness.

Face to face with these facts, the popular theory,
namely, that whatever people and young children see
in the pictures will glide off their minds like foam, falls
precipitately to the ground. And Dr. Holaday is enter-
taining no idle fancy when he says: *"My private guess
is that pictures play a considerably larger part in the
child's imagination than do books."* The implications
of these words, which we purposely underline, are, if
we pause to think of them, simply stupendous. And if
this guess of the investigator be true, as the writer believes it to be, then the present situation, into which a
welter of movies coming constantly in a wild ceaseless

cataract has plunged us, is an unprecedented condition. And the survey, whence these facts are drawn, though but the first glimmer of light in the dark skies of our general ignorance upon the subject, must instantly enlist the attention of every one of us.

3

The general knowledge test, so called, as described above, was only the first part of the "information" experiment. Further tests undertaken bore more directly upon the material of the picture itself—the plot, the incidents, the characters, all its values, that is, as a story and a dramatic presentation. For though our stock of general information is modified by the movies, as we have seen, our object in going to them is not general information, but rather entertainment and amusement. We are all well aware of a probably inborn craving for dramatic presentments of life. No need to go back to the Greeks, with whom the drama was a high, almost a religious cult, to sustain us in our love of dramatic and theatric presentations. By our own intuition and experience we know that what we derive through the avenue of our imaginative faculties colors and often enriches our characters, our views, our ways of looking at life and meeting it, our specific gravity as individuals. And if that be true, how supremely important that what we see should be both beautiful and true!

The tests arranged by Drs. Holaday and Stoddard for dealing with the imaginative part of the material had to be constructed with the utmost care. The questions had to be selected in such a manner that they could be answered by children of the various grades as well as by adults. Take, for instance, these specimen questions upon the picture of "Tom Sawyer":

"The first present Tom received for letting a boy work on the whitewashing of the fence was (1) a watch (2) a whistle (3) a dead cat (4) a compass (5) a tooth."

Clearly a question like this can be answered just as well by an eight or nine-year-old child who had followed the picture as by an adult. Or, another question:

"Felice said that when she married she would be of help to her husband because she had (1) a wagon and horses (2) a lot of linen (3) some money (4) a number of furs (5) some furniture."

Anyone who saw the picture, "Fighting Caravans," whether child or adult, could easily answer that question. Each one of the twenty-six tests consisted of anywhere from thirty to sixty-four items. All were aimed to establish how much of the picture was retained. The results were illuminating. The very youngest children, the eight and nine-year olds, were found to have retained sixty per cent as much as the adults.

If you attend the movies with your nine-year-old son or daughter you may be assured that out of every five points you have noted they will have noted at least three. Our favorite theory, then, that children instantly forget what they see in the movies, suffers a rude, and quite disturbing shock.

What surprised the investigators even more, however, was the amount of retention over longer periods of time. Ordinarily, the tests were given the day after the picture was shown. When, however, a test was repeated without warning after a period of six weeks, they were astonished to find that these second and third grade children, the eight and nine-year olds, still remembered ninety-one per cent of what they had originally retained from the picture, or almost all they had carried away. Fifth and sixth grade children remembered ninety per cent, and the high-school children eighty-eight per cent. The adults, strangely, had the lowest rank with eighty-two per cent.

Now, this fact is of almost incalculable importance. While it is true that if children retain sixty per cent of what an adult would retain, they miss forty per cent— a condition which often leads to many misunderstandings of facts and implications—it means, nevertheless, that not only do children carry away in their minds a vast deal of what they see in a picture, but they remember it for a long time afterward. After three months the averages were found to be virtually the same, with even occasionally a slight *increase* in the amount recalled upon the part of the youngest children. If, briefly, they had received whatever they had gleaned from the screen with the pliability of wax, they were found to be retaining it, as the phrase goes, with the durability of marble.

So powerful had proved the visual images of the screen impinging on the minds of the youngest children, that sometimes the amount they remembered after a lapse of time ran over one hundred per cent. That is, they occasionally remembered more after one month, or even after three months, than they had remembered the day after the showing of the picture. And that these percentages of their retention are conservative is probable from the known fact that children at best find diffi-

culty in expressing all that they know. Their com-
petitors, moreover, were progressively older, ranging up
to such mature persons as graduate students working
for Masters' and Doctors' degrees at the University and
young professors and their wives.

This expanding memory of the younger children as
regards motion picture content is exceedingly interesting. It is possible that the realistic attitude with which
a child is likely to view events on the screen, the intense
reality which characters and incidents assume to his
young world-exploring eyes, as well as the childish day-
dreaming induced by these vivid images—all of these
things may be responsible for the apparent intensifica-
tion of their picture memories. The parent reading this
may be imagined saying in astonishment:

"But why don't *my* children come home from the
movies remembering so much?"

The answer is simple. They do! Ask your child to
answer your specific questions about the story of a
movie you and he have seen together, and then listen
to him rattle off. "If the proper stimulus (in the experiments, the tests) is applied," declares Dr. Holaday, "the
answer is prompt. Your child may go to a generation
of movies and never meet this stimulus—never repeat
all he has observed and concluded in regard to the
pictures he has seen, but the embers are there." And
embers, as will be shown later, have a chance of flaming up.

Clearly, in the light of these facts, what the screen
becomes is a gigantic educational system with an instruction possibly more successful than the present

text-book variety, but with a content which, in view of the facts presented in he preceding chapter, makes us disturbingly reflective.

Interesting as sidelights are some of the peculiarities of the different age groups and the types of items that tend to cling longest to their memories. All the way from the second grade to the second year of high school children seem to remember best such items as sports, crime, acts of violence, general action and titles. The passage of weeks, or even months, seems only to enhance the memory as to these favorites. With adults, sports are not nearly so vivid and seem to decline to fifth and ninth places respectively in long-range tests.

Sad and weakly emotional items are well retained by all groups, from the eight-year old to the educated adult —thus testifying perhaps to our native sentimentality. Of humorous action, however, adults tend to forget the details swiftly; but these items are strongly retained by the children. And possibly this may prove to Mr. Sinclair Lewis and Mr. H. L. Mencken our intense provincial-mindedness: scenes of home and school and generally familiar exteriors, such as have figured in the youth of most of us, are retained best by all, from the eight-year olds to the professors. Scenes, on the other hand, which the experimenters group under such headings as "cafés, frontier scenes, hotels and ships" are retained least by all age groups. In this last fact there may be a crumb of comfort for parents in rural areas.

For convenience the investigators classified the information derived from the movies by their spectators into ten divisions or categories. The headings they used for these were as follows: emotional; humorous; mysterious; revue (dancing, vaudeville); crime; fighting and violence; romance; sex, love-making, etc.; drinking; general conversation; general action. The gain in information on the part of the younger children took place in all of these divisions, no one of which failed entirely to register with even the youngest, the eight and nine-year olds. No single category, that is, entirely passed over their heads or was entirely lost. Now, as we have seen, seventy-five per cent of the movie output deals with love, sex and crime, presenting often shoddy goals, pursued, frequently, by highly objectionable human beings. It is not difficult to guess at the view that parents must take of too frequent going upon the part of their children to movies of this type. Children in an institutional home used in the experiments, it was found, retained what they saw at the movies as effectively as children living in normal homes and surroundings. There was no difference. The movies, evidently, speak to all more or less alike. They are universal. Suddenly we are awakened to the fact that for over two decades, for almost a generation, we have given least attention to what demands it most.

A universal medium—the screen! Books, according to Holaday and Stoddard, cannot vie with it. The school must be of a very superior sort to excel it. Exaggerated? Pictures, as the investigators point out, have two means of reaching the human consciousness, both the visual and the auditory. How indirect, by comparison, is the medium of books! Seventy per cent retention! When could an educator count upon so much? The screen becomes one of the most powerful single instruments in the education of our population. Yet an African tribe could scarcely have used it more irresponsibly.

With the school and the home, as we have seen, the movie has become a dominant influence in the lives of our children.

"Considerable legislation," observe Drs. Holaday and Stoddard, "affecting the age at which children may go to the motion picture theatre is on the statute books. Several American states and cities, at least one Canadian province, and nearly all the countries of Europe have laws on the subject. Legislators, agencies and leaders who advise legislators on subjects affecting child welfare will wish to scrutinize the intellectual content of a medium that finds as open a road into the youthful mind as does the theatrical picture, and that remains in memory as tenaciously. The fact that scenes of crime, fighting and other acts of violence are among the items most noted and best remembered, even by the youngest children, may well add to their concern over that large portion of the film output that specializes in these realms."

How large the portion of such pictures we have already seen. How active will be the concern of the legislators and agencies mentioned by Holaday and Stoddard remains yet to be seen. Certainly, for censorship boards, for legislators, for parents, and for producers, carefully arrived at data are now available. When we reflect that the world movie audience is said to consist of about 250,000,000 people weekly, it becomes clear that the entire world has ample reason to be seriously concerned as to the mental material presented by the movies. Other phases of the survey will support the inescapable conclusions sequent upon the study presented in this chapter. But were none others available, were this the only one, with its ineluctable facts, that not only do even young children retain half of what they see in the movies, but often show an increased volume of their memories and impressions after a lapse of months, even in that case the attention of legislators, educational and cultural societies and public opinion generally should be instantly riveted upon the problem. Much has been done by way of safeguarding the purity and integrity of water supplies, of food and drugs. The motion picture presents itself as nothing less than a food universally but confusedly ingested by the human mind.

Seeing, however, as do Drs. Holaday and Stoddard, but little hope of any great change in the film content at present, they feel compelled to urge the most careful selection of motion pictures for the young.

CHAPTER V

MOVIES AND SLEEP

WHAT do we know about sleep? What do even the most careful parents among us know about the sleep of our children? We assume that there are a number of agents, such as coffee or excitement, which may keep them wakeful. But actually very little is known about them. Even our own testimony as to whether we have slept well or ill is not reliable.

To the psychologist sleep is a positive form of human behavior just as are walking and talking. Characteristic of the sleep of all of us is a continual *motility*, or restlessness, expressed in turnings, tossings, movements, changes in posture of the body or limbs throughout the entire night. Not even the most perfect sleep is so perfect, but it is checkered by this inherent motility. There is never complete immobilization.

In the comprehensive survey of motion picture influence upon the young and adolescents, this question presented itself as of capital importance: Do movies of various sorts produce effects upon sleep in a way injurious to normal health and growth, or do they not?

The fact that mental and moral results, as will appear later in this volume, are the aristocracy of movie effects upon the young, must not lead us to lose sight of that other cardinal fact, namely, that the movies produce definite and positive physical effects upon the spectator. Anything that produces mental effects just as certainly produces physical effects. This truism is repeated, because, so far as concerns motion pictures, not only had we laymen neglected the point, but even scientists had omitted to study it.

In the bibliography of the monograph resulting from a special research upon sleep disturbances by Professor Samuel Renshaw, Drs. Vernon L. Miller and Dorothy P. Marquis, are listed no less than two hundred and fifty-five works upon the subject of sleep. Yet none of those forerunners had investigated the effects of motion pictures upon sleep, which a poet has called "chief nourisher at life's feast." In view of our vast national movie audience of 77,000,000 weekly, of whom over 28,000,000 are children and adolescents, in view of the emotional content of the run of motion pictures and of their powerful visual impressions that remain long in the memory, it became obvious that the subject of sleep needed immediate investigation. If the sleep of children is sufficiently affected by movie going to influence not only their school work and tempers, but also their health and growth, then concrete and positive knowledge upon the subject becomes of paramount importance to all of us. If, however, movies do not affect sleep, that is a matter of equal importance.

How to approach the subject? If the sleep of all of us is checkered by a certain amount of motility, then, clearly, the first step in discovering the effects of any external influence upon sleep would be to find out the amount of restlessness normal to the habit of body of any one of us. Large numbers of individuals would have to be investigated before satisfactory answers to the various questions upon the subject of sleep could be obtained.

The investigators, as a matter of fact, set themselves a number of questions, some of which we should never even have thought of asking. A few, which perhaps any one of us might have posed, were these:

Is it true that sleep during the fore part of the night has greater recuperative value than that indulged in toward morning? The old saw about beauty sleep dies hard in our consciousness.

How much sleep does a child of a given age need in order to maintain normal health and growth?

Do certain types of motion pictures produce effects which delay the onset of sleep in children? If so, what types?

What kind of changes in motility (restlessness) follows the viewing of definite types of motion pictures?

To what extent is impairment of the normal sleep pattern prejudicial to health and growth?

Simple and innocent as this handful of questions appears, the task of answering them scientifically, accurately, loomed enormous. Notwithstanding, the investigators went to work. Their results form not only a major contribution to the scientific knowledge touching sleep, but also a massive pillar in the entire structure of movie effects upon the young.

The first thing Drs. Renshaw, Miller and Marquis required was a measuring apparatus. Science consists largely in measuring. Not having any such apparatus immediately at hand, they proceeded to perfect one which would supply them with data of unusual exacti-

tude in their study. But the main things for us is, that
it has brought at last some knowledge, and thus, as they
observe, "we have made new use of a very old psychological principle in examining the nature and amount
of the change in children's sleep after they had seen
movies as compared to their own normal sleep patterns."
Their aim and hope, they declare, is that their work
may help to solve that part of the motion picture
problem, "and that the new apparatus and methods may
contribute to the more hygienic regulation by parents,
physicians and others, of children's sleeping habits—
which are so often neglected, but are of such high importance to the process of developing sound minds in
sound bodies."

2

The apparatus they perfected was the hypnograph.
Who of us has ever heard of the hypnograph? It means,
the sleep recorder. This little apparatus, the first of its
kind devised to work electrically, with its brush contacts and brass inlays, is comparatively simple, and an
electrician could construct it from the specifications they
give. It can be attached to a cross-bar under the bedspring, midway between the head and foot of the bed.
A small bakelite rod of the contrivance is so sensitive
in design that it moves with each change of the sleeper's
posture.

Imagine for a moment your child asleep in its cus-
tomary bed, in its own room, unconscious of the little
apparatus beneath its bedspring, while a pen in your
room is travelling over paper and recording the child's
tossings and restlessness, showing you by morning the

loss it has sustained out of its nine hours' sleep, its necessary recuperation for the ensuing day. Would not such a record, if out of the ordinary, stir you to immediate concern? And would not that move you to take at once all possible remedial measures? In our private lives, however, such measures are not yet feasible. Possibly, as the investigators hope, they soon will be. In the meanwhile, their pioneering work is the first news of the possibilities.

In casting about for a suitable field for research, the experimenters found that in the average home, even in the average good home, the irregularity of habits of eating, playing, time of retiring, and so on, would be disadvantageous to accuracy. What they needed was a place where many children were available at once and where the living schedules were more uniform than even in a private home. Boarding-schools and convents presented numerous difficulties, owing to the range of ages of inmates, the frequent presence of room-mates, the rigidity of institutional rules. Finally, however, they found their ideal material for the experiment in the Ohio State Bureau of Juvenile Research at Columbus.

During the two and a half year period of their research, the Bureau offered them extraordinarily favorable facilities. It is not an orphanage or a reformatory. It is a place established for the observation of children who are referred there by Juvenile Courts or Probate Courts, or, as is often the case, are voluntarily brought by parents seeking advice, or by people intending to adopt a child and desiring an expert report on its possibilities. The age range of the children is from five to nineteen, and the Bureau is in possession of the family, medical and scholastic history of each child, its intelligence quotient and the results of psychological examination by the staff.

"It is significant," declare Drs. Renshaw, Miller and Marquis, "that the Bureau actually furnishes kind treatment, clean beds, good food—in a word, more hygienic and probably happier conditions than most of these children have had in their homes in which they found difficulty."

Observation over a period of two and a half years showed them to be no less happy and contented, under no greater tension, than any sampling of similar size in any ordinary public school population. In fact, what with regularity of habits, attention to diet and health and daily routine, many of these children were better off than some in so-called good homes. Only children in good health were chosen for the experiment, and if a child developed illness during the process, its record was not used. Children of different intelligence levels were utilized, and even the heredities were available to the investigators.

Twenty beds at the Bureau were equipped with the hypnograph apparatus, the first ten boys and ten girls were selected in their respective departments and the work of testing the effects of the movies on sleep was begun.

Altogether one hundred and seventy of these boys and girls from six to eighteen years of age were studied during a period of 347 nights. Each group of twenty remained in the experimental beds about fifty consecutive nights. Their records yield the results observed in a total of 3,591,000 minutes, or 59,580 hours, or 6,650 child nights of sleep. In the two and a half years of observation these children were exposed to fifty-nine different motion picture programmes.

During all this time, every movement and change of posture, every sign of restlessness in their sleep was unfailingly recorded. Wires forming cables from the apparatus hidden beneath their beds led through the wall to a recording room in which were located the batteries, relay box and a polygraph recorder. This polygraph unit, or writing apparatus, simultaneously registered the twenty records throughout the night by twenty stylus pens which kept moving upon a paper tape at slightly over an inch a minute. As soon as each child got into bed, a small signal light went out and the writing upon the tape began. In case a child left the bed, or if the mechanism was otherwise interrupted, the observer in the recording room was made aware of it by the flash of the signal light. While ignoring respiratory movements or heart-beats, the mechanism was sensitive enough to record movements even so slight as a bending of the elbow or a turn of the head.

The groups of sleepers usually occupied the experimental beds for a period of from three to five nights without any recorded observation, merely to allow them to become accustomed to sleep naturally in the new beds. Once the researchers were satisfied upon this point, they began to take records, ordinarily for about fifteen consecutive nights, in order to establish what was the normal sleep pattern of each one of these children.

We have already seen that no such thing as absolutely motionless sleep exists. When any of us declare that we "slept like a log" or "slept like the dead," we are merely using language carelessly. Not even the soundest sleep of the healthiest child is without some movement. The investigators, of course, knew this and proceeded to measure the relative amount of disturbance in every young sleeper's night. What they found, briefly, was this:

Only about one child in a hundred ever sleeps a full hour without tossing or movement of some sort. Sleep is a succession of quiet periods alternating with restless periods. The average length of the quiet periods for all children for the entire night is not quite eleven minutes. During fifteen per cent of the minutes of the nine hours passed by the child in bed he makes bodily movements. This is on the average 8.7 active minutes per hour, or about one and a third hours of the sleeping night. And since these are averages, it means that one-half of all children do not attain a figure so comparatively satisfactory. In fact, one-half of all the quiet periods are less than five minutes long.

The popular belief about beauty sleep is justified by science, since the point of the minimum of restlessness always occurs early in the night. Though the greatest period of restlessness, or motility, follows immediately upon getting to bed, yet, after a period varying from fifteen to ninety minutes, that motility gradually decreases until a minimum for the entire night is reached.

For boys the quietest hour of sleep is the second hour after they go to bed; for girls, strangely, it is the third hour. Are those hours, we may ask, absolutely quiet? No, but the quiet periods in these halycon hours average as long as nearly seventeen minutes. They diminish steadily from that point, however, until in the ninth hour, the hour before rising, quiet periods average only about seven and a half minutes. In children between five and ten no sex differences are noted in respect to these sleep peculiarities. Beginning with puberty, however, and throughout adolescence, the differences are marked. Boys of eighteen, for instance, are sixty-four per cent more active from ten to eleven o'clock, their quietest hour, than are boys from six to ten. Similarly, the oldest girls are thirty-two per cent more active than the youngest girls during this hour. Not only are younger children less active, but those between six and ten have quiet periods twenty-seven per cent longer than the age group immediately following theirs, eleven to fourteen.

All this is detailed to the reader because most of the information is new, irrespective of movie going or any other influence. Many curious facts were discovered incidentally. As an example, it is known that winter is the period of slow growth and of minimum physical strength for children. From January to June is the period of slowest growth, while that of greatest growth is between mid-July and mid-December. During the slow growth period the activity in sleep also lessens. Summer and autumn, the time of rapid growth, is also the time of greatest restlessness in children. Boys, it was found, are most restless in autumn, showing an increase of all the way from fourteen to twenty-six per cent over winter. Girls, oddly, are considerably more restless in the summer months than the boys even in autumn. The cause for this is unknown. Experiments were made with such factors as temperature, humidity and extra coverings as influences in sound sleeping. None of these makes any appreciable difference, excepting a swift and sudden change in temperature as, for instance, twenty to fifty degrees within a few hours.

Even the temperaments of the different children were studied, because those, too, entered into the conditions. The sleeping habits of any one of us are a highly individual affair. On-coming illness, which parental solicitude detects from restlessness in sleep, was confirmed by the investigators. In a number of cases under observation, they found that at least one night, and sometimes two or three nights, before active symptoms appeared, the child showed increased motility. Normally, however, the hourly motility during sleep for any given child is stable to a high degree, and that made it all the more possible to study with considerable accuracy the effects of such an excitement as the motion picture upon the sleep of children.

Motion pictures undoubtedly furnish a certain excitement to the young. But are they all that goes to make that excitement? Is not the mere fact of going somewhere, of going into a crowd, of music, lights, bustle, movement—are not all these factors at least as exciting as the pictures themselves? Such an objection could be justly raised and to anticipate it, as well as to satisfy themselves, the scientists tried still another experiment. At six-thirty, following supper, they assembled twenty children just as though they were going to the movies. But instead of to a picture theatre the youngsters were taken in automobiles to the crowded downtown section of the city of Columbus, where they were enabled to "window shop," to enjoy the lights, the crowds and the scenes presented to them in a trip to the city, the University campus, the beautiful river drive, the wealthy suburbs. The time occupied was about the length of a movie programme, but no movie was included in this junket. Then, taken back to the Bureau, they went quietly to bed. An analysis showed that eighteen of the twenty children slept just a shade more quietly following the trip than was their normal. It certainly had produced no effects of excitement, notwithstanding that the children had been thrilled by the experience of going down town at night.

The experimentation with actual movie going was then taken up. The children were assembled at about six-twenty after supper, and walked the two blocks to the theatre, arriving there about six-thirty. They saw, as a rule, what any other spectator sees at a movie—a feature picture, a comedy and a news-reel. The programme lasted about two hours. The children returned to their home at about eight-forty-five and went to bed promptly at nine. In general, they had precisely the same conditions under which the average child sees the movies.

The programmes were unselected. The children saw whatever pictures happened to be shown at one of the two neighboring theatres. In every way the investigators aimed to keep normal and typical living conditions surrounding the experiment. And just as their sleep restlessness was recorded when no movies had been seen, so now the automatic stylus pens charted the restlessness *after the movies* of these children for many nights, extending, as has been said, over two and a half years of observation. By way of careful check upon the procedure, the investigators bracketed *two* series of normal nights with the movies series of nights.

What was the result?

To the writer, in examining the result of these experiments, it appears that the influence of motion pictures upon children depends upon various factors—upon the kinds of picture they see; upon the age, sex and mental "set" of each individual child. Not all pictures affect all children alike; girls are often affected differently from boys and older children from younger children. Within these limits certain highly significant facts emerge.

Take first a single instance, one motion picture and the record of one boy, eight years old. Before seeing a film called "Movietone Follies of 1930," his restlessness, or motility was thirteen per cent. After seeing the film it registered twenty-six per cent. That is, it was twice as much as his total normal restlessness for the night when he had seen no movie. Similarly, a boy of ten showed almost the same increase in sleep disturbance after seeing a picture entitled "Strictly Unconventional"; and another, eight-and-a-half-years old, showed an increase of thirty per cent, or a third more of restlessness for only half the night after seeing the picture, "Concentration Kid."

In almost every case, the observers found, the change was greater in the fore part of the night, between nine and two, than between two and six, though in some cases the movie acted as a depressor, inducing less motility in sleep. This, as will be shown later, proceeds from the same cause as increased motility. The percentage of those showing neither increase nor decrease appears as practically negligible.

Elaborately the investigators proceeded to record the effects of particular pictures upon their young charges, discovering in the process how unexpected are some of the results and how individual are the influences upon children. Where one boy, aged eight, after seeing "Remote Control," showed an increase above normal restlessness of only about thirteen per cent, another boy aged fifteen-and-a-half after the same picture registered an increase of sixty-two per cent above normal. One girl of twelve, after this picture, recorded the astonishing increase of eighty-five per cent above normal, virtually doubling her sleep movements. Yet, other girls aged eighteen, eight and sixteen showed only about twenty per cent increase over normal after this picture. Though all showed increases, personal idiosyncrasies ranged wide. A girl of sixteen, after seeing the film "Just Imagine," actually registered an increase of ninety per cent, or all but double her normal motility. Yet most of the other children were comparatively cool to the story. To them it was like any other picture.

The strange effects of particular pictures both impressed and intrigued the psychologists. "Billy the Kid" is a movie concerning a notorious young western killer, presented in a glorified light, and there is much gunplay, rough-riding and excitement in the plot. Here, certainly, was a picture that ought to excite boys to a high pitch. Yet, only one boy of fifteen was moved sufficiently to register an increase of fifty per cent above his normal motility. Of the girls seeing it, however, two-thirds were to such an extent stirred that they actually recorded more than half again their normal restlessness. The excitement of one of them showed up to seventy-five per cent above her normal quota. That is, she practically doubled her normal restlessness every hour of that night.

To the majority of boys, however, "Billy the Kid" proved to be like any other picture.

Altogether, basing their observations and calculations upon the recorded results of seeing fifty-eight different picture programmes, the investigators arrived at some striking facts which cannot but be of interest to parents careful of their children's health and, indeed, to all of us.

Briefly, they found that, though the variety of effect upon different individuals is considerable, *boys, after seeing a movie, showed an average increase of about twenty-six per cent, and girls of about fourteen per cent greater hourly motility than in normal sleep!* So great were the variations in individual cases, that fifty, seventy-five and even ninety per cent of increase in restlessness were recorded! But even the general averages are astonishing and their importance can hardly be over-estimated.

A child's sleep, remember, is made up of a succession of quiet periods and active periods, so that, assuming, for instance, that a child moves in six different minutes distributed throughout an hour in activity, that will leave fifty-four quiet minutes, each quiet period averaging nine minutes in length. Increase the number of active minutes to twelve and the quiet periods shrink to four minutes each! Those quiet periods, as we have seen, are longest about the second hour of the night and decrease steadily until morning. The marked increase in restlessness after a movie, it emerged from the experiments, has the positive effect of preventing the child's full recovery from his fatigue. The increased restlessness in the earlier part of the night, when sleep is at its best, is not made up in the latter part of the night. It remains a total loss.

An indulgent excuse might be that, granting these facts, a single night of impaired sleep now and then cannot be so very damaging to the child. True, his health might suffer a little, his work in school might suffer, and even his temper, the next morning. But then it would be all over and forgotten. In a preceding chapter we have seen how powerful is the retention of movie impressiohs on the part of children and how the scenes and images gain rather than lose in the child's memory after a lapse of time. Though not in the same way as the mental effect, the physical effect also was found in many cases to persist after the first post-movie night. For as long as four or five nights after the children had seen a movie the sleep of some was still disturbed by a greater than normal restlessness, dependent upon the age, sex and mental set of the individual child. For nearly a week, that is, after the movie some children still showed the adverse influence upon their sleep and recuperation. The scenes of sports and exciting action which, as Holaday and Stoddard found, cling longest to the memory, play their part in the physical organism as well. And from their general observation, though they did not especially study this particular phase, the investigators believe that matinee attendance should show as great an effect on motility, or restlessness, as evening attendance, or even greater.

These post-movie effects, it was found, have nothing to do with whether a child is bright or dull, stupid or quick. The nervous system, allowing for individual variations, responds more or less alike in all. The fullest effects seem to accrue when the child spectator is about the age of puberty. But it is inadvisable to make

sweeping generalizations. Certain pictures may have
salutary effects, both sedative and instructive, depending
upon the type of film or the type of child (excepting,
of course, abnormals.) "For certain highly sensitive or
weak and unstable children," nevertheless observes Dr.
Renshaw, "the best hygienic policy would be to recom-
mend very infrequent attendance at carefully selected
films."

3

Now, though the great majority of children show
that increase in sleep restlessness upon which we have
been dwelling, it is nevertheless true that an appreciable
number actually show the opposite after movie attendance. Roughly, Drs. Renshaw, Miller and Marquis
found, about two and a half times as many children
showed significant increase from all types of films as
showed corresponding decrease. What, we may well
ask, does this mean? Does it mean that forty per cent
of the children actually obtain a more restful night's
sleep as a result of seeing a movie before going to bed?
That your child or your friend's may be among that
fortunate number that actually sleep more soundly after
a movie? To find an answer to this the investigators
undertook an elaborate study upon the effects of loss of
sleep. Many scientists in the past have studied this subject. For instance, three experimenters observed the
effects upon rabbits of fatigue to the point of collapse
and death by sleep deprivation. The symptoms of collapse were a sudden fall in temperature, a rise in the
pulse followed by a marked drop, then a gradual slow-
ing down of respiration. Adults experimenting upon

themselves and upon other adults reported an increase of errors in mental arithmetic and other mental tests as a result of lack of sleep, a pulse pressure indicating a load upon the heart, a lack of inhibition, irritability, light-headedness, nervousness, a feeling of mild intoxication, blankness of mind, and fatigue that in some cases became positive pain.

Among all these scientific records of experiments, however, the psychologists studying the movie influence were unable to find a single study on experimental insomnia in children. Once again they were obliged to become pioneers. Wishing to find out to what extent insomnia is related to the impairment of normal sleep by motion picture attendance, the investigators, having at hand the necessary children at the Juvenile Research Bureau, proceeded to experiment.

First, without warning, after the usual period of normal nights, the children were allowed to stay up late, to prolong the day's activities, in their respective recreation rooms, by engaging in games, reading, solving mechanical puzzles and similar occupations between the hours of nine and twelve in the evening. This play was as nearly normal as the experimenters could keep it and, at a few minutes before midnight, the children were prepared for bed and allowed to sleep until their usual time of rising at six in the morning.

This reduction of sleep, from nine to six hours, was continued for three nights, thus causing the children in a period of this length to lose a complete night's sleep. Following this process with five nights of normal sleep, the children were asked to rise at three in the morning. Three hours, that is, before their normal time of getting up. After dressing and making their toilets, they engaged in play activities until breakfast time. Altogether forty children participated in the experiment, covering a period of two hundred and eighty child nights of sleep, in which their normal sleeping period was shortened by one-third.

While most of the children remained fully awake and quite alert, enjoying the unusual experience, children under ten naturally became very drowsy. Soon, however, it became necessary to restore all the children to the ration of nine hours. The matrons and attendants at the Bureau reported that many of the children had become peevish and irritable and the problem of conduct had become acute. The younger the children, the worse the results.

But what interested the scientists still more was to find that the motility, owing to this sleep deprivation and added fatigue, *decreased* about twenty-eight per cent in the boys and some twenty-three per cent in the girls. This, at first sight, may appear as an advantage. If the restlessness of the children is so significantly reduced by loss of sleep, then does it not follow that the less they sleep, the better they sleep? It was found, moreover, that though all the children had been awake for eighteen hours, and though some declared themselves tired and sleepy, others were *apparently* fresh and ready to prolong the period of wakefulness. This freshness and alertness, however, is a characteristic of certain degrees of fatigue and is a commonly known result of many so-called stimulating drugs which are in reality depressants. The loss of sleep, in short, is a means of prolonging and increasing the fatigue state.

Fatigue, in reality, is a state of partial asphyxiation, until the bodily cells in the presence of oxygen have had time to recuperate. Definite changes in behavior are associated with even a moderate degree of fatigue. There is considerable likelihood, the investigators conclude, that emotional instability from fatigue is similar to the effects produced by alcohol, cocaine, heroin, hashish and other narcotics, differing only in degree. The first effects of fatigue, like those of alcohol, or asphyxiation, may be "stimulating." But this is a false stimulation. The real effect is always depressant. There is a kind of inertia about fatigue which tends to keep the fatigued person doing the same thing. Dr. H. M. Johnson has reported that a tired driver near the end of a long journey becomes unable to stop driving, and he curses stop lights and becomes irritable. A drunken person cannot be silenced, or diverted, and a fatigued person often exhibits a craving for the very cause of his fatigue. We all know that it is the tired children that are the ones who fight hardest against being put to bed, precisely as certain of the children in the experiment asked to prolong their wakefulness. Every effect of alcohol which has any social significance can be produced by some degree of fatigue. Physiologically the two conditions are the same —special instances of cell asphyxiation.

What follows from all this, insofar as it bears upon our special inquiry, is that decreased motility after a movie, or after loss of sleep, is a manifestation of the same cause as increased motility, namely, fatigue; partial asphyxiation; oxygen starvation; partial anesthesia. Any change in motility beyond the normal range of fluctuation peculiar to the individual is therefore an indication of

fatigue. As Drs. Renshaw, Miller and Marquis put it,
"If a child shows decreased motility after a movie or
sleep loss, this greater quiet may be a quiet of the same
type *produced by soporific drugs,* not a more restful,
recuperative sleep." Not only that, but whereas an adult
can usually make up loss of sleep in a single night of
normal length, the sleep deprivation in the case of children extends into several nights following the deprivation. And some movies, declare the investigators, yield
as great effects in the production of immobilization as
those following the experimental insomnia. Restlessness
or a drugged stupor—the choice is unimportant.

"The significant increases of fatigue," they declare,
"whether induced by sleep impairment following the
movies, from overwork, from narcotic drugs or alcohol,
or any source of oxygen deprivation, are detrimental to
health and growth, not only because of their known
physiological consequences, but also because of the fact
that the important inhibitions which serve to prevent
misconduct are weakened. Frequent indulgence may
lead to the formation of the habit of craving further indulgence. The best hygienic regulations for children
should therefore include, among other things, only infrequent attendance at selected types of motion picture
programmes."

Clearly, these investigators are not alarmists, nor does
any such attitude enter in the slightest degree into their
work. They give the considered and carefully calculated
results of their findings. They paint no pictures. Yet
every reader can so easily paint the picture for himself.
Imagine the children from the age of six on, exposed to
the flood of movies pouring across the screen, loaded

chiefly with the well-known movie trinity of love, sex and crime; with all the violence, vulgarity and false values that so many movies have. It is a question whether this child will have become so excited as to lose sleep for a week, or that the other child will be so drugged and exhausted by emotional fatigue that his sleep will be a kind of stupor. Whichever of the two happens, the price we pay is exorbitant.

In view of all this, is it surprising that Drs. Renshaw, Miller and Marquis express a hope that parents, physicians and others will examine their study in the hope of organizing a better hygiene for the vast numbers of America's children, 11,000,000 of whom, thirteen or under, weekly attend the movies?

Sleep plays a tremendous rôle in the growth and health of children. The effect upon it of the movies we have briefly examined. This, however, is not the only physical effect. There are others, which may partly explain the changes in sleep motility and doubtless play an important part in physical influence upon the young organism.

CHAPTER VI

OTHER PHYSICAL EFFECTS

A TRAINED nurse, whose function it was to open and put in operation children's play-rooms and first-aid rooms in a chain of motion picture theatres in a large midwestern city during a period of two and a half years, describes in a statement of her experience some of the curious movie habits of certain present-day mothers. Some mothers, she declares, would take extremely young children with them into the motion picture theatre. When a child became nervous or tired, the mother would send it to the play-room, where, in extreme cases, it remained for as long as nine hours at a stretch. She recalled cases of children left until one in the morning. That play-room became a sort of parking-place for the children of careless mothers bent upon shopping, bridge-playing, or other errands. The movie house, especially the neighborhood theatre, is frequently so used. However undesirable the lot of these children, they were still in better case than some of the infants compelled by their unintelligent mothers to remain in their seats and watch the unfolding of the screen play.

"A very bright, sensitive girl named Gloria," recounts Mrs. R., the trained nurse, *"three years old,* frequently got so wrought up and hysterical that it required an hour and a half to quiet her. Gloria's mother was trying to break her in to attend the movies. During 'The Phantom of the Opera' children would scream all over the theatre; many of them would dash out and mothers would leave the theatre with frightened and hysterical children clinging to them. And at times the children would vomit as a result of their emotional condition."

Mrs. R. was not only an experienced nurse, but the widow of a physician with whom she had read medicine. And as her husband had been a pediatrist, she was particularly experienced in the observation of children. In the first-aid rooms which she established in the theatres she instituted a system of clinical cards for use in recording history and disposition of cases precisely as in a doctor's office or in a hospital. The only additional feature was that they carried a record of the movie attendance of the patient in the particular theatres under her charge. Most of the children cared for in the playroom were under the age of twelve, the youngest, she remembers, being but seven days old. Adults, however, were also cared for in the hospital rooms, the oldest case in her recollection being that of a woman of eighty-seven.

Among the many pictures which frightened children and horrified adults, she remembers "The Phantom of the Opera" as conspicuous. It caused, she declares, eleven faintings and one miscarriage in a single day. Four of the eleven who fainted were men. The average was three or four faintings a day during the run of the picture. Ushers were especially drilled and prepared to deal with cases of fainting and hysterical collapse. "While adults," she adds, "would faint, children would become hysterical. I have had as many as three in my arms at

once and it required an hour or more to quiet them.
These were generally children six to eight years old."
But, as we have seen in the case of three-year-old Gloria,
many were younger. Their number of an evening in the
play-room, ranging in age from six to seven or eight
years, was sometimes as large as forty-five or fifty.

While the Lon Chaney pictures were often the most
horrifying to children, many others, including wild west
and war films, frequently had similar effects. She remembers "The Dawn Patrol" as causing children to
leap from their seats, jump up and down and scream
with excitement. Serial pictures, she observed, kept children wrought up from week to week while waiting for
the next instalment, the excitement growing intensely as
the serial proceeded. After seeing wild west films that
contained hold-ups and robberies, boys of from five to
twelve would come out into the play-room and excit-
edly re-enact the scenes.

This, admittedly, is a highly specialized, even a spectacular case, not included in the Payne Fund studies,
but it does indicate a certain condition—that many motion picture theatre owners are prepared for this kind of
thing, as attested by their preparation of such rooms and
nurseries; and, also, it illustrates the emotional effect
upon young children of horror pictures in their most
intense form.

But even if we grant this to be a concentrated collec-
tion of emotional disturbance of children in the experience of one theatre nurse, the fact remains that what is
here recorded in sharp outline appears at times in milder
shape in numerous cases scattered throughout motion
picture audiences. These effects, like those upon sleep,

are largely physical, and light upon one of them relating to eyesight, and notably to what is called visual flicker in watching motion pictures on the screen, was worked out in Dr. Renshaw's experiment.

Strictly speaking, as we know, there is no such thing as a really "moving" picture. It is a series of little "still" pictures that give the effect of motion upon the screen. Flying before the eye at the rate of twenty-four a second, these tiny photographs achieve the semblance of movement and life. The curiosity of the researcher was aroused: Did the forty-eight interruptions of light and shade between the twenty-four little pictures produce a result of flicker greater in children than in grown-ups? His experiment convinced him that there is very little change as between children and grown-ups. Children who suffer from loss of sleep doubtless feel the effects of flicker more and probably suffer more fatigue or eyestrain. But Dr. Renshaw's final conclusion is that children between the ages of six and nineteen are not any more affected by flicker than are adults—and that neither group is much troubled by it.

Under the International Educational Cinematographic Institute of Rome, however, an organ of the League of Nations, a wide inquiry was started to discover whether watching pictures on the screen brings visual fatigue. The experience of anyone accustomed to watching pictures in a projection-room is that eventually the eyes do get tired. Dr. Park Lewis, of Buffalo University, reporting to the Institute at Rome, declared that he found 28.62 per cent of the children he had examined, irrespective of age or sex, complained of visual fatigue after seeing a movie; 4.41 per cent experienced this fatigue only occasionally. Most of those who suffered from visual fatigue he found to be children under twelve. This fatigue, however, is not necessarily due to the rate at which motion pictures pass before the eye.

Without any reference to such experiences as those of Mrs. R., mentioned at the beginning of this chapter, of whose very existence they were probably unaware, psychologists by means of careful research set out to investigate emotional effects of pictures upon children. We have already seen the effects of movie going upon the sleep of the young. Further research, from other angles, records other physical facts that are related to the emotional reactions of children. The problem was, can such emotional conditions be studied in the sense of being measured and compared?

It appears that they can. An instrument—called a psycho-galvanometer—exists which can indirectly measure the intensity of emotion. It has existed for some time. So far back as 1888 Féré had already begun to investigate the electrical effects from the body in connection with emotion, and as early as 1907 Dr. Frederick Peterson, the New York neurologist, and the Swiss psychoanalyst, Dr. Jung, jointly published a paper upon the use of the psycho-galvanometer in recording emotion. The human body is known to offer resistance to certain small electrical currents. The degree of this resistance, owing to changes in the chemistry of the body, is raised or lowered under stress of various emotions. The electrical currents used are so faint they cannot be felt, but, in the presence of the varying degrees of emotion, the body's resistance causes the delicately poised needle of the galvanometer to oscillate and to give an index of the amount of that resistance. So, if you thrill at a feat of Douglas Fairbanks, or recoil from the horror of a Mr. Hyde or a Frankenstein monster, the deflection of the needle of the galvanometer promptly indicates the intensity of the emotion involved. Equipped with this instrument, Dr. Christian A. Ruckmick, professor of psychology in the University of Iowa, and his assistant, Dr. Wendell S. Dysinger, set out to make a series of observations upon the emotional effects on children of exposure to the movies.

Since, of course, the only way movie effects can actually be measured is in the presence of genuine movie scenes and performances, the experimenters were obliged to make arrangements with the theatres, so that the seats supplied for the children under observation should not be too obtrusively located. First of all, however, they had to measure the particular resistance to the small electrical current of the young bodies under observation without the distraction of a motion picture. That was the normal reading, or zero. It was the change in this reading under the stimulation of a movie that the scientists were after. This they recorded and photographed, registering at the same time the pulse rate of the subject. The work was done partly in the laboratory where pictures were shown and partly in the theatre, where the apparatus was installed. The children used in the experiment were supplied by the schools of Clinton, Davenport and Cedar Rapids, Iowa, and they ranged in age from six to eighteen. Normal children only were chosen. Where intelligence quotients were available, children with an I. Q. of 90 to 110 were preferred. Where I. Q.'s were not available, the school record was used in determining choice and thus a group a little higher than normal was assembled. In the theatre experiments sixty-one persons were used, nineteen of about nine years of age, twenty-four about sixteen, and eighteen about twenty-two, that is, young adults. Altogether some 5400 readings were taken, of which 2150 were in actual theatre conditions.

In the laboratory part of the experiment two fifteen-minute exposures were shown to each subject in a single day. In the theatre they saw pictures at their regular showings. The experimenter sat near the subject and communicated by means of a signal system with his assistant, who was in control of the recording apparatus some distance away. The method was simple enough, requiring no elaborate description. The subject of the experiment had the second and fourth fingers of his left hand washed with alcohol and wrapped above the first joint with adhesive tape. The tips of these fingers were placed in liquid electrodes, (a normal salt solution), the arm on the arm-rest. By chatting with the children he was observing, the experimenter quickly put them at ease so that they soon forgot they were part of an experiment in their eager anticipation of the picture. The heart apparatus was placed over the pulse of the right arm, and all that was asked of the young people was as little movement as possible. In the preliminary laboratory investigations the experimenters went over the pictures carefully so that only the most typical motion pictures were chosen, no unduly harrowing ones being included. In the theatres they took whatever pictures were shown at the time.

"We were careful," the experimenters explained, "to

establish normal conditions by getting into rapport with the subject, in order that his attention should be directed not at the simple apparatus, but at the picture itself. In most cases experimental conditions were forgotten by the subject and the enjoyment of the film was as genuine as under normal every-day circumstances. The results simply show to what degree excitement or emotion affect the different age groups."

With all these preparations, what did the experiment yield? It yielded this:

"Hop to It, Bell-hop" is a humorous picture with no great depths of plot and with very obvious situations. It does not specialize in emotional scenes. Yet, for all three groups, young children, adolescents and adults, the little instrument, the psycho-galvanometer, gave an indication of emotional excitement, or what the scientists called a deflection index. It showed, for example, that adolescents were twice as much excited as the adults. (Where the reading of the adults was 1.2, that for adolescents from sixteen to eighteen was 2.0.) The surprise, however, came with the youngest group, children between six and eleven. These registered a reading of 3.6, or precisely three times as much as adults!

What this means is, that the intensity of emotion of the youngest children viewing a motion picture is so far greater than that of adults, that now we can understand somewhat more clearly why certain pictures register so intensively on their memories. This is undoubtedly a factor in explaining Dr. Holaday's results and an explanation of why their sleep restlessness increases, as discovered by Drs. Renshaw, Miller and Marquis. Now, too, we can see why that restlessness extends into the fourth or fifth nights. The scientists did not attempt to correlate those various studies, but to us the correlation emerges clearly enough. The seeing of a motion picture is for young children a powerful emotional experience that affects their young brains and nerves with almost the force of an electric charge. Here, too, as in the sleep motility, we see that each child has his individual peculiarities. But that virtually none remains unaffected and all are powerfully affected by what they see on the screen, is a fact not only of scientific importance, but of the highest hygienic significance.

Among the older children, the thirteen to fifteen group, some were found to give a zero reading in the "danger" pictures. On the other hand, certain ones are emotionally stirred to such an extent that in several instances were recorded readings of 10.0, or eight times the emotional reaction of the average adult! What that would do to the sleep of these children for some nights to come may be easily conjectured. And interestingly enough, boys seem to show a somewhat more vivid response than girls, which mothers of daughters and sons will recognize as confirming their usual judgment. Their masculine offspring may be in reality more excitable than the feminine.

And let it be repeated that the pictures shown to the children in the Ruckmick experiments were not especially selected for thrill, terror or anguish. They included such ordinary specimens as "Hop to It, Bell-hop," "The Feast of Ishtar," "The Iron Mule," "Charlie Chan's Chance," "The Yellow Ticket," "The Road to Singapore" and "His Woman." Among all these "The Yellow Ticket" alone was at all outstanding in thrill and excitement.

Yet, it certainly did not compare for harrowing visions with such highly intense movies as "The Phantom of the Opera," "Dr. Jekyll and Mr. Hyde," "The Lost World" or "Frankenstein."

We have already seen, in the statement of the theatre nurse, some of the extreme effects of such pictures on young children in the ordinary course of her observation. Measurements of Dr. Ruckmick and Dr. Dysinger indicate what results might have been obtainable had they exposed children to the bloodcurdling scenes of such pictures as "The Phantom of the Opera" or "Frankenstein." Later, as we shall see, some young people were found to shudder even at the memory of what films of that type had done to them in childhood. For years, a number of high-school and college students confess, they grew chill at the very thought of those films and fearfully avoided dark places. "I went home and could not sleep that night and many nights," wrote one high-school girl for Dr. Blumer. "I would wake up from my sleep and scream for fright." Scarcely surprising, this, when Dr. Ruckmick's instrument indicated the results it did in face of such commonplace pictures as "Hop to It, Bell-hop" and "Charlie Chan's Chance."

The experimenters grouped their findings in a variety of ways. In scenes of danger and conflict, as we have seen, nine-year-old children are more powerfully affected emotionally than are their parents or their older brothers and sisters—more than any other age group in the entire range. Next to them comes the sixteen-year-old group. Apparently the effect of "danger" pictures decreases with the maturity of children; but for young children attending the movies is a very exciting affair.

Drs. Ruckmick and Dysinger also studied the effects of love scenes and suggestive or erotic incidents upon the emotions of children. When showing "The Feast of Ishtar," a picture containing much oriental suggestiveness, the subjects were divided, as in the "danger pictures," into nine-year-old, sixteen-year-old and adult groups. Here it was found that the younger children were least affected, although the figures denoting effects show as large as those for adults. The investigators felt, however, that owing to the difficulty of separating the danger elements entirely from all the erotic scenes, the figures for the young children should be scaled downward. It was clearly obvious that the sixteen-year olds were the most widely and powerfully affected by those erotic scenes. In fact none of this group failed to be affected, and their reactions were stronger than those of either the younger children or the adults. The adults were affected only about one-half as much.

Particularly significant, as emerged upon analysis of the data, is the presence of individual differences. Some nine-year olds were affected by the erotic scenes while some thirteen-year olds were not. Some adults were less responsive than others. The effects upon children, in other words, is not uniform. In the earlier years a few are affected and most are not. As they approach fifteen to seventeen years the number of those affected grows. In that period, it is apparent, all are affected. In the eighteen-year group the amount of excitation again varies with the individuals and, in general falls from the level of the sixteen-year olds, but does not disappear up to the limit of the ages studied. As between boys and girls there was no clear difference in the response to love scenes.

Adults, as we should expect, are the least disturbed of all by what they see on the screen. To most of them it is "only a picture." The adult's mature realistic point of view, what has been called the "adult discount," takes into consideration the acting, the direction, the characterization in a picture. In short, it is critical. But it is the absence of criticism, the wide-eyed acceptance of the screen as a transcript of life which makes seeing a movie so thrilling and soul-stirring an experience to the young.

2

Just as in the talkie picture and dialogue synchronize, so Dr. Ruckmick's apparatus photographed the little chart made by the subject's heartbeat while the emotional disturbance was being recorded by the galvanometer. The normal heartbeat of people varies slightly, but generally it is somewhere between 70 and 80. The experimenters, we must remember, were not in a position to expose the children to abnormally harrowing pictures. The pictures used, as has been pointed out, were of the most ordinary variety. Nevertheless, even in these the pulse rate of the children watching them ran up from a normal of 75 or 80 to 125 and 140. A sixteen-year-old boy, whose normal beat is 80 per minute, while watching a stirring prison scene in "The Yellow Ticket," ran up to 154, or practically double his normal pulse. To what height the pulse might have risen with such pictures as "The Bat," or "Frankenstein," we cannot say.

One investigator outside the group conducting the Payne Fund research, Dr. T. B. Homan, of Kansas City, independently made a study to determine the results of the emotional reaction of an adult to the average motion picture. We shall not here enter into the entire scope of his experiment, but will present an unusually striking case which he describes, to supplement the findings of Ruckmick and Dysinger.

The young woman selected by Dr. Homan for experimental purposes was duly tested as to heart action and brain reaction. She was twenty-two years old. "She seemed," he explains, "to be perfectly normal physically and mentally, interested in life about her but never going into the extreme emotional stage in either her joy, sorrow, disappointment or any of the emotions." Comfortably seated in the theatre, she had upon her arm a sphygmomanometer, that is, a mechanism measuring the heart action.

The observations extended over a considerable time and various results were brought to light. It was found, for instance, that in a variety of cases of fear induced in the subject of the experiment, the sphygmomanometer would hesitate before changing its beat. In case the emotion was joy, however, there would be no hesitation but the mechanism would accelerate rapidly. Anxiety was a swift and powerful accelerator of the heartbeat. In tense moments of the picture viewed rising of the pulse from 80 to 140 was quite common. The remarkable feature of the experiment, however, was the curve precipitated by the film entitled "The Mysterious Dr. Fu Manchu." All readings were high, many of them over 150, several of 168 and one of 180. One scene close to the end of the picture, when the heroine begs for mercy from the sinister Chinese doctor, shot up the young woman's heartbeat to 192, or nearly two and a half times the normal rate! It now becomes apparent that the statements of the theatre nurse as regards faintings and hysterics before certain pictures are probably not exaggerated.

Dr. Homan found that "a picture of extreme emotional content, whether it be tragedy or fear, leaves a physical imprint upon the human being lasting as long as seventy hours!" Seventy hours—three days to recover normal composure! Small wonder that Drs. Renshaw, Miller and Marquis discovered the effects upon children's sleep to linger on in some cases for nearly a week after seeing a movie. It becomes obvious, too, why, as Drs. Ruckmick and Dysinger declare, "so-called nervously, neurotically and hysterically inclined children should not be over-stimulated emotionally, especially during adolescence," as they are likely to be by indiscriminate, ill-advised or too frequent movie going.

Too frequent stimulation of children may be interpreted as over-stimulation. As Drs. Ruckmick and Dysinger put it: "They are sitting quiet; there is no chance to express the emotion in activity: yet they are intensely stimulated. Such a situation is bad for health, represents a deplorable mental hygienic situation and might easily contribute to the habits which are popularly called 'nervousness' in children. Where the boy or girl has a chance to work off emotions in the open, in exercise or play, it is splendid. Such excitement in a darkened theatre is by no means splendid."

And since the concept of the "nervous child" is popular rather than scientific, the writer turned to an authority outside the Payne Fund survey, Dr. Frederick Peterson, a noted neurologist, as to how injurious he considers scenes of horror and tense excitement in the movies.

"If sufficiently strong," was the reply, "they have an

effect very similar to shell-shock, such as soldiers received in war. A healthy child seeing a picture once in a while will suffer no harm. But repeating the stimulation often amounts to emotional debauch. Stimulation, when often repeated, is cumulative. Scenes causing terror and fright are sowing the seeds in the system for future neuroses and psychoses—nervous disorders."

CHAPTER VII

HORROR AND FRIGHT PICTURES

How intense may be the emotion bottled up in children before the screen and seeking an outlet is illustrated by many cases cited by Professor Herbert Blumer of the University of Chicago. Chiefly, he finds, it is in scenes of suspense and horror that the intensity of emotion and anguish, when it comes to the surface, shows itself in the clutching of seats, wringing of caps and handkerchiefs, biting of lips and fingernails and the utterance of groans. It is where the child can see no hope of escape from danger for his favorites that agony consumes and terror ravages his nerves.

"Children," suggests Professor Blumer, "have been subjected to needless torture by the failure to recognize this simple point in constructing the plots and scenes of thrillers." A scenario writer, of course, would have a very definite retort to this suggestion. But Professor Blumer is thinking in terms of children rather than in that of scenario technique.

The whole problem of terror and excruciating elements in pictures has been conspicuously ignored by producers and censors alike. That this is true, we can hardly fail to see from some of the evidence presented in this chapter. Even in the comparatively innocuous films used in the Ruckmick-Dysinger experiments, the intensity of

emotion of young children, three times that of the average adult, is a sufficiently telling indication.

"So intense is the response of some youth," observed
the psychologists, "that the galvanometric deflection ran
off the scale." They simply mean to convey that the
effect on the boy was exceptionally sharp.

That a boy in that case leaves the movie he has been
seeing in a "nervous state" is simply a bald under-
statement. What such results may do to the sleep of the
young we have already seen. What they can do to the
mental states we shall presently see, at least in part. It
becomes irresistible to cite a case among a group of
problem boys studied in a congested area of New York
City under the direction of Dr. Thrasher, of New York
University, author of "The Gang." A nervous boy, emotionally unstable, recounts his movie experience:

"Sometimes I go to shows and see mystery pictures
and after, at night, I dream about them. . . . They
come nearer and nearer and after I feel like they are on
top of me, I holler . . . My mother and father get up
and say, 'What's the matter, what's the matter?' "

"Do you ever have the same dream over and over?"

"Yeah, the dreams about the man . . . He comes to
sleep next to me . . ."

"Do you ever see him in the daytime?"

"Yeah, sometimes in the yard . . . He runs after me."

His mother tells him it is his imagination and he admits it. "But," he declares, "he looks like a real man."

No wonder, as Ruckmick and Dysinger put it, "such
excitement in the quiet darkened theatre is by no means
splendid." Upon this point all the authorities seem to
agree.

"Were you ever frightened or horrified by any motion picture or scene in any motion picture?"

Professor Blumer asked this question of 237 school children in the fourth to the seventh grades. Ninety-three per cent of them readily answered "Yes!" Only seven per cent answered in the negative. In 458 high-school autobiographies which he secured, sixty-one per cent of these adolescents recorded to what extent they had at various times been terrified by movie scenes. So large a percentage, clearly is not likely to be wholly made up of nervous or unstable children. The sleep disturbance measured by Dr. Renshaw, the high psycho-galvanometric index of emotion and the rapid pulse so often found by Ruckmick and Dysinger, and also by Dr. Homan—these are the phenomena that interpret themselves in the answers and autobiographies of the young people so carefully investigated by Blumer and Hauser. No effect upon the brain and nerve cells is, as we know, in strict scientific literalness, ever wholly wiped out.

In the smaller towns, as these lines are being written, there is still current a certain picture entitled "Sky-Scraper Souls." Among the spectators in one of these theatres there is a four-year-old child. His sophistication still naturally falls short of the point of knowing that the body of a girl hurtling down twenty stories from an office building to the pavement below is no girl at all, but a skillfully prepared dummy. To his childish eyes a living, breathing human being, as human as his mother or sister, has hurled itself to a violent death. From his little heart and throat issues an eldritch shriek of terror.

The adult spectators frown and stir uneasily in their seats. They are made far more uncomfortable by that infant's scream of agony than by the falling of the girl. They, in their adult wisdom, know that the picture is illusion and the falling girl a bundle of stuffed clothes. To the child the scene is as real as life, as real as death. What business, everyone feels, has that child to be there at all? He has none, for in his case a crime has been committed—a serious wound inflicted upon a little child's consciousness.

Some of the autobiographies and case histories collected by Professor Blumer and Mr. Hauser hark back to experiences as vivid and to ages as immature as that child's when they suffered those experiences. A nineteen-year-old girl, a sophomore in college and by now well able to put her early impressions in writing, contributes this memory:

"I don't even remember where I saw my first movie, but it was in some very small theatre in Englewood (Chicago). I don't know who the heroine was, but I do remember that at the most dramatic part she was bound, laid on a pile of sticks and burned. At this point I became hysterical and had to be taken from the theatre. I never knew if the unfortunate girl was rescued or burned to death but I never forgot the smoke and flames curling around her slender body. This little episode characterizes to a great extent my reactions to my early movies. I never could be convinced that the actors were not really suffering the horrible tortures depicted in many films and my sympathy knew no bounds."

There, again, we see the excrutiatingly realistic attitude of the child toward the picture. To the adult it may be good art or bad, it may be clever mechanism, good photography, effective direction, successful or unsuccessful story telling, a good movie, or hokum and trash. To the young child it is reality itself—the diffuse, chaotic reality of every-day life, intensely concentrated within the limited area of the screen. And if a child, as we know, can identify itself with an animal, or even a plant, and commune with these subhuman creations as though they were friends and brothers, how much more closely is it apt to identify itself with the screen presentments of living, active and speaking human beings!

The "adult discount," a phrase first used, so far as we know, by the investigators in this survey, may yet have a whole literature growing up about it, so important is the effect it expresses and the need it represents in safe-guarding children against exposure to these traumatic shocks from fright pictures to the young nerves, of which the entire movie research is so eloquent.

To a twenty-year-old college girl the memory of horror from such a film is still so present that she can describe with vividness her childhood impression of "a horrible hairy ape with a habit of breaking into people's houses," which came in through a window and ran off with the heroine. "After seeing this picture, I was afraid to go into a dark room at night because an ape might be just coming in through a window and carry me off. I was a nervous child, anyway," she continues, "and in the course of an exciting movie like this I would bite the fingernails on both hands until my fingers would bleed." Nervous children, as we have already seen, and shall have occasion to see further, need special attention from their elders with regard to pictures.

Some recall such experiences as, "I had horrible night-mares"; "I was horror-stricken—for several nights I had terrible dreams about that awful Chinaman"; "my screams when a Negro slave cowered before his master and the whip touched his back, made it necessary for me to be taken home." That is doubtless one of the factors in the findings of the Renshaw experiments upon sleep disturbance, and is closely related to the flying heart and accelerated pulse and sharp emotional reactions in the Ruckmick-Dysinger experiments. "A deplorable mental hygienic situation" was the descriptive phrase used by those investigators. In plainer language, does that not mean simply an outrage upon young nerves and brains? A college girl telling her experience of one of the ape pictures, after seeing which she was obliged to sleep with her mother, declares: "I do not believe I cried but I became speechless, powerless, rigid, staring wide-eyed into the dark, and the fear did not leave me for several days."

Such pictures as "The Phantom of the Opera," "Dr. Jekyll and Mr. Hyde," "The Gorilla," "The Cat Creeps," "The Lost World," and doubtless many of that variety of which we have no record, seem to be responsible for more fright caused to children than many times their number of ordinary pictures. As a fourteen-year-old school-girl puts it: "I was so frightened by 'The Phantom of the Opera' I could not scream . . . I could not move for two or three minutes . . . it was a mysterious sensation, and my blood became cooler." Another girl declares that she can never forget the chill of terror and that she still shudders at the thought of the "Phantom," and a college boy admits that it took him two or three years to get over the fear of dark places inspired by "Dr. Jekyll and Mr. Hyde." Dr. Whitley similarly, in the study under Professor Thrasher, found boys who

dream of the horror pictures they have seen and that
certain motion pictures "do aid and abet emotional instability." All of which would tend to support Dr. Peterson's opinion that shock of this character is virtually the
same as shell-shock. Many boys and girls confessed to
expressing their emotions before danger pictures not only
by biting their finger-nails, twisting their caps, hiding
their eyes, as we have already seen, but by jumping out
of their seats, getting under the seat, running home,
being terrified by shadows, avoiding dark streets. One
boy was afraid, after a particularly gruesome picture,
that a trap-door would open in the pavement and swal-
low him. A girl declared with positiveness that the sidewalk rose up behind her as she hurried home. Approximately one-third of the children in one class examined by Dr. Blumer, "mention having had bad dreams
following upon their experiences, including shock, night-
mares, keeping one's head under the blankets, asking to
sleep with mother or father, crying out in sleep and
falling out of bed."

Many parents even today laugh at such childish fears
and alarms! The elders reassure themselves, these things
will pass quickly. But do they? In many cases, doubtless, they do. There is evidence, however, that some of
these shocks of fright and terror abide for a long time,
and in some cases, it may be, permanently, precisely as
Dr. Peterson suggests. Many young people testify that
some of these early frights, seared upon their childish
brains and nerves by certain harrowing scenes in the
movies, remain with them and had not left them at the
time they were questioned. A college student, recalling
a picture she had seen in childhood in which a mad-

woman in an insane asylum tried to stab the heroine, declares that to this day she has a horror of crazy people. A Negro high-school girl relates that as a result of seeing a picture called "Earthbound," her nerves "became shattered" with an effect she had not been able to cast off. A college sophomore of nineteen, as we have already seen, needed years to get over his fear of the dark after seeing "Dr. Jekyll and Mr. Hyde," and one young woman of twenty was so horrified by a showing of Dante's "Inferno" that for a number of years no threat or cajolery could induce her to enter a movie theatre.

The resiliency of childhood fortunately makes most of these frights and terrors seem of but temporary duration, but many of them may become fixed and abiding. The sensitiveness of the individual child is naturally a factor in the results. Certain fright pictures, as has been indicated, become so many chambers of horrors for young spectators, and the fact that many young persons will eagerly go to "creepy" or "spooky" pictures by no means alters the results. Dr. Blumer tells us that out of one class of forty-four children, thirty-eight gave instances of being frightened, yet thirty-one of these young worshipers of gooseflesh declared that they liked to be frightened.

Dr. Blumer is the only investigator in the research who sought facts pro and con in the matter of children being frightened by pictures. In his samplings he found not only that children declared they had been frightened, but that the fright persisted for days or much longer periods. On the other hand, he found some who say they were not frightened, or that the fright was short-lived. Some, as we have seen, disconcertingly declared that they like being frightened by certain pictures. Here, obviously, is a difficulty. To what extent can we trust their liking as an allowable indulgence? In scanning the findings and studies the writer can only conclude that once again it is upon the parents that falls the obligation of carefully studying their children for tendencies to over-stimulation and of devising a rigid regimen as to the types of motion pictures they may be allowed to attend.

2

"The very effort," observe Blumer and Hauser, returning to the subject of fright, "taken by the child or youth to explain to himself that what he saw was only a picture and that it is foolish for him to feel afraid, points to the condition of *emotional possession.*

"When impulses which are ordinarily restrained are strongly stimulated, a person under this heightened emotional state at times suffers some loss of ordinary control over his feelings, his thoughts, and his actions. The individual identifies himself so thoroughly with the plot or loses himself so much in the picture that he is carried away from his usual trend of conduct. His mind becomes fixed upon certain imagery, and impulses usually latent or kept under restraint gain expression, or seriously threaten to gain expression. This emotional condition may get such a strong grip upon the individual that even his efforts to rid himself of it by reasoning with himself may prove of little avail." That is what Professor Blumer means by emotional possession. Children are more likely to be subject to it than adults, but it is not confined to any particular age group. Some cases of this kind of possession, under the impact of shock to the nerves by certain scenes of terror and anguish, we have already seen. There will be instances of others.

Some of the researchers, it will be recalled, point to the "adult discount" as a salutary method of mitigating at least a part of the shock to the young mind in face of horrifying pictures. The reason is that an adult soothing and reassuring a child after a vivid impact of a terrifying scene is not the same as a frightened child telling himself that it is "only a picture." The child's own effort is but a whistling in the dark to keep his courage up. The adult's reassurance is not only comforting, but steadying. A twenty-year-old girl, for instance, tells of a certain picture which ended sadly and which nearly broke her heart as a child, so unused was she to an unhappy ending in a film:

"Finally I went to my mother and told her all about it. She did not laugh. I often wonder why. She talked to me for a long time and told me I must not take movies too seriously. They only show a few experiences of lives of imaginary people both pleasant and unpleasant. She told me I could pity people who must live as some do who were represented in the movies, and at the same time by contrast appreciate my own opportunities." That was a sensible mother.

A young man, similarly grateful for parental enlightenment, recalls that "rather than see me perturbed by these post-movie moods, they impressed upon me the untruth and unreality of the movie and thus corrected my former impressions. This change took place at the age of ten." Otherwise, the dread effects may linger for a long time, as they are found to have done in many instances. A college girl presents a circumstantial account of one of these:

"About four years ago (I was then fifteen) I saw 'The Lost World'—a movie portraying the prehistoric animals which were supposed to have been rediscovered still living in the African jungles. An American sportsman and his wife believed they could still find dinosaurs of enormous size. . . . We see them hunting and searching everywhere for this great reptile at one time seen by a native. Tracks are discovered and finally they come upon the dinosaur which is about seventy feet long, with an ugly scaly body, and a nauseous slimy neck upon which is perched a little wriggling pointed head. . . . I had to cover my eyes to prevent dizziness. As the story goes the hunters succeed in trapping the beast and getting him crated for the homeward journey. . . . A special raft-like ship was built and the trip goes well until about ten miles from port. Then the dinosaur succeeds in breaking loose and plunges into the sea. He hits the bridge and breaks it to pieces; upon reaching the port he smashes things right and left with his huge tail, tears upon the city, waves down office buildings, crushing and eating people on the street. A panic follows; people get down on their knees to pray; everyone thinks the world is coming to an end. I think the picture ends with the dinosaur's plunging into the ocean never to be found again, and leaving the city in a turmoil about its return. 'The Lost World' was probably the most terrifying picture I ever saw, and it certainly left me with a bad imprint for a few days. After I got home I knew that I could not sleep; therefore I sat in the living-room and decided to read a book; only the reading lamp was burning and I still insist that I saw all sorts of huge strange shadows on the wall. Every little noise made me jump. Finally I dozed off and suddenly began to kick and struggle as if I were trying to get away from being crushed; my entire night was spent in that manner and the next day I could not concentrate on my work at school. I knew perfectly well that it was all imagination, but try as I might I could not get the picture out of my mind. Even now as I write about it (after four years!) I shudder and feel the tension of my nerves."

The important point in this illustration is the length of time the fright suffered by the girl remained in her consciousness. After four years she still experienced some of that loss of control and shuddered at the thought of the picture. That is a marked phase of what Professor Blumer calls emotional possession.

This deep impress of emotion is not, however, confined to fear alone. Pathos and sorrow and sentiment are other emotions that may flood the young spectators, or even the older, and cause them to weep unrestrainedly. Professor Blumer does not bring up the point as to whether such catharsis is good or bad for a child. In the opinion of the writer such emotional catharsis was never meant for children, especially very young children. In any case, out of 458 high-school autobiographies, nearly three hundred students, sixty-four per cent, describe experiences of irresistible weeping at such pictures as "The Singing Fool," "Beau Geste," "Over the Hill" and "Coquette." The effect of these sentimental pictures is transient compared with the grisly shapes of fear that linger in the young mind after viewing scenes of the gruesome and the terrifying. Now and then, fortunately, a picture that moves the young spectator to sorrow and pity is accompanied by a resolution "to be good," as, for instance, "Over the Hill," a story of filial neglect of an old mother. Such emotionally pitched films sometimes have the effect of what is ordinarily understood as religious conversion, with effects more or less abiding.

"I resolved never to leave my family to such an old age," declares a girl after having seen "The Old Nest." Another, speaking of "Over the Hill," recalled:

"I saw it with my mother, and during the picture I cried profusely and promised mother that Mrs. Carr's fate would never be her own as long as I was alive to do my share. I don't believe the effects of that picture will ever wear off."

Now, however crude the art or the means inducing these resolutions "to be good," however remote from the Greek dramatic ideal of catharsis, or the purging of the emotions, however inappropriate even this type of purging may be for the younger children, few people will be disposed to quarrel with it. It is for parents to decide whether or not they desire to have their children so affected. Certainly, these sentimental pictures are not in the category of crime and sex which, as Dr. Dale showed us, figure so largely in the production programs.

But of the undesirability of exposing the young promiscuously to scenes of fright and terror and raw anguish, as in the case of many motion pictures here mentioned, there can be no doubt. We have seen to what extent the physical organism is affected by such pictures in the careful observations of investigators with measuring instruments. We have seen in a flood of testimony, of which only a small portion is here presented, the interpretation of some of these experimental laboratory data in terms of memories and reminiscences on the part of the young people themselves. We know, too, that psycho-analysis abounds in cases of psychoses and neuroses traceable to fear and traumatic shocks in early childhood. Lastly, we have seen the virtual necessity of explaining harrowing and ravaging scenes, of minimizing terrifying effects by pointing out that the content of most films is remote from life, inartistically contrived, with only a distant semblance to reality. In view of all this, it would seem we have sufficient data to show us the necessity for guidance both in the choice of movies for our young and in our decisions as to whether or not to expose them to any and all motion pictures at haphazard. To Dr. Thrasher the question somewhat resembles the use of alcoholic beverages. They certainly are not meant for all, or even for most children.

Adult guidance, in short, the "adult discount" becomes virtually imperative. Dr. Ruckmick, who has continued his experiments, found that children "were largely interested in and moved by the scene of conflict or of danger or of love rather than by the picture as a whole. We might almost state this," he adds, "as an inverse relationship. The younger the children the more they appreciated and emotionally responded to the separate items in the film, and the less they appreciated or even assimilated the continuity of the story, to say nothing of the moral or ultimate outcome of the picture. This outstanding fact is becoming even more evident in the work which we are doing now with abnormal patients."

In a picture of horror and fright the total effect may be almost ludicrous, or at least comic, and yet a child cannot see that effect, but can only react to the separate scenes of horror and of fright, as of an antedeluvian monster, or a giant ape. Similarly, in the case of sex and crime pictures it is the isolated scenes and episodes that rivet the attention and engage the emotions. "Abstract ideas," observe Ruckmick and Dysinger, "and general concepts begin to accumulate only as his experience grows and the power of generalization itself develops. Consequently, we have no right to expect that very young children, or even adolescents, will make the same synthesis of a motion picture that the adult does."

He concludes: "But a more serious consequence of this psychological fact is that many of the claims of the motion picture industry by the same token fall to the ground when these pictures are viewed by very young children, early adolescents, and sometimes during the late adolescent years. An exciting robbery, an ecstatic love scene, the behavior of a drunkard, and the like, cannot be toned down by the moral situation at the end of the picture when the episode is justified in terms of the hand of the law or the retribution of an outraged Providence. It is not altogether clear, therefore, that the claim made in terms of a mature mind can hold for the growing mind. The ultimate outcome of the story, the moral that honesty is the best policy, the assumption that the way of the sinner is hard, are adult generalizations and belong to what we have called 'the adult discount.' Even if the picture clearly depicts this outcome it very seldom strikes the attention of the younger generation with anything like the force that it does the adult mind."

In the same way, doubtless, the picture of a prehistoric monster smashing a city, or a fifty-foot ape carrying a woman to the top of a skyscraper, may be a thrilling, even a delightful, fantasy to the adult. To the child or early adolescent it may be a harrowing experience of reality.

The immense number of hours thus spent in a darkened theatre, often with no ventilation at all, when they might be engaged in healthful outdoor play, cannot, aside from all other considerations, but have an effect upon the young bodies and nerves. In outdoor play they are active. In the movie theatre they are merely instruments, all too immature, for the emotions of the screen characters and scenes to play upon. The inpouring of emotion has no vent except in subsequent physical behavior and conduct patterns. As Dr. Peterson put it, "On the playing field or play-ground stimulation is healthy exercise and has a different physiological foundation. There is an outlet for emotional tension. In the theatre it is all suppressed."

Without pretensions to exhaustiveness, the research upon which these pages are based has brought together more data bearing upon health and physical effects of children and adolescents in connection with the movies than has ever before been available. They should prove a powerful factor in shaping the attitudes and policies of parents and the public generally as regards their choice, selection and regimen touching motion pictures. The effects on conduct, for which even more data are available, will be studied in subsequent chapters.

CHAPTER VIII

"UNMARKED SLATES"

"This industry must have toward that sacred thing, the mind of a child, toward that clean virgin thing, the unmarked slate, the same responsibility, the same care about the impressions made upon it that the best clergyman or the most inspired teacher of youth would have."

Surely, a lofty ideal for motion pictures!

Those words were uttered before the Los Angeles Chamber of Commerce by the head of the Motion Picture Producers and Distributors, Inc., Mr. Will H. Hays.

Now, the present writer is willing to believe that Mr. Hays meant what he said at the time he said it. Slates, however, if we are to use Mr. Hays' figure, sooner or later get written upon. Just what it is that is written, how it is written, and whether it can ever be wiped off —these are of the agitating questions upon which data can be found in the Payne Fund investigation.

We have already been told, in the impressive figures of Dr. Dale, that of the national weekly audience thirty-seven per cent is made up of minors,—28,000,000 of them, of whom 11,000,000 are thirteen years of age or younger—very much one would say, in the category of unmarked slates. The writing upon them, judging from Dr. Dale's analysis of 1500 motion pictures, appears sufficiently legible, but not wholly edifying. To the extent of seventy per cent and over, the slates retain what is written upon them for a considerable time and in many cases, doubtless, permanently. But there is more to it than merely these facts.

During the War, mature readers will remember, motion pictures were in use by virtually all belligerents as an instrument of propaganda. That is to say, it was recognized that motion pictures could be so used as to change the opinions and sympathies of people with regard to any desired topic. If that is true—and it was found to be true—the motion picture becomes an instrument so potent as to be in effect a weapon.

If a motion picture can change sympathies and attitudes and affect conduct, it becomes of enormous importance as a factor in our education, in our standards, in all the social fabric of our lives. So important does it become, that if it did not exist, we should incontinently desire to invent it; and so significant that if it falls short of the best and highest quality attainable, the entire country should feel instantly moved to eradicate whatever defects it carries, in view of its influence upon the young, and to make it, as nearly as human agency can, perfect.

The investigators concerned in the Payne Fund research set about finding some reliable data indicating to what extent motion pictures can and do affect mental attitudes. Two types of study were carried out: one, by Professor L. L. Thurstone and Miss Ruth C. Peterson, of the University of Chicago, sought to measure changes in the attitudes of groups of children toward certain social values after those children had viewed a selected motion picture. Drs. May and Shuttleworth of Yale University aimed to study the differences between children who attended the movies very frequently and those who never attended. So small, however, was the number of those who never attended that the investigators were compelled to contract their study, and to compare "movie" children, who attended on the average 2.8 times a week, with "non-movie" children, who attended less than once a week. They desired to observe whether or not there were any characteristic differences between the groups which could be attributed to movie influence.

Now, inter-racial contacts are exceedingly fruitful of prejudice. Various cases cited in the present volume indicate the marked, generally unreasoning, prejudices that exist among children (and others) against the Chinese, the Negroes, the Indians. Dr. Herbert Blumer, of the University of Chicago mentions a number of such cases, and the survey made under direction of Professor Frederick M. Thrasher, of New York University, in a congested area of New York, finds that movies "serve as a means of strengthening certain racial prejudices." "In my childhood," declares one boy, "the movies developed in me a prejudice against Chinese, Mexicans and Indians, as they were usually all 'bad men'."

The Thurstone-Peterson survey began by reviewing between six and eight hundred films in order to find material suitable for their experiment. Then, having found their material, they proceeded to develop their technique, "an instrument for measuring attitudes," which cannot here be dwelt upon, and to find communities where experimental groups of grade-school children, high-school students, and, in one experiment college students, were available under the best possible conditions for their particular study.

The prejudice against the Chinese is of common and frequent occurrence among American school children. When the investigators tested 182 children in the Geneva (Illinois) High School for their attitude toward Chinese, they found only small percentages endorsing such statements as "I consider it a privilege to associate with Chinese people," and a larger percentage subscribing to opinions such as, "I hate the Chinese"; "the Chinese are aptly described by the term 'yellow devils';" "I dislike the Chinese more every time I see one." Those children, briefly, showed themselves to be what can only be described as anti-Chinese.

Tickets were then distributed and a week later the children were given the opportunity of seeing the regular evening performance of "Son of the Gods." "Son of the Gods" is a film telling the story of Sam Lee, who was brought up by an admirable Chinese, one Lee Yeng, whom Sam believed to be his father. Sam Lee is a fine attractive person whom people generally like and admire. But being Chinese, Sam is naturally left outside the social life of the community. The presentation of Chinese life in the picture is friendly and the Chinese characters are shown as admirable people.

On the following morning after seeing this picture the children were again tested for their attitude toward Chinese. The shift in this attitude was striking. The curve dropped low at the "unfavorable" end and rose high at the "favorable." "The conclusion that the film 'Son of the Gods' made the children more favorable toward the Chinese," declare the investigators, "is undoubtedly justified."

Here then is a clear concrete case not only that movies can affect children for good, depending upon their content, but that quite definitely they have a propaganda value and can alter children's mental attitudes. Five months later, much of the gain in friendliness still persisted. More than. that, in this particular instance the experimenters were able to test the children again after an interval of nineteen months after the picture had been shown. Still the favorable effect, that is, a better attitude toward the Chinese, was present in the mind of these children!

Let us bear this case in mind when we think of the power and influence of motion pictures.

The investigators found in Illinois a town with a population of 5700 people which had no Negroes. According to the superintendent of schools, very few children in Crystal Lake, the town fixed upon, had ever known or even seen Negroes. Upon the subject of prejudice, therefore, for or against the Negro, here obviously were some slates from which much could be learned.

Theoretically, we fear most what we know least about. Like many theories, however, this one is not always supported by facts. A test administered to a group of 434 Crystal Lake children, from grades six to twelve, that is, including seniors of the high school, showed a pronounced liberality toward the Negro race. Only a very small proportion of the group betrayed prejudice by agreeing with such statements in the test as "The white race must be kept pure at all costs, even if the

Negroes have to be killed off." Or, "The Negro should be considered· in the lowest class among human beings." On the contrary, they gave large endorsement to propositions such as this: "I believe that the Negro deserves the same social privileges as the white man;" or, "by nature the Negro and white man are equal."

Such were the slates. The next step was to write upon them. Not so long ago "The Birth of a Nation," a picture considered as a powerful example of anti-Negro propaganda, was revived with sound. The test on general attitude toward Negroes having been administered to the children, it was decided to show them that film, the "Birth of a Nation," which is anti-Negro. Here was a way of writing upon virgin and unmarked slates with the assurance of being able to read scientifically what was written thereon.

The day after the showing of the picture the children were once again tested on their attitude toward the Negro race. One wishes the reader could see the curve of graphs plotted by the psychologists on the before and after readings. If you compare the "before" readings to a peak, then the "after" readings sink almost to a crater. Where before the picture had been seen the favorable attitude curve rose to a height of, say, nearly 200 units, it dropped after "The Birth of a Nation" had been seen to well under 100, the unfavorable attitude rising correspondingly. The unmarked slates, in other words, now bear definite record of a shift toward anti-Negro prejudice. After five months, when the test was again administered without a further showing of the picture, simply upon the recollection of the past, the effect of prejudice against the Negro still remained.

Still sixty-two per cent of the prejudice found the day
after seeing the adverse film was present in these young
minds. Even after eight months, the effect was still
definitely there. Prejudice against the Negro had been
quite clearly increased in these children's minds by the
movie, "The Birth of a Nation." The virgin unmarked
slates had been all but indelibly written upon with a
pencil of peculiar force. The motion picture, which can
be a tremendous power for good, can as obviously be a
powerful force for evil, depending upon its content and
use.

2

Typical as were the experiments with "Son of the
Gods" and "The Birth of a Nation," they were, of
course, not isolated cases, but merely two in a pro-
longed research.

Genoa, Illinois, for instance, has a population of only
twelve hundred. It is not much disturbed, clearly, by
the cross-currents of metropolitan life. To its 133 junior
and senior high-school children was shown a picture entitled "Four Sons." This picture is friendly and favorable to the Germans and it also carries implicitly within
its plot some anti-war propaganda. The normal attitude
of the children toward the Germans having been previ-
ously established, they were all invited to see the film,
"Four Sons."

The psychologists constructed two ladder-like graphs
illustrating the place of Germans among fifteen nationalities in the children's estimation. Where before the
picture the English naturally led, with the Germans
trailing behind the Irish, French and Swedes, the post-

showing graph finds the English still leading, to be sure, but on a lower rung of the ladder, with the Germans risen high above the other nationalities and quite close to the English. Very definitely, after seeing the picture, these children showed an attitude both more favorable to the Germans and less favorable to war. These virgin slates were found to take the writing with astonishing ease. It all depends upon what one chooses to write on them.

In one case presented, however, the result was not what might have been expected. In Mendota, a town of 4,000 population, a study was made to test the children's attitudes toward gambling. A group of 240 high-school children were given the opportunity of seeing a movie entitled "Street of Chance," which depicts the life of a gambler in such a way that their attitudes upon the subject might be affected. Now, the gambler appeared in the film as an interesting and rather likeable character. Other crimes, or misdemeanors, with which gambling was compared in the tests, included such categories as bank robber, gangster, kidnapper, smuggler, bootlegger, pickpocket, petty thief, drunkard, speeder, etc.

Before they saw the picture, the children ranked gambling well toward the bottom of the scale as a "crime," that is, as less serious even than such occupations as those of pickpocket and petty thief. After the picture, however, their feeling of condemnation of gambling not only did not lessen, but moved up several units in the scale. As an occupation, that is, gambling was still ranked as less serious than bank-robbing, kidnapping, smuggling or bootlegging. But now it was appraised as more grave than picking pockets or petty thieving. "The film 'Street of Chance' may be said," conclude the investigators, "to have a socially approved effect since it made the children more severe in their judgment of gambling." They offer no explanation of this phenomenon, and the only conjecture the writer can suggest is that a prejudice against gambling is more solidly ingrained in our national mores than many of us would suspect.

Various other experiments were made. In one town children saw a picture entitled "Welcome Danger." This is a Harold Lloyd comedy, full of slapstick farce but still, a story of Tong conspirators and Chinatown lawlessness and therefore anti-Chinese. The anti-Chinese feeling in these spectators showed an increase, not significant, but as the experimenters phrase it, "in the expected direction." Similarly, In Geneseo, Illinois, 500 school children were exposed to "The Valiant," a picture calculated to influence one against capital punishment. The result is judged by the investigators as "not statistically significant," though the effect on the children's attitude was to make them slightly less favorable to capital punishment. In like manner, "The Criminal Code" made children more lenient than they had been before in the matter of the punishment of criminals, and "All Quiet on the Western Front" definitely turned their attitudes in favor of pacifism.

The experimenters even went on to study the cumulative effects of more than one picture upon the same theme, or aimed in the same direction. They found that where the effects of seeing separately "Big House" and "Numbered Men" were small, the effect of showing both pictures to the same group of children produced a significant change in their attitude toward the punishment of criminals. Three films upon the same issue produced a still more marked effect.

Briefly, by dint of careful experiment, the investigators discovered that not only do motion pictures leave a definite imprint upon the minds of children who see them, but that this effect, or mental influence, is *cumulative,* in accordance with the substance of the picture seen. Repetition definitely enhances the effect. The investigators do not arrive at the following conclusion, but to the writer, from these and other data in the studies, it appears not impossible: Show several pictures with gangsters as heroes, or with questionable mores, and may not the gangster at last seem a hero to the young mind and the mores in time increasingly a matter of course?

The effects of pictures on the mental attitudes of children, moreover, persist for a long time. They were found by actual experiment to persist after two months, after four and five months, after eight and nine months, and even after nineteen months. Nineteen months is the longest interval measured for effects by this particular research. But in concluding the summary of their work, the investigators significantly add: "The data presented indicate that the effect of the motion picture on social attitudes probably persists for a much longer time."

Whether or not we are a part of all we have seen, all we have seen, by experimental proof, remains a part of us. And since that is true, Mr. Hays' poetic metaphor of the slate falls completely to the ground and remains shattered. The writing upon a slate, however virgin, can be erased in an instant. The writing of the movies upon children's minds, on the other hand, appears to be fairly indelible. There seems to be no such thing as wholly erasing what is written there. After two years, the scientists found it to persist in measurable quantity. It may be overlaid, but the probability is that it abides forever.

3

The May-Shuttleworth approach to the subject of motion picture influence upon children's attitudes was wholly different. Professors May and Shuttleworth made what is known as a general survey of the field. Unlike Professor Thurstone and Miss Peterson, they did not show actual motion pictures to the children they studied, or administer tests on attitude before and after selected pictures. They sought to gain light upon the subjects of character and attitude in two classes of children—"movie" and "non-movie." This classification in itself, as has been pointed out, proved difficult, owing to the almost entire absence of "non-movie" children in the schools in which they obtained their information. What the classification became then, was a grouping of children who go to the movies once or twice a month, never or rarely; and another group, who go to the movies two, three, or four times a week. The latter are designated as the "movie" group and the infrequent attenders as the "non-movie" group. The 101 non-movie and 102 movie children were approximately the same in age, sex, school grade and cultural background.

In the result of questionnaires, of teacher ratings, conduct records and a "Guess Who" test, in which children were invited to fill in blanks in a descriptive sentence about a classmate, the investigators summarize their findings thus:

"We have found that the movie children average lower deportment records, do on the average poorer work in their school subjects, are rated lower in reputation by their teachers on two rating forms, are rated lower by their classmates on the Guess Who test, are less co-operative and less self-controlled as measured both by ratings and conduct tests, are slightly more deceptive in school situations, slightly less skillful in judging what is the most useful and helpful and sensible thing to do, and are somewhat less emotionally stable. Against this long record of disadvantages the movie children are superior on only two measures: they are mentioned oftener than the others in the Guess Who test and are named more frequently as 'best friends' by their class-mates." Tests showing no differences by this technique include honesty ratings and honesty as measured in and out of school situations, persistence, suggestibility and moral knowledge.

The attitude tests used by May and Shuttleworth, in the absence of actual picture-seeing to base them on, cannot be reproduced here in any degree of fulness. This is the type of question used by the investigators:

All Most Many Some Few No Chinese are cunning and underhand; or

All Most Many Some Few No Chinese are frank and fair and square.

They used similar forms touching other nationalities, touching prohibition, ministers, prize-fighters, athletes, college professors, professional dancers, and so on, the children being asked to check the word which they believed to be truly applicable.

All told, they declare, "we have compared the responses of movie and non-movie children to well over a thousand specific questions. Of all these only 45 show clearly reliable differences in the attitudes which are revealed, . . . less than one half of one per cent. . . . The absence of difference does not of course prove that there is no difference. The single test questions may not be sufficiently sensitive to show them."

The significant differences in replies, as we have seen, are only a handful. "Undoubtedly motion pictures have an influence," declare the investigators, but the extent of this influence is, by the technique they used, uncertain. How great it is, or how powerful in relation to other factors, is difficult from this study to determine. As the experimenters themselves put it, "The single test question may not be sufficiently sensitive to show them" [the differences in attitude]. This particular technique, or manner of procedure, shows no differences in the matter of moral, social and political questions, and, on the whole, reveals no differences of significant import.

All in all, after scrutinizing the various studies searchingly, the writer feels that Thurstone has established a case for the direct and powerful influence of motion pictures upon the mental attitudes of children. Drs. May and Shuttleworth, with technique not so sensitive, under conditions not so clear-cut, have been able to discover few indications illuminating the problem. The Thurstone-Peterson study, on the other hand, with its own technique and carefully selected pictures used in the tests, obtained results of a remarkable incisiveness.

One significant conclusion of the May-Shuttleworth study, supported by Drs. Blumer, Hauser, Thrasher and Cressey, is that the motion picture is only one of various important influences, such as the home, the school, books and companions which makes impact upon children. These men conclude that each category, including the character of the spectator, reacts upon the other. Thurstone, however, by means of his finely-devised technique and his carefully chosen cases, shows that the viewing of the movie may be a *cause* and the child's social attitude an *effect*.

4

Even those of us who are not scientifically trained observers know that the *mores* of a nation are, if not the greatest, one of its greatest assets—or liabilities. The mores constitute society's moral code. What we call morality is conformity to the mores. A nation may be possessed of the mores of Sodom and Gomorrah, or of the highest in the domains of culture and spirituality. The choice lies with the nation. Failure to conform to the existing standard of mores is immorality. We have seen to what an astonishing extent the attitudes of the young are modified by pictures seen on the screen. What is a good picture? A picture, leaving aside the quality of its art, is good if it complies with the national mores and bad if it conflicts. To what extent do the current movies either comply or conflict with the mores of today?

Dr. Charles C. Peters, professor of education and director of educational research at the Pennsylvania State College, was sufficiently moved by this query to make an elaborate enquiry into the subject. Not much of it can here be cited, and still less of his exceptionally interesting technique or method of research. What he undertook was a study of four specimens of conduct upon the screen in order to see to what extent they are in conflict with the national mores. With the object of testing approval or disapproval of motion picture scenes involving such action as kissing and caressing, aggressiveness of a girl in love-making, as well as some other points he desired to test, he secured evaluations from thirteen groups of widely diversified categories of human beings. They included such varieties as social reformers, university faculty members and their wives, ministers, college students, factory hands, young society women and girls, Negro school teachers, business men, miners and their wives, and young adolescent sons and daughters of miners—virtually a cross-section of the nation.

For purposes of illustration, it will be best, perhaps, to cite two scenes from different pictures and to record to what extent the scenes were approved or disapproved by the widely different human beings of these assorted groups. First, let us glance at a scene of kissing from the film entitled "Young Man of Manhattan":

Toby and Ann, a young married couple, both writers and a little jealous of each other's success, have had a quarrel which led Toby to sleep through the night on a couch. While he was asleep Ann softly covered him with a quilt. The scene shows them in the morning cautiously greeting each other.

"Hello!" Ann remarks quietly as she sees Toby's reflection in the dressing-table mirror.

"Hello, Ann," he replies in a subdued tone of voice. "Working?"

"Yes, I am trying to get a start on my first article for Dwight Knowles." She resumes her typing while Toby watches her in silence, then tells him, "The coffee is on the stove."

"Thanks," he says, then offers hesitantly, "Awfully sweet of you to put that cover over me."

Ann turns around and smiles. "I didn't want you to be cold." Toby, who has been looking dejectedly at the floor, brightens as he sees Ann's smile. She stands up, and he smiles in return, then they impulsively run to each other and embrace.

"Toby," Ann cries.

"Oh, Ann darling!" he exclaims, kissing her affectionately, and she returns the kiss.

"Mmm. Oh, Toby, I've been so unhappy."

He kisses her hair, then they both sit down on the edge of the bed, Toby keeping his arm about her. "Oh, what was it all about, for the love of Pete?" he demands. "Case of masculine egotism, getting up on its ear because you're going to make more money than I am."

"Oh, silly, not more than you *can*," Ann protests. "Only more than you do right now."

This scene was admired, or, at least, approved, by eighty-three per cent of even the most conservative group which consisted of faculty members of Pennsylvania State College, and by ninety-four per cent of the most liberal, that is, the working boys and girls.

Now let us look at another scene—involving aggressiveness on the part of a girl in love-making taken from the picture, "Young as You Feel":

Lem Morehouse, a wealthy middle-aged meat-packer who has hitherto led a very conventional and highly regimented life, is dancing with Fleurette, a French singer who is trying hard to vamp him. As they dance, she snuggles down against his chest and sings in a low voice to the accompaniment of the orchestra:

  . . . "Out of sight is out of mind
     With others I have met—
     This I find, that you're the kind
     I never do forget.
     No one else without a past
     Could look so slow
     And work so fast—
     The cute little way you do
     And the cute little things you do."

Lem is grinning ecstatically, and she puts her head down on his shoulder and declares, "Oh, you're doing much better, dear."

Now we know what songs the Sirens sang. This, though a scene in a farce, falls far below the approval of each individual group used by Dr. Peters, and of all the groups combined. In other words, it illustrates a type of conduct which is contrary to the collective mores of these thirteen widely varied groups in the nation.

Dr. Peters believes that characters in attractive rôles tend to make the conduct they enact attractive and characters in unattractive rôles generally make for a tabooing of their acts. Dr. Dale, we recall, found many attractive characters in criminal rôles. In the 142 feature pictures studied by Dr. Peters and his staff were listed 726 scenes of aggressiveness in love-making. Of these 549 were enacted by characters in attractive rôles, and

177 by characters in unattractive rôles. Nevertheless, so flagrantly did these scenes of aggressiveness offend the mores, or standards of conduct, of the thirteen widely different groups who saw them, that seventy per cent of all scenes of aggressiveness would be disapproved. Two-thirds, that is, of these scenes were offensive to the general taste of the public, consisting of adults and adolescents. And eighty-three per cent of all the feature pictures studied contained some such disapproved and offensive scenes. And lest it should be charged that the groups were overburdened with too many mature and austere adults, it should be mentioned that among the most tolerant and liberal was the group of social workers, social reformers and leaders, people, many of them, of national reputation. Even the young miners and factory workers were less liberal in accepting "naughty" scenes.

Now, just as the scenes of aggressiveness were disapproved, so certain others selected by Dr. Peters met with a different reception by the groups. The general question to which he sought answers is whether the patterns of conduct presented in the movies were such as the people would be willing to have imitated under like conditions in life. The scenes of what Dr. Peters calls democratic practices, treatment of employees and subordinates, treatment of persons based on social or occupational status, treatment based upon racial discrimination, in all of these, the movies show up somewhat better than the conditions to which people are accustomed in every-day life. In the matter of treatment of children by parents motion pictures are at their best, seventy per cent of all parent-child scenes having

been found by Dr. Peters to be such as to challenge the
admiration of all his groups combined. Scenes of
companionship between parents and children and those
showing tolerance of the point of view of children were
especially admired—all of which demonstrates what
the screen can do, if it will.

Returning, however, to the disapproved scenes, such as
aggressiveness, and recalling Dr. Dale's findings as to
the excessive iteration of the themes of crime and sex,
we readily see how much that is contrary to the national
mores is constantly presented. Though May, by his
technique, shows but little influence, Peters finds generally against the movies with respect to mores.

It becomes, therefore, a matter of fundamental and
critical importance to the parents of the land that what
their children see should build up rather than break down
the principles of conduct which have made the American
nation. The only excuse for tolerance of the objectionable
is our ignorance, in that hitherto no reliable data existed.
While all of us were shaking our heads in vague surmises, the power of the motion picture in influencing
and shaping young minds had not before been definitely
measured.

"A generation of film-going children is learning to
pick up points and impressions on the screen very quickly
—how quickly and how permanently we do not know."
This was the statement of a British Commission on educational and cultural films made in London, in May,
1932. We, in America, have been equally ignorant. In
the light of the work of Stoddard, Holaday, Thurstone
and other investigators under the Payne Fund research,
we now know a good deal more. We know, in the words

of the British Commission, that the points are picked up by the film-going children with astonishing quickness and with a degree of permanency most of us never suspected. We realize, in brief, that their minds and attitudes are being influenced and modified by the films. The case, to the writer, therefore, appears something like this:

As a nation we believe in high standards of living. We believe in sanitation, in pure food, in pure milk, in the best obtainable hygiene, instruction and education for our children. Is it possible that the color and content of their minds is a matter of indifference to us? We pay for our school system. We pay for our water supply. We also pay for the motion pictures. What would we say if any questionable character were to be allowed to come in suddenly and take charge of our children's schooling? Or, if suspected water were even occasionally turned into our mains? What an outcry goes up if a milk supply in a town is suddenly discovered to be in the least degree tainted! The vast haphazard, promiscuous, so frequently ill-chosen, output of pictures to which we expose our children's minds for influence and imprint, is not this at least of equal importance? For, as we cannot but conclude, if unwatched, it is extremely likely to create a haphazard, promiscuous and undesirable national consciousness.

CHAPTER IX

MOVIES AND CONDUCT

Motion pictures are a school. The investigations of Drs. Dale, Holaday, Thurstone and Blumer have definitely proved to us not only that much, indeed, most, of what this school teaches remains in the memory, but that it remains there for a long time, perhaps permanently, and that it colors the attitude and conduct of the pupil. In view of this, it is hardly surprising that some of the investigators gathered a store of data upon the widespread extent to which movie heroes, heroines, villains, indeed most of the characters and also the situations are imitated by children and adolescents.

The mirror held up by the movies is gazed into by myriads of adolescents and even young children in their secret thoughts, in their broodings, their day-dreaming and fantasies—they want to be like the people in the movies. One can hardly refrain from smiling at such a passionate outburst as this upon the part of a young Negro high-school girl:

"Oh, to possess what Miss Bow has—that elusive little thing called 'It'! After seeing her picture by that name, I immediately went home to take stock of my personal charms before my vanity mirror, and after carefully surveying myself from all angles, I turned away with a sigh, thinking that I may as well want to be Mr. Lon Chaney. I would be just as successful."

Even before this adolescent stage, however, with its beginnings of love-making and love technique, movie impersonations already assume shape and color in the minds of the young with marked influence upon the variety of their play. Imitation is quite natural for children. They have always been imitators, imitating everything that is of interest to them. Much of this sedulous imitation is quite harmless, often amusing and sometimes useful. Movies, because of their concreteness and vividness, are one of the great sources of patterns for imitation upon the part of children and here as elsewhere some of them are innocuous. Mixed with these, however, are many objects and patterns of imitation quite serious in their nature.

Who, for instance, is not familiar with the cowboy band, the robbers, the Indians of the back-yard or playground? Often enough it is quite healthy and harmless amusement, as in patterns of domestic life, beautification, dressing-up and imitating favorite actresses upon the part of little girls. When a young woman recalls that "I had a great desire to have curls like Mary Pickford, and improved my appearance with the aid of shavings from new buildings near by," it is merely amusing. Or, when another tells how she tried to impress her brothers to play as her adoring beaux, the while she preened before them with a curtain for a train—and she would go off to her mother and cry when the young male brutes laughed at her—that also is still in the domain of the harmless and the humorous.

When a college boy, similarly, confesses to the painstaking, persevering imitation of Bill Hart's narrowing of the eyes, twitching of the facial muscles, his menacing, murderous look, it is again merely amusing. "After months of torture, vain sweating before the mirror," he concludes sadly,—"and interrupted on different occasions by my mother or father, sister or brother,—I gave it up. I didn't decide that Bill's look wasn't worth while. I finally concluded that I didn't have the stuff. It was Bill's alone." There are, however, less ordinary cases presenting a different account. As clear an indication as any of this childhood movie influence is the following account from the autobiography set down by a young convict:

"As soon as I got to be old enough to wander around a little without getting lost, my first thing I done was to get acquainted with the other neighborhood tots and we would all get our nickels together and go to see the thrilling western or crook pictures that happened to be shown in the neighborhood. It was a great thrill to see the guns in action in a big train robbery or cattle rustling breakup. As soon as we got tired of looking straight up at pictures we would decide to go back to the neighborhood and start our evening game of 'cops and robbers.' It used to be hard for us kids to decide as to who would be the 'coppers' because everyone wanted to be the bold robber they just saw in the moving pictures.

"As a small lad I did not have much use for a copper in crook plays. I always hoped the robber would get the best of the copper. I got a kind of grudge up when I saw the copper conquering the robber. I decided some day to grow up and show the coppers something, but

I was only a child then. The boys always used to choose me for their chief robber, because I was the biggest and strongest, and if they wouldn't choose me as chief, I would punch a few of them and break up the game. I was always a very bad man for the kid coppers to catch and if they would corner me I'd fight my way out. So you see the motion pictures were responsible a little in bringing or starting me up in the racket."

2

That quotation is given at some length because it indicates a positive influence of childhood movie experience of the less happy variety in subsequent life. Fortunately they are not all like that. When a girl describes how she imitated a graceful pose, or sought to copy a particularly winsome facial expression of one of her favorite screen heroines, it is scarcely different from imitating a dress or a costume from a stage star, a species of imitation almost as old as the stage. The process of adjustment to the world they live in is a serious business to the young. Where their own environment does not supply them with models of dress, deportment or carriage, mannerisms of the screen stars will be as inevitably copied as were once those of Rachel, Bernhardt or Ethel Barrymore.

Just as many a girl experiments with the enhancement of an unimaginative given name, and a Mary Ann becomes Marian or a Nora, Leonora, so it is quite natural for a girl impressed by the wide-eyed air of innocence of a movie star to try to convey to her world that she too is both wide-eyed and innocent. As a fifteen-year-old high-school girl recalls, "I remember one movie star,

Mabel Normand, who had large eyes, and from admiring them I gradually began to stare at others with wide eyes. My friends thought there was something wrong with my eyes."

"I simply adore Greta Garbo," cries out another. "She wears her clothes so sporty, and the way men fall for her! Boy! I'll bet every girl wishes she was the Greta Garbo type. I tried to imitate her walk. She walks so easy, as if she had springs on her feet. But when I try to copy her walk, I am asked if my knees are weak. How insulting some people are!"

"One acquires positions, such as standing, sitting, tipping one's hat, offering one's arm to a lady," confesses a sophomoric Romeo in praise of the famous John Gilbert. And another aspirant, aiming to shine, tells how he "tried to express disapproval by delicately arching my eyebrows, and I practiced drawing my fingers together languidly while I smoked an (imaginary) imported cigarette with my monogram upon it. I even attempted to cultivate a slow drawl." And a girl, in the line of her progress, tells of learning "that when I cry I should not even attempt to wipe away the tears, as they are so much more effective rolling downwards."

"I got my first striking illumination through the movies," recalls a girl, "of the difference clothes may make in appearance. It was in 'Daddy Long-Legs' where Mary Pickford paraded for five scenes bare-legged, in dark brown cast-offs, pig-tailed and frecklefaced, good, sweet but hardly beautiful; and then in the final scene, after a visit from Daddy and a bath in milk, with her curls down, the gangly knees covered, the ankles silk-shod, in a pink satin, pearl-studded dress, a re-born,

gorgeous queen, she emerged as striking as the cater-
pillar of the butterfly transition. At home that night
I tentatively hinted at putting my daily glass of milk
to better use, wound my straight black hair in tortuous
curl-papers, draped myself in red gauze and compared
effects."

Absurd as is the picture this young girl paints of herself as a silly flapper, with "ankles silk-shod," it nevertheless indicates an urge to beautification which is, after
all, inalienable from woman; and for many girls like
herself the screen is probably the only source of enlightenment, or, as this girl calls it, illumination. Others desire dresses like Clara Bow's or Joan Crawford's, and
still others learn how to wear earrings, how to make
the most of their physical advantages, or how to cover
disadvantages; how to put perfume on their ear-lobes
like Norma Talmadge whose husband "kissed her
aside on her ear." If movies did no more harm than
that, few would have any quarrel with them.

Young swains, similarly, admit learning their etiquette from the movies. "I watched for the proper way
in which to conduct oneself at a nightclub," declares a
stately college senior, and another concludes with almost
spiritual fervor, "I am very thankful that the movies gave
me some education along certain lines of etiquette—
ways of dress, conduct at table, et cetera." For many
in the congested areas of cities, as Dr. Thrasher's research will show, notably those of immigrant parentage,
the movies are a large part of education. The family
background, the play-group, the school, the "hangout"
and the gangs are for large percentages probably more influential than the movies. Yet for considerable numbers,

under certain conditions, the movies, in the Thrasher-Cressey study, are shown to form an important element in social education. Hence their merit if they are good, and their danger if they are objectionable. The educational angle, however, is not confined either to congested areas or to the offspring of immigrants.

When a girl tells of learning to handle a cigarette like Nazimova, to smile like Norma Shearer, to use her eyes like Joan Crawford, or to tilt her head like Anita Page, she is not necessarily an immigrant's daughter. She is merely a daughter of Eve. "I have learned from the movies," a high-school girl boldly announces, "how to be a flirt, and I found out that at parties and elsewhere the coquette is the one who enjoys herself the most."

Man is by nature an imitative animal, and the types of imitation mentioned are as common and inevitable as any in the human curriculum. The aim in adducing them is to emphasize that the movies are a school, a school of conduct, a sort of supplementary system of education. And if the movies are that, they cease to be nobody's business.

If, for instance, as Dr. Dale shows in his analysis of 115 movies, winning another's love is a principal goal in at least seventy per cent of those pictures, it becomes obvious how great a proportion of the spectator's attention will be focussed upon that particular emotion. If seventy-five per cent of all pictures deal with love, sex and crime, then, obviously, the curriculum of this particular school demands wise, discriminating and urgent attention.

Though young children do not frequently choose love

pictures as their favorite form of screen entertainment, we know that it is difficult to find any pictures devoid of this element, and we know that once they are exposed to them, the impression upon the young minds remains fixed to a comparable degree with other forms of dramatic presentation. Ordinarily the very young children, where they have a fair choice, do not consider "wasting" their money on love pictures. What they crave is the promise of action.

"Love stories in pictures," as one student records, "never held much attraction for me at this time (age twelve). I had a cousin, however, who was extremely fond of them. As she was one year older than I and was much stronger and bigger, I had to do as she wished. She would make me go with her to see Francis X. Bushman and Beverly Bayne in some of their silly love pictures; and then when we returned home, she made me make love to her as she had seen the other two do on the screen. I did not appreciate this at all."

Once they are a little older, however, ways and manners in love-making assume a definitely more enthralling aspect, and the copying of love technique suddenly becomes a preoccupation of major importance. Adolescence brings a new group of interests, childish things, if not utterly put away, tending to fade out.

From a sampling of nearly 500 autobiographies written by high-school students, thirty-three per cent report definite imitation from the pictures of ways of love-making. Nearly forty per cent did not give information. Knowing, as we do, however, the self-consciousness of adolescent girls and boys upon this particular subject, at once so intimate and so new to them, it is reasonable to assume that the percentage of love-technique copyists from the movies is considerably larger than the thirty-three per cent mentioned by Blumer.

"I soon lost my enthusiasm over western pictures and developed a sudden appreciation of love pictures," is the way one he-man explains it; and another, towering at eighteen in the dignity of a high-school senior, states it squarely thus:

"The first interest in love pictures came when I was about fourteen . . . I became more interested in girls and began to love them. I sometimes practiced making love to my friends after I had seen a love scene. I have seen plays of love and passion where children were not admitted and from these I got ideas of how to make love to a girl." "The technique of making love to a girl received considerable of my attention," reveals another square-shooter, "and it was directly through the movies that I learned to kiss a girl on her ears, neck and cheeks, as well as on her mouth."

The name of these young scholars in the school of love is legion, and how lavish is the instruction! No wonder intelligent foreign observers have more than once expressed the idea that, judging from our films, we as a nation must be largely, if not wholly, given up to eroticism and sex. We have seen the figures arrived at by Dr. Dale. The statements of young people in this and subsequent chapters appear as at once elucidations and confirmations of these figures. Over and over the young testify to their schooling in life by means of the films.

"When I had my first 'puppy' love affair," confides a young miss, "I was very much disillusioned in my Prince Charming because he merely pecked me when he kissed me. In fact I was quite disgusted—I thought him bashful and a fool for not knowing how to kiss after seeing so many movies." And this sly maiden of fifteen: "When with the opposite sex I am rather quiet and allow them to tell me what to do. When they go to make love, to kiss or hug, I put them off at first, but it always ends in them having their own way. I guess I imitated this from the movies because I see it in almost every show I go to."

There may possibly be parents who desire this species of schooling for their daughters, but their numbers, one would think, must be small. Yet the constant reiteration of the theme and the infinite varieties of love scenes cannot but have an effect upon the conduct of young people. If, according to the Dale findings, winning another's love is the goal of one hundred and fifty-eight persons in 115 pictures, that may become tedious to intelligent adults, and produce the effect it did upon the author of "Purilia." But to young adolescents involved in the first unfolding of mating instincts, what can all that eroticism constitute but a school of patterns of conduct? As one sixteen-year-old girl so pertinently, so pathetically, puts it:

"A young couple sees the art of necking portrayed on the screen every week for a month or so, and is it any wonder they soon develop talent? I am not allowed to have dates at home so I know how true this is." Some of the more serious results of this type of schooling will be considered later. The aim of the present chapter is merely to present evidence that the movies are, as some of the young people have described them, "a liberal education in the art of love-making." That it is for many

young people the one available school of its kind only
enhances its importance. A twenty-year old student,
with an unconsciousness that appears naïve for a college
girl, writes:

"Movies are a liberal education in the art of making
love. Every young person probably appreciates a love
scene subjectively. I never learned any ways of flirting
because flirting is against the family code. I did learn
something about the art of kissing, however; that the
tableau looks far more graceful if the young lady puts
more weight on one foot than on the other; the effect is
softer. It is helpful, too, to see how two screen lovers
manage their arms when they are embracing; there is
a definite technique; one arm over, the other under."

Others tell freely how much of technique in flirtation
they learned from the screen, the come-hither glances,
"vamping," kissing, necking. "Such techniques are very
necessary," a nineteen-year old youth declares, "and I
feel that the movies are performing a real service."
Though touched with humor as some of these illustrations are, they are none the less real instances of studied
imitation. As one college boy who attempted to imitate
John Gilbert in love-making puts it,

"I place the blame not on my inability to imitate what
I have seen on the screen, but on someone else's inability
to imitate Greta Garbo's receptive qualities." And another youth confesses:

"Once I tried to imitate Bill Haines' smart-aleckness
at a dance by kissing the girl I was dancing with.
She gave me a 'sock' in the jaw." He adds that the girl
did not appear to like his technique. To many, however, it is not a matter of choice. Realistically they assess

their own potentialities and what they can learn from the screen to aid them in the objectives in which they are interested. A college girl of nineteen illustrates this with admirable sobriety:

"I am especially interested in those closest to my own possibilities in all points about them, but especially with the more perfect actresses, (I pick them for their acting now,) their carriage, conduct, and particularly love-making technique—I find this much more suggestive and effective than I could possibly find any book by, say, Elinor Glyn, on 'How to Hold Your Man'."

An equally sober male collegian is still more business-like and judicial in summing up his profit and loss in the matter of movie-schooling with:

"I am not sure whether this influence has been wholesome or otherwise. Without it I might have become an unbearable prude; with it I was encouraged into indiscretions which I have later come to regret. On the whole I think it was an evil, but as with most evils, it was not unmixed with elements of good."

3

Day-dreaming is a practice in which nearly everyone of us indulges at times. But for day-dreaming there would probably be no poetry, or art, or much else in life that is good. The crucial point lies in the forms which day-dreams assume and the direction in which they tend. They divide themselves, as I review these studies on motion picture influence, into two chief types: Day-dreams that appear normal; and, second, a kind of day-dream that is dangerous.

"For days after I had seen them," writes one girl

of a set of movie characters, "I acted just as they had done." "How often," writes another, "I have wasted time day-dreaming, picturing myself as the heroine of those wonderful pictures." And a college girl recalls:

"I think it was during early adolescence that the movies had their greatest effect upon me. I spent the time just before I slipped off to sleep in planning and dreaming about the pictures I should play in, my clothes, my admirers and suitors, my cars, my jewels, and even the home I should have, which was to be the most magnificent structure in all Beverly Hills. . . . I never told anyone about my brilliant future, but I felt quite superior, all to myself, over other girls who were not to have such a glorious career as I was to have. Then one day I confided in my best friend and was distinctly surprised to hear that her future was to parallel mine, and that she, too, was going to be a star of the first magnitude."

Love scenes play a prominent rôle in these day-dreams, more particularly in the lives of girls, though the boys are not immune. One boy confesses to dreaming of Joan Crawford by the hour, and even of writing letters to her. And a college girl makes this admission:

"I always put myself in the place of heroine. If the hero was some man by whom I should enjoy being kissed (as he invariably was), my evening was a success, and I went home in a dreamy frame of mind, my heart beating rather fast and my usually pale cheeks brilliantly flushed. I used to look in the mirror somewhat admiringly and try to imagine Wallace Reid or John Barrymore or Richard Barthelmess kissing that face."

"At one time," a girl records, "it was even the height

of my ambition to marry Dick Barthelmess. I spent much Latin grammar time thinking up ways of becoming acquainted with my various heroes." And a colored girl confesses, "I fell in love with Gilbert Rolland. I would imagine I was the leading lady in the pictures he played in. I used to sit and day-dream that one day I would marry Gilbert Rolland and we would have a lovely time until I went out with Ramon Navarro and Gilbert would catch me kissing Ramon. Then there would be a lawsuit and my picture would be in the paper. I would win the lawsuit and marry Ramon Navarro. I would keep on until I had married and divorced all of my movie actors."

This amoral confession carries its own comment, as do the various testimonies of identification with the hero or heroine. They may be foolish and even absurd, as doubtless they often are. Something of them, however, remains for a long time and perhaps permanently in the consciousness of these girls.

"I can picture," says a girl, "John Gilbert and Greta Garbo rehearsing a love scene right now, but in my mind it isn't Greta Garbo, it's me!" "I picture myself," says another, "the recipient of Gilbert's kisses. Folded in his arms I could forget all my school worries."

Rudolph Valentino still lives in the hearts of many young women, and women not so young, as the ideal lover. "After seeing 'The Sheik'," declares one girl, "I was in a daze for a week." Girls record how they dreamed of Valentino, of his kisses and embraces. "Buddy Rogers and Rudy Valentino have kissed me oodles of times but they don't know it, God bless 'em!"

Many people, including some psychiatrists, believe

that day-dreaming, or fantasy, tends to soften the harsh contours of life in a world of antagonism and frustration. There is, however, another side to it. Day-dreaming is a turning inward of action, correspondingly leading to a deadening of incentive and capacity for outward action. "In this sense," observes Professor Blumer, "day-dreaming becomes a method of escape, a sign of failure to meet one's problems and of an unwillingness to work out one's frustrated impulses into some form of social adjustment. . . ." In other words, this type of day-dreaming becomes in reality a sort of drug.

"In forming a judgment," adds Professor Blumer, "one should not forget that indulgence in day-dreaming may stimulate impulses and whet appetites. To this extent, the condition of day-dreaming may pass over into patterns of thought, intention and desire, and accordingly encourage overt forms of conduct, or at least become closely linked up with such forms."

4

The aim of these varied quotations is to illustrate to what an extent the movies are actually a school of conduct for the young in some of their major concerns, play, amusement, love-making. There are, of course, many other types of interest. All forms of conduct presented on the screen are subject to imitation and have their imitators.

"If an individual sees some form of conduct which promises to aid the realization of one of his aims, it is likely to be chosen," is the conclusion of Professor Blumer. And that, briefly, is the psychology of imitation.

Add to that the fact that motion pictures are not text-books, but romantic and dramatic presentations of life, apparently—vivid with color, emotion and appeal, and generally demonstrating *successful consequences of action*. The more vivid the appeal, the more certain the emotion. Copying the movies thus appears for the young as inevitable. Much will be rejected, much out-grown. Yet there is evidence of an astonishing amount being taken over and incorporated into conduct. Inevitably the young boy seeking for patterns of play will acquire screen patterns of both good and bad action in proportion to their frequency and spectacular interest, just as certainly as the young girl seeking popularity will select details of beautification and conduct which she has seen to be successful on the screen. As Dr. L. K. Frank, of the General Education Board, suggested to one of the researchers in this survey:

"The æsthetic appeal which the motion pictures make causes the typical young person to accept their sugges-tions and associations in a way which he or she would not do otherwise. The motion picture is for the great masses a more significant educational influence than most of the school work done in the country."

It is fortunate that there are other influences which counteract the distressing patterns of conduct put before children by so many pictures and, as we have seen, slav-ishly followed. The mores of the community, the family, the home are not without their potent influences. Un-happily, however, those long-established agencies find themselves obliged to combat with increasing vigor that powerful, vivid, direct influence of certain types of mo-tion pictures.

The aim here is neither to argue for motion pictures, nor to moralize against them. It is merely to convince the reader that what the last quarter century has really given us is another educational system, alluring, persuasive, cogent and appealing, which involves all the childhood and youth of the country as completely, as thoroughly, in effect, as our long-built up educational system itself. We often express deep concern about textbooks, about whether or not they should instill patriotism, belittle or whitewash national leaders and heroes; whether school teachers should be married or single; whether spiritual and character instruction should or should not be included in curricula, and so on, endlessly—because education is of vital interest, perhaps the most vital of all. Here, however, is another educational system equally vital and perhaps more far-reaching in its results than any we call by that name.

CHAPTER X

MOLDED BY THE MOVIES

WE have long suspected, most of us, that the movies are seriously affecting the mores and ways of our children and young people. The conversation of any group in the country abounds in surmises, vague impressions and cloudy suspicions. But that the movies are actually *molding* their habits of mind, their imagery, their outlook on and adjustment to life, supported as it is by numerous facts gathered by the Payne Fund research, is a discovery of the most vital importance in all the field of social study. The fact that good pictures may be as permanent in their influence as bad only makes the infrequent occurrence of the good the more regrettable.

In approaching the subject of movie-influence and movie-effects, obviously, neither Professor Blumer nor any of the other investigators could examine all the 77,000,000 that constitute the weekly movie audience, nor even the 28,000,000 minors. In most of social study samples of the population have to be taken, and Dr. Blumer took large samples. While what is called "suggestibility" is possible in some cases, the numbers examined by Blumer are so large that the facts must have validity. Not only did Dr. Blumer check his facts after several months, but his method markedly illustrates the impersonal and impartial quality of the research. And the variety of the answers, both affirmative and negative, indicates their reliability rather than "suggestibility." Throughout his survey Blumer sought not for opinions but for facts.

Now, when we pause to consider for a moment what that discovery, of the molding quality of the movies, means, it appears as nothing less than awe-inspiring. The long centuries of culture and civilization striving for expression in morals, literature, art and science; the aim with which great teachers have taught, great poets sung, great novelists written and great artists and scientists created—all that long history of mortal effort and human endeavor has culminated in the shapes, creations and images of our haphazard movies! Homer, Aeschylos, Sophocles, Dante, Shakespeare, Keats, Newton, Farraday, Edison—what were they, after all, but fore-runners to the creators of "The Perils of Pauline," "Dr. Fu Manchu" or "Our Dancing Daughters," no less than of "The Covered Wagon" and "Ben Hur"?

The first reaction of many readers may well be that such a question upon the part of the writer is absurd. But, let us see. The aim of a culture, at long last, is so to shape human behavior that it rises in a steadily ascending curve from low beginnings to heights of human conduct and attainment. Our interpretation of life to-day should, if we have progressed, be on vastly higher planes than that of the caveman, of the nomadic man, of the Roman Empire, or of the middle ages. As a result of this extensive study of motion picture influence, however, Professor Blumer finds that "a large part of the average child's imagery used for interpretation of experience in every-day life has its source in motion pictures." Whole classes of school children were asked by Blumer to do a variety of things in which the contents of their minds and fancies would emerge freely without constraint or external compulsion. He asked them, for instance, to draw pictures of action, of any interesting phases of life that came into their heads and out of their imaginations—with no further suggestions. What emerged in the sketches almost invariably were "the cowboy, the Indian, the airplane combat, mystery characters and other familiar motion picture types or themes."

Similarly, when such children were asked to write stories or essays, what usually came to light were movie themes—characters, situations, plots, conceptions made familiar by the movies. Like an atmosphere, a movie world surrounds our young, and a movie world, to a great extent, fills their heads.

Motion picture scrap-books, motion picture photographs of favorite stars profusely decorating the lockers of high-school girls and boys, motion picture conversation, motion picture imagery—what else is this for the young people but a motion picture world? A college girl tells how Dickens was spoiled for her because the illustrations, possibly Cruikshank drawings, were remote from the movie types she had been accustomed to seeing. Another explains that whatever books she read were acted out in the theatre of her mind "as the movies would have them." "Even now," she adds, "that persists. I can read plays and short stories and enjoy them as such but there is always a subconscious picture of how they would look when produced" (in the movies). In the study of Stoddard and Holaday we have seen to

what an extent the contents of motion pictures are retained in the memories of young people, and in the
work of Professor Thurstone and Miss Peterson we have
had it proved to us how relatively permanent are the
stereotyped impressions of the movies written upon the
brains, how fecund they are in resulting mental attitudes. And if all this is true, if this is the upshot of
the march of history, cultures and civilizations through
the ages, I ask any fair-minded reader whether the
only description for the phenomenon is not "awe-inspiring."

Approaching the matter in another way, Dr. Blumer
seems amply to confirm their findings. A serial seen by
one student in his childhood upon "the yellow menace"
made him for years fearful of every Chinese laundry-
man. "To this day," declares a girl—a college senior—
"I do not see a Chinese person but what I think of him
as being mixed up in some evil affair"; and one student
in whose mind motion pictures engendered prejudice
against Japanese and Germans says, "I am afraid that in
all cases where a picture has been presented from a
prejudiced point of view, I jumped too readily to the
conclusion that it was all true." His fear is quite justified, assuming he was of the age of those examined by
Dr. Thurstone and Miss Peterson. He virtually could
not choose but jump to such conclusions.

A Negro high-school boy, himself a member of a race
suffering under prejudice, naïvely and roundly reports:

"I think all Chinamen are crooks because I have seen
them in the underworld of pictures so often. I have
seen a picture where the Chinaman almost burned a
lady to death, trying to make her tell a secret. This pic-

ture and similar ones have made me afraid of Chinamen." And a college girl, early fed upon serials with
Pearl White and Warner Oland in them, writes:

"He, Warner Oland, was always wicked in the canny,
cunning, heartless mandarin who pursued Pearl White
through so many serials. I carried over this impression
to all Asiatics, so that they all seem to conceal murderous
intent behind their bland features, their humble attitude—merely a disguise until the time was ripe to seize
you and kill you, or, worse yet, to make you a slave.
I never pass by our Chinese laundry without increasing
my speed, glancing apprehensively through the window
to detect him (the Chinaman) at some foul deed, ex-
pecting every moment one of his white slave girls to
come dashing out of the door. If I heard some undue
disturbance at night outside, I was certain that Mark
Woo was at his usual work of torturing his victims. *I
have not been able to this day to erase that apprehensive
feeling whenever I see a Chinese person, so deep and
strong were those early impressions.*"

In italicizing the last lines of this statement, we wish
to point to the fact that not only was the result of such a
picture in the mind of a sophisticated college girl virtually the same as in that of the naïve Negro high-school
boy, but that her attitude, notwithstanding her greater
knowledge, is permanently qualified by the ideas of the
movies she had seen in childhood—which more than
bears out the findings of Thurstone and Holaday.

In the same manner some girls cannot dispel the notion gained in their early movies that a man with a
mustache is sinister because movie villains wore mus-
taches. On the other hand, just as many declare their

attitudes towards Germans and Chinamen affected by
the films, so equally appreciable numbers record the
birth within them of hatred of war by such pictures
as "Wings," "Mother Knows Best," and "The Big
Parade." They support, in short, the fact that the motion picture has become an instrument of civilization,
and that it depends upon us how we permit the instrument to be used.

2

In the heart of anyone surveying all these materials
arises an immense sympathy for the young. In all
times the young have faced the difficult situation of adjustment to life. What, however, with the war and some
of its sequential conditions, economic, ethical and social,
upon the one hand, and upon the other the vortex of
ceaseless exhibition of ill-considered, ill-selected, often
absurd and preposterous motion pictures, with good ones
too sparsely represented, surrounding them with a
largely misshapen movie world of ballyhoo and vulgarity, leaving upon their minds a whole farrago of
confused and conflicting impressions, one cannot but be
appalled by the shattering creation we have prepared
for them. Moiling and milling in this confusion, we
demand that they be wise, noble, firm and far-seeing.
We desire them to be not only brave and good, but
filled with austere purpose and high character—by the
law, one supposes, of contraries.

Anyone believing that the place of motion pictures in
the lives of the young is exaggerated by such considerations, needs but to study the materials gathered by the
research, of which only a small portion can here be

cited. Truly, as a thoughtful nineteen-year-old college girl expresses it:

wrong impressions "I think that movies make adjustment to life and understanding of people and their problems more difficult, because of the wrong impressions which they give. The understanding should come first—then the movies. Also I think that the movies over-emphasize the sex interest and get people's minds to dwell on sex out of all proportion to its importance." That is pretty clear thinking for a girl of nineteen.

It would matter little to how great an extent the movies over-emphasized certain things were they rare occurrences, were they not so prevalent and all-pervasive. A circus, with its vivid and often violent scenes, with its barkers and ballyhoo, with its side-shows and monstrosities, comes, after all, but once a year. The movies, however, as we have seen, have a weekly attendance of 77,000,000 people in the United States, with 28,000,000 under twenty-one and 11,000,000 thirteen and under. These minors average an attendance of at least once a week and in many cases two, three, four and more times a week. Scarcely surprising that movies change the manners and affect the mores.

"When I go to see a modern picture like 'Our Dancing Daughters'," writes one high-school miss of sixteen, "I am thrilled. These modern pictures give me a feeling to imitate their ways. I believe that nothing will happen to the carefree girl like Joan Crawford but it is the quiet girl who is always getting into trouble and making trouble."

And there, for that girl, go by the board all training and all efforts at rearing her in a particular way to a particular set of mores which society, up to this point, has decreed as good and useful for her sex. She is sanctioned in her view and justified by that beacon of light, "Our Dancing Daughters." Another girl finds in that film and in Joan Crawford the embodiment of the true spirit of the younger generation: "No matter what happened she played fair. She even lost her man and in the eyes of the older generation; they think that when a modern young miss wants her man back, she'd even be a cutthroat, but Joan Crawford showed that even in a crisis like that she was sport enough to play fair! And 'play fair' is really the motto of the better class of young Americans."

From the same picture a girl of sixteen derives an almost complete and compact social philosophy which must have been of concern to her parents:

"The movies have given me some ideas about the freedom we should have. For instance, in the pictures the wildest girl always tames down and gets the man she loves. Why not in real life? My notion of the freedom I should have, and I have it, is to go out and have a good time, but watch your step. . . . On the screen, when it shows a party with the heroine included, they are generally the life of the party, and I believe that 'when you are in Rome, do as the Romans do.' I used to think just the opposite, but after seeing 'Our Dancing Daughters' and 'The Wild Party' I began to think this over, and I found out that it is the best way to act."

Social philosophers have often wondered why not only our machines and our clothes but even our manners and morals have become standardized. A whole literature has arisen on the subject. The extracts from the autobiographies just cited should supply some valid data for the answer. Throughout these studies the matters of love technique, all conceptions of life, the relations between the sexes, all sex morality, play a tremendous part. It could hardly be otherwise when over seventy per cent of 115 pictures analyzed present as a major goal the winning of another's love. The movies present many patterns; in fact, they constitute a vast schooling in sex. Fifty per cent of the high-school students examined by Professor Blumer indicated that their ideas about sexual love came from the movies. Thirteen per cent denied that they had so obtained their ideas.

"As far as I can remember," writes a college freshman who had been too strictly reared, "almost all of my knowledge of sex came from the movies. There was no other place where I could have gotten it. Ideas about kissing definitely came from the movies. This is absolutely true; the first time I ever kissed a girl was after I saw Greta Garbo and John Gilbert."

A seventeen-year-old high-school girl not only learned what she knew of love-making from the movies, she tells us, but, "that bad and pretty girls are usually more attractive to men than intelligent and studious girls. The seemingly "free abandon to the fact that love-making is perfectly all right" came to the wisdom of another directly from the movies, and a college girl recites how the movies taught her that "men place a high premium on the physical aspect of woman," and that "a considerable quantity of 'it' may be attained by pretty clothes, risqué clothes." The engaging frankness of these girls, particularly of young high-school students, is as instructive as it is charming—and alarming. Here is the philosophy of a sixteen-year old:

"No wonder girls of older days, before the movies, were so modest and bashful. They never saw Clara Bow and William Haines. They didn't know anything else but being modest and sweet. I think the movies have a great deal to do with present-day so-called wildness. If we did not see such examples in the movies, where would we get the idea of being 'hot'? We wouldn't."

3

The aim in presenting these documentary excerpts is not so much for the purpose of drawing conclusions —that seems scarcely necessary—as to show what a tremendous part the movies play in the major as well as in the minor things of life of American youth. Our educational system is one of our national glories. It is for us to consider to what extent the superimposed system of the movies at present satisfies us as a "glory."

Possibly some parents may be willing to have their children acquire their attitudes, manners, morals, ideas of love and sex from the movies. But how many of us would like to have our children become dissatisfied with their homes, or rebelliously resentful of parental control, in consequence of the teachings of what we may perhaps call our movie Bible? Not that in pre-movie times a certain number did not tend to be dissatisfied or rebellious, or even to run away. Formerly the reading of particular types of narratives created the incentives. Now, the motion pictures, so easy to see, showing as they do certain delightful and alluring experiences, doubtless enhance those desires. Many of the cases cited illustrate both the dissatisfaction and the lure. Twenty-two per cent of the high-school boys and girls studied by Professor Blumer declared that they had experienced feelings of resentment against parents as a result of certain motion pictures, and twelve per cent confessed to occasional experiences of actual rebellion. As one boy put it, "The movies depicting social life at first disturbed me. I wasn't satisfied with my environment; I expected too much from my parents in the way of comfort and leisure."

The young sybarite! But how can he help it? How can he know, stimulated by the vivid presentations of the movies, that these shifting scenes deal only in the exceptional? To a young mind and imagination, as we have seen, they are reality itself. They often present, as Dr. Blumer phrases it, "the extremes as though they were the norm." In the constant race for the startling and the novel they have long lost sight of the norm. Many of the young are bewildered by the stream of scenes and stories. One cannot but sympathize with the poor colored high-school girl who naïvely unburdens herself thus:

"Since I have gotten old enough to realize what good times really are I am dissatisfied with my clothes and my home. I see the girls in the movies going out in cars to road-houses and to balls, cabarets and many other things that put me in the habit of wanting to go, too. Sometimes I feel like stopping school and going to work for myself, so I can go any place I want, do anything and get anything. I think the young girls of today should be given privileges to go and have a good time.

Not all of the time, but very often, so they can enjoy themselves as everybody else."

She is fifteen and her color does not make her by any means unique, only a shade more pathetic. The movies "put her in the habit" of wanting to go and they put her in the habit of demanding privileges and good times and similar things. Many of her white young sisters seem to be irresistibly put in like habits. "I think a girl of seventeen," protests one, "should be allowed to go anywhere. I think she knows what to do and how to act." Subsequent disclosures will show that many of her sort falter and stumble in this type of knowledge. A boy admits that "the movies have made me dislike restraint of any kind. They have also made me dislike work," he adds, and he, too, as documents will prove, becomes one of a numerous host that often comes to grief. A coeval of his, a girl of seventeen, is equally frank:

"After seeing a wonderful picture full of thrills and beautiful scenes, my own home life would seem dull and drab. Nothing unusual would happen and I would become dissatisfied and wish I could run away. My clothes were never smart enough and I felt that my parents were far too strict with me. The girls in the motion pictures nearly always had far more privileges than I." Those girls in the motion pictures are enjoying more privileges than any community, either in Paradise or in an African jungle, but, as Dr. Blumer puts it, there the extremes are shown as though they were the norm.

Now, what becomes of so many of these yearnings and dissatisfactions? The ready answer will be that they fade out and dissipate themselves under pressure of life.

In many cases, as Blumer has elsewhere indicated, that is true. In examining certain phases of delinquency traceable to the movies, however, we shall see that many of these dissatisfactions and rebellions do not remain static or repressed, nor do they vanish. Often they have results in positive acts and conduct unhappy in their consequences. But this fact appears clear—the widespread extent of the movies has brought a multiplicity of temptations within reach of the masses.

That pictures may, however, be the cause of other and more worthwhile emotions in the young supports our general contention that good movies could be of enormous service. To that extent motion pictures share in the characteristics of the theatre, which many believe to be one of the best forms of education mankind has devised. Now and then, with the showing of such films as "Ben Hur," "The Ten Commandments" or "The King of Kings," a powerful effect is found to have been left upon young minds, and there is evidence of proportional influence upon their moral conduct. If it does not endure for long, it is due perhaps chiefly to the infrequency of such pictures and to the overwhelming frequency of other types which portray quite opposite schemes of life as the general and normal thing. One boy records that he saw "Ben Hur" three times. "That picture," he says, "made me want to live an unselfish, self-sacrificing life." These ambitions, he adds somewhat disillusioningly, used to last for two or three weeks. After which, he confesses, "I have gradually lapsed back into normal again." Similarly, "The King of Kings" made him want to be "a great religious leader," and "Sorrell and Son" made him more appreciative of his father. A high-school girl, with all the ingenuousness of fresh discovery, asks why in face of such pictures everyone cannot be good. "I think," she adds, "these pictures are wonderful and there should be more of them." As to the general question of endurance in the case of these comparatively rare effects, it is perhaps best to answer by the statement of a sixteen-year old girl who expresses her experience in this way:

"After seeing Janet Gaynor in 'Seventh Heaven' and 'The Street Angel,' I resolved to be as kind and sweet to everyone as she was. But before long the pictures died from my thoughts—also my resolution." Now, she may be exceptional and in some these favorable results may persist longer.

Family affection, however, when successfully portrayed on the screen, seems to find not only a ready response in the hearts of young spectators, but in the case of many of them a promise of longer duration. A high-school girl declares that after seeing "Beau Geste" she made a vow to love her sister as the young people in "Beau Geste" loved one another. "I am still," she adds, "trying to keep my promise and hope to continue." A college girl, referring to the effect of the same picture upon her love for her brother, goes into greater detail:

"After seeing 'Beau Geste,' though, our love turned into something more beautiful. One seemed more willing to sacrifice something for the other. If I asked my brother to do me a favor it seemed that he did it with much more willingness. Possibly this was imagination on my part, but I know that I for one was changed and could 'go through anything' for my brother." Still another girl records the enduring effect of this film after four years—"My brother and I are the ideal brother and 'kid sister'."

4

There are even records of ambitions being stirred up and kindled by pictures, or nascent desire to imitate some fine or laudable character attractively presented, thus supporting Dr. Dale's plea for more of such inspiring pictures. The cases where such effects occur are few, to be sure,—less than seven per cent of the young people examined refer to such an experience. But possibly the reason for this slender showing is due to the paucity of pictures presenting the elevated strain and the mold of greatness. The film depicting the life of Abraham Lincoln, for instance, is cited as having a powerful effect upon one boy, and several tell of forming musical ambitions after seeing "Humoresque." One student describes how movies depicting law-court procedure fired him to a desire for distinction in the law:

"I picture myself in the position of the presiding judge, a source of justice, then in the rôle of the prosecuting attorney, freeing society from the scourge of gun-play and violence, and finally as the counsel for the defence successfully maintaining my client's innocence. . . . This, I believe, has been the most lasting beneficial effect that I have derived from motion pictures."

This, let us remember, is also a form of day-dreaming. In the light of the experience of so many of a different character, that youth is fortunate. Another, who had been physically weak, attributes to a picture of circus life the blazing up of his ambition to grow stronger. Emulating a performer in feats of strength, he practiced progressive weight-lifting until he put on forty pounds of muscle, cured his lung trouble and attained to perfect health.

Fifty-nine per cent of Dr. Blumer's high-school material tell of a yearning for travel that came to them from the pictures, and fifty-one per cent answer affirmatively the question—"Have the movies developed in you a desire to go to college?" Some of these desires take on a more or less grotesque shape, to be sure, but any prompting in a good direction deserves to be recorded, even applauded. "When I saw 'The Campus Flirt'," writes one girl, "I was determined to go to college and become the heroine of campus activities." And a colored boy, oddly, derived his inspiration toward the higher learning from seeing Clara Bow in "The Wild Party." "So much so," he explains, "that I had to go to see the picture again; because I realized that if a girl could get along so nicely and have so much fun, the boys would have much more fun than that."

Now and then, as in the cases of those who were stimulated to a warmer affection or to giving birth to a fine ambition, you hear of a case where the incitement toward the laudable is quite as powerful as so many recorded urgings toward its opposite. A boy who had had no thought of going to college, who had already registered in a business school, recounts this as his personal experience:

"One evening I attended the theatre alone. A college picture was being shown which was different, however, from most pictures of this type in that it did not stress football and the inevitable campus romance unduly. Instead, it was a real worthwhile story of a young man's struggle to get a college education and his final success. The picture showed both the value of a college course and the pleasure derived from the social functions.

"I did not have to ponder over this picture after I had seen it. Instead, the answer to my problem came very suddenly while I was watching the screen. One thought flashed through my brain: 'I've just got to go to college'."

Many, however, record their bitter disillusionment upon coming to college, owing to the fact that a college or university is so different from what the movies had led them to expect. The public view, speaking generally, of college life is to a large extent molded by the movie presentations of it. Professor Blumer secured a virtually verbatim record of an illuminating and amusing conversation bearing upon this point of four college girls living in a dormitory—the conception of college life held by some of the youth of our nation.

"—Her idea of college is Bebe Daniels and Richard Dix."

"One Minute to Play?"

"Yes, that combined with 'Flaming Youth'."

"Well, you know a lot of us have that in mind when we come away to college."

"It doesn't take us long to get rid of it, though. But the ones who never get there are the ones who idealize the rah-rah stuff. They really believe college is nothing more than a big house-party."

"High-school kids are like that."

"Yes, and working girls. I worked in ——'s (a department store) and I learned a lot. When they discovered I was a college girl, you should have heard the questions they asked me. They were *pathetic*."

"What, for example?"

"Well, the girl that worked beside me was particularly thrilled. She asked me if I lived in a sorority house, and if there were a lot of good-looking men, and did we drink much."

"I wondered the same things myself, when I was in High School."

"But that wasn't all. This girl wanted to know if we had dirt sessions, and did the college students pet all the time. Not a word about classes or studying, just the social side. She said, 'Oh, do you really go to house-parties? And do the men and girls wear their pajamas when they're together'?"

"Good Lord, where did she think of that?"

"Movies."

"She might have gotten it from these sizzling books— '*Unforbidden Fruit*,' and so on."

"No, these girls don't read much. The movies are about their only source of enlightenment. They dote on college pictures, too. The University campus—Youth's Playground"!

"You know, I had a few of these ideas myself, somewhat toned down. And I lived in a college town."

"I think we all have, to a certain extent. After seeing every collegiate show from 'The Freshman' to 'Varsity' we're all ready to have just a big frolic through the fields of higher education."

"Yeh, and we find out soon enough"—

Perhaps the vast increase in college enrollment is not wholly due to a love of learning? . . .

5

It is to be expected, in view of the numbers of motion picture spectators, that differences in interpretation, in accordance with peculiarities and points of view, must emerge. A picture like "The Birth of a Nation" may to most people be virulent anti-negro propaganda. To some, as to this Jewish college girl, it may bring a feeling of indignation and rebellion. "For weeks," she says, "I looked with sympathy at every colored person, and got eleven cents together within two weeks and gave it to a little Negro boy."

Many adults and notably parents protested that "Our Dancing Daughters" would be likely to lead to harmful and immoral attitudes upon the part of the young. Yet many young people discovered in that film a representation of fair play and legitimate independence for themselves. The attitude of one's own group often determines the attitude of the individual. There comes a time, generally at about the age of sixteen, when love pictures become much more the topic of conversation and therefore much more enticing than other kinds of pictures. All the numerous experiences and histories, however, tend to show to what an amazing extent the movies loom as a sort of unsystematized system of education.

There are those (though Dr. Blumer does not pass judgment upon this point) who believe that motion pictures must be levelled down to the twelve-year-old intelligence. Usually the films are of approximately that level. And that very fact makes it so natural and easy for the young to absorb the images and form their ideas of life from the movies.

"This point," says Professor Blumer, "can be better appreciated when we realize that the display in motion pictures is a visual display. Images are supplied, so to speak, ready-made. They have a vividness and a clean-cut character which makes easier their absorption in whole-cloth fashion. This, it may be inferred, is particularly true in the case of those who are visually minded."

The clear-cut visual distinctness, the very universality of the pictures, carry with them a kind of sanction for the things shown—for good or ill. We have seen in Dr. Thurstone's experiment how frequently screen images shape the minds and opinions of the young. The images that fill the mind are, after all, a tremendously important part of the mental furniture, and determine how an individual will conceive and interpret phenomena and experience.

The screen is the most open of all books. And when the young see pictures presented in a certain way, it is small wonder that the vividness of the reception of those scenes, owing to the youth and freshness of the spectators, makes of the movies a peculiarly incisive and important factor in schemes of conduct. The less experience the spectators have, the less selective they naturally are. Coming to the young, as pictures do, in the most impressionable years of their life, the effect becomes of extraordinary weight and potentiality, and amounts often to a shaping and molding of their character.

Could we but have an equal emphasis upon high ideals, how tremendous would be the beneficent effect upon our children! That is the thought that is left in the mind of the writer as he surveys the possibilities and shortcomings of the movie output. So far as concerns adults, they are their own masters to choose as they wish. Children, however, are another matter. They deserve to be imbued with the best ideals that civilization affords.

CHAPTER XI

THE PATH TO DELINQUENCY

ANYONE considering the revelation of the findings by the group of scientific investigators in their survey of the motion pictures is moved to rueful laughter at the topsy-turvy quality of our civilization.

Quite definitely emerges the fact that the movies are a school, a system of education virtually unlimited, untrammelled and uncontrolled. It could be an immense and unprecedented instrument of civilization. Whenever what is called a good picture is produced, evidence is plentiful to show that those who see it, notably the young, are instantly affected by it. That type of picture, however, continues to be far too rare.

We used to smile at the goody-goody quality of what was called Sunday-school literature. Our pendulum has certainly swung far the other way when we reflect for a moment upon the evidence presented as to the contents of the volume of pictures daily emitted from Hollywood. When we recall that in 115 pictures presented to our 77,00,000 audience, as Dr. Dale found, 406 crimes are actually committed, and an additional forty-three attempted; that many of their characters are not only far from being models of human conduct, but are, many of them, highly objectionable in their occupations, in their goals, in their lives; that in thirty-five pictures fifty-four murders are committed, and in twelve pictures seventeen hold-ups successfully carried out—what can we possibly expect our young people to derive from all that?

If their minds, to use the old figure, are not precisely slates, but rather wax in their receptivity and fairly marble-like in their retention, as the writer must conclude from the Holaday and Thurstone studies, is it any wonder that the all too long procession of crimes, illicit enterprises, misdemeanors and techniques of delinquency presented in the movies should leave a certain deposit of impressions upon young minds? Yet constantly, in our ignorance, we have gone on exposing them to movie patterns of conduct and at the same time gone on wondering why the rising generation is restless, unruly, hard to control, and why crime waves are increasing in intensity. It is the present writer's hope that the very publication of these findings may contribute to better conditions.

We are all of us, it has been said, potential criminals, and the movies, some psycho-analysts believe, provide the spectator with opportunities for vicarious killing. It follows that the young, being more malleable, are likely to be more subject to influences than the adults. In the back of all our heads there has for some time been a vague notion that in some manner movies have a relationship to delinquency and crime. Substantial data upon this subject have been gathered and will presently, at least in part, be set forth. But even if we went no farther than this point, would it not suggest itself, in view of what has already been said, that, if the motion pictures analyzed by Dr. Dale did nothing else, they would, by sheer force of iteration, at least make young people more tolerant toward crime and delinquency? Even adults must come under such influence in view of the endless play upon these themes. The question is, then, how much effect and what manner of effect do the motion pictures have in influencing tendencies toward delinquency?

Delinquency is no new thing; it has always existed. It would be absurd to say even now that Al Capone and his organization are products solely of the movies. Numerous forces of present-day civilization play constantly upon characters and tendencies of youth, of which the movies are doubtless one, and movies are what we are here considering. What do the movies contribute to an alarming condition? Through facility of seeing them is created a tolerance of criminal patterns and a ready stimulation to those either predisposed to delinquency and crime or to those whose environment is too heavily weighted against them. The seed is supplied all too lavishly to the fertile ground.

Before proceeding to the study of actual delinquency and criminals, Professor Blumer and Mr. Hauser endeavored to find out to what extent the usual run of boys and girls are made more tolerant of crime and criminality by the pictures dealing in those subjects. They found that high-school boys and girls often not only expressed sympathy for the criminal, but that a few drew the conclusion that mere hard, plodding work is not desirable. Sympathy for the criminal, it is the present writer's observation, often implicit in the plots of motion pictures, is naturally quite common among the young. To cite some of the cases listed by Blumer and Hauser, a sixteen-year-old girl writes:

"Movies have made me less critical of criminals when I consider that all are not as fortunate as we. Starvation has been the cause of more crime than anything else as I see it in the movies. As a result, I believe crime should be corrected instead of being punished for the latter encourages more crime." "Usually," says another, "crime pictures make me feel sorry for the criminals because the criminals probably do not get the right start."

"A lot of crime movies I have seen," declares a sixteen-year-old boy, "made me feel more favorable towards crime by depicting the criminal as a hero who dies protecting his best friend against the police, or some movies show them as a debonair gentleman who robs at will from the rich and spares the poor. I have thought I would like to be a Robin Hood." "Many times o'er," one lad poetically phrases it, "I have desired to become a crook—and my ideal is Rob Roy, Scotland's greatest honorable crook, with Robin Hood close behind him." Even young girls assert that motion pictures create desires in them to become "benevolent criminals." "I have always felt," announces a fifteen-year old miss, "that being a character like Robin Hood would be *the* life."

The Robin Hood model of criminal, or the "Alias Jimmy Valentine" type, appears as attractive to many youngsters. Now, all this does not mean that these young boys and girls have been definitely incited to crime by the pictures. It does show, however, how the sharp barriers between right and wrong, built up by other institutions and training, as in the home, the church and the school, are progressively eroded and undermined, and some young people are made more tolerant toward crime and the criminal. As Professor Blumer expresses it:

"Merely to see, and to be attracted toward, a Robin Hood in motion pictures does not mean that one conceives all criminals as courageous and honorable persons, or all crimes as a worthy enterprise for the benefit of the poor or distressed. . . . Yet it should be apparent that views of particular types of crime and criminals, as have been formed by the writers of the accounts given, do exert some influence on the general stereotyped conceptions of crime and criminals. Many of the writers of the accounts admitted this to be true."

A number, on the other hand, declare that the movies showed them that crime does not pay and set them against it. Some are even vehement in protest that movies could not make them want to become criminals. Roughly, however, about one-fourth of all the high-school boys and girls who wrote on this subject indicated that motion pictures have made them on occasion more favorable to crime and criminals.

2

Now, the boy who stated that films depicted the criminal as a hero and made him more favorable toward crime has perhaps unwittingly put his finger on one of the most important bearings touching this point. Herein, to the mind of the present writer, lies much of the danger of crime movies to the young. Life, it is true, is not geometrical in its patterns. It is difficult to draw lines sharply and clearly between good and evil. The world, however, has agreed that for the young a certain austerity of conduct is indispensable. Otherwise, if that austerity is blurred or waived, if the child or adolescent is treated as though he were the mature philosopher, or at least the mature adult, there are certain to follow the irresponsibility, the bewilderment, the confusion so characteristic of our day. Many an educator has declared that the college generation of today is more responsible in various respects than were the generations of his forebears in the same institutions. But even if this be true, we must not forget that the total college population is but a small portion of the total minor movie population of 28,000,000.

"*Quod licet Jovi,*" said the medieval schoolmen, "*non licet bovi*"—a Latin jingle, simple enough, expressing merely that what may be suitable for some is not suitable for others.

One of the easiest gateways to blurred and confused conduct is the ready assumption, frequently derived by the young from the movies, that luxury, extravagance, easy money are the inalienable right of everyone. The recent economic depression has shown us one result of an almost universally accepted concept that wealth is easily attainable. The study of the case of various young delinquents shows to what an extent the same concept derived from the movies has played havoc with the youthful lives.

"The creation of desires for riches and suggestions for easily realizing them," observe Blumer and Hauser, "may dispose many, and lead some, to criminal behavior." In his study Blumer found that among criminals, delinquents and what they call "marginal delinquents," the appeal of a life of ease plays a markedly important rôle. A fourteen-year old boy in a Chicago area where delinquency runs high, expresses these influences briefly thus:

" 'No Limit' is a picture about gangsters. They always played dice and held people up and took the people's money. I felt like I was one of those and was getting some of the riches they had." Another, two years older, from the same area, declared, "Seeing gangsters having lots of money and big cars and being big shots makes a fellow want them. . . ."

These boys, however, are still only aspirants and their expression is as yet no more than a pious hope. The maturer tendency toward realization is exhibited in the terse statements of some reformatory inmates, sentenced for various crimes, who have already done and dared and come within the range of the Blumer-Hauser survey:

"As I became older," bluntly admits a lad convicted of robbery, "the luxuries of life showed in the movies, partly, made me want to possess them. I could not on the salary I was earning." Another, working off a burglary sentence, is even more explicit:

"The ideas that I got from the movies about easy money were from watching pictures where the hero never worked, but seemed always to have lots of money to spend. All the women would be after him. . . . I thought it would be great to lead that kind of a life. To always have plenty of money and ride around in swell machines, wear good clothes, and grab off a girl whenever you wanted to. I still think it would be a great life."

A great life!—the ideal held up to view in so much of

our public entertainment—"lots of money to spend"—
"swell machines"—"women"—the cheapest and the shod-
diest vulgarity even when it is not criminal. A large
percentage of movie characters, as Dale has shown us,
have either illegal occupations or no occupations—patterns tending to sensitize such material as these boys to
suggestions of a similar life.

"The pictures that they show of this sort," mouths a
young robber, "shows how the man that is a crook gets
his money and how he out-smarts the law and it looks
very easy."

But these, someone may object, are young criminals.
True, they are young—but once they were not criminals,
although many of them doubtless came from delinquent
areas or unsuccessful homes. Even in a good neighborhood one-fifth of the boys examined, indicated on a questionnaire response that motion pictures moved them to
the desire of making "a lot of money easily." In a high-
rate delinquency area, that is, an area where there are
frequent arrests, the percentage of such flashy ambitions
rises to thirty-nine or nearly double the percentage of
the other boys, while among the truant or behavior
problem boys, it runs up to forty-five per cent. The conclusion appears inescapable that to show certain types
of pictures—so numerous in the current output—in what
are known as high-rate delinquency areas, in cities, is in
some measure like selling whiskey to the Indians, against
which there are quite justly severe laws and sharp
penalties.

The natural protest would be that in that case no film
depicting wealth, no so-called "society" drama could
ever be shown upon the screen, since it might move

many young people to yearn for easily acquired money. Upon investigation, however, it was found that it was not the society dramas, but the "gangster" or "crook" type of picture that caused the trouble. In a high-delinquency area, as Professor Thrasher and Mr. Cressey found, it is the gangster picture that points the way to wealth, and thereby the way to "high society." The themes and characters of such pictures are more familiar to the people concerned, the atmosphere more natural and kindred to their environment and interests, and as Thrasher puts it, "the boy of this community can with ease identify himself with the character portrayed." They exhale possibility within reach of the aspiring among themselves, whereas the film of wealth and fashion embodies a world remote and alien, in the realm of the unattainable.

The Blumer-Hauser investigation showed that more than one-half of the truant and behavior problem boys examined, fifty-five per cent, indicated that pictures dealing with gangsters and gun-play stirred in them desires for wanting "to make a lot of money easily." Only five per cent, however, believe that the wealthy type of picture, or the type indicating a wealthy social background, provoke in them the desire "to make lots of money easily." The crook pictures are the sort that suggest direct and comprehensible ways of making easy money. Twenty-five per cent of a sampling of 110 boys in a penal institution mention "hold-ups" as the high revelation they gleaned. Eleven per cent cite stealing, and twenty per cent give the vague but all-embracing "crime" as the royal road to fortune brought to them by the message of the pictures.

To some of them the themes and plots of such pictures bring an appeal and an urge all but irresistible. The kind of poverty that used to be called "decent" is not fashionable in the pictures. Instead there are those engaging characters found by Dr. Dale of "illegal occupation," or "no occupation." An eighteen-year-old lad in a reformatory, sentenced for robbery and rape, virtually traces his own derivation from such pictures:

"I would see the 'Big Shot' come in a cabaret. Everyone would greet him with a smile. The girls would all crowd around him. He would order wine and food for the girls. Tip the waiter $50.00 or more. After dining and dancing he would give the girls diamond bracelets, rings and fur coats. Then he would leave and go to meet his gang. They would all bow down to him and give him the dough that was taken from different rackets. When I would see pictures like this I would go wild and say that some day I would be a Big Shot that everyone would be afraid of, and have big dough. Live like a king, without doing any work."

In a nut-shell, the above is the most striking anatomy of the "gangster" or "racket" picture and of its influence upon such as that boy, and, to many of us, one of the answers to the question of why crime is so prevalent in our cities. Dale has shown us how considerable is the percentage of crime pictures in the total. Compared with their continuous production, the sale of whiskey to reservation Indians is a trivial offense.

The Big Shot! Symbol of the spread of vulgarity in our troubled age, that seems to grope for solutions of its difficulties in all directions except the right ones. It will spend billions for frantically attempted "cures" and nostrums, but, in the domain of social malady, hardly anything for prevention. It is safe to say that not even Imperial Rome at its most decadent held up such symbols or images for its young to ape and copy. Even very young grade-school boys of ten and eleven in certain areas of cities actually crackle with bravado when they refer to some of their cinema obsessions.

"De 'Big House,'" says a ten-year-old lad, "made me feel like I was a big tough guy. I felt just like Machine Gun Butch." And an eleven-year-old Italian boy chortles, "When I saw Jack Oakie in 'The Gang Buster' I felt like a big gangster." "I feel like the big shot that knows schemes and hiding places," confessed another, "and knows how to kill and capture cops and get a lot of money."

All of these avowals and many more like them come from boys living in an area where delinquency is frequent. After allowing for the element of boasting, "they seem," says Professor Blumer, "to be captivated by the daring, adventurousness and toughness shown in the pictures. Even in narrating their experiences the emotional influence was evident in their increased excitement during the interview and their apparent re-living of the scenes." Who says that we fail to educate our young in the ways of democracy? Even in the normal neighborhoods thirty-one per cent of the schoolboys declare that the movies incite them to do something daring. In one penal institution twenty-six per cent of the inmates answered that pictures taught them to act "tough," or to act like a "big guy." They call it, some of them, feeling "brave"!

"I feel tough and go home and lick my little nephew,"

brags a twelve-year old, and, "when I see an exciting picture," declares another, "I get all nervoused up. I don't know what I do then. Sometimes I feel like a tough and if a guy comes up to me I bang!—punch him in the nose and without even asking him what he wants." Another tells of emerging from a "gang-land" picture and beating and robbing of all his money the first small newsboy luckless enough to come in his way. He has since landed in the reformatory for robbery and rape.

When they testify, as does one boy, that "pictures about gangsters enabled me to become one," or, as another, a reformatory inmate, puts it—"A picture that is pretty exciting and adventurous makes me want to do something and when I come out of a show . . . I would go with another fellow and break in some store that looked like it had a few dollars in it"—when pictures produce particularly significant effects like this, it would appear high time that protest and responsibility take the place of apathy and irresponsibility.

"If," conclude Blumer and Hauser, "it is true that in much delinquency and crime there is a spirit of bravado, boldness and 'toughness,' it seems to be a not unreasonable assumption that the inducement of this spirit by motion pictures may help to initiate or reinforce criminal activity. The declaration by some delinquents and criminals that this has been true in their cases suggests that it may be true in others."

3

While day-dreaming, as we have seen, may operate for good, it may, also, in certain circumstances tend de-

cidedly toward evil. Fantasies of criminal behavior are
one of the forms of day-dreaming, and where inhibitions
are not strong and where so many pictures present scenes
of crime, it is not astonishing to find many boys admit-
ting that forms of violent action have filled their dreams,
and that fully twenty per cent of a sampling of 110 convicts studied admitted that they had brooded upon being
gangsters or burglars after they had seen an adventurous
burglar, gangster or bandit picture. How reliable are
their assertions is for the reader to judge. Pathetic are
some of their confessions. It all looked so feasible in the
movies!

"I have seen pictures," writes a young forger of nineteen, "and imagined how easy it was to cash bunk
checks, and I have done that very thing." Easy—but
he spoke from behind bars.

"As a child," writes a lad of twenty-two, "I always
wanted to be the bad guy and always wanted to get into
the racket, and would always lay in bed and think of all
the money that the bad guys would make. There were
also a few pictures that I saw that caused me to think
that I was a bold burglar, and I always thought of pulling a job, but when I got to the place I always got cold
feet." Cold feet, or not, this particular day-dreamer is
serving a sentence for burglary in a reformatory.

The game of "cops and robbers" figures as a pastime
among boys of all classes, but it is an especially favorite
pastime among the young in what is called high delinquency areas. For this game certain of the gangster
and crime films are replete with images and suggestions.
"When I was a small boy," recalls one lad, "I used to be
crazy about seeing a cop-and-robber play. After the play

I would go home and act as if I was a robber and sometimes my brother or my chums would be the police.
Then later in my years I would break in a store and
make off it was a bank or some big place to rob."

At the age of fifteen he was in a state institution under
sentence for burglary. He goes on with vivid circum-
stantiality—"In my mind I felt good for the bad guy
and always wished he would pull a job and never get
caught. I would always take the part of the bad guy
and think in my later years I would be some big gangster and be the leader of a big gang. Have a nice home;
make off I am in a business, but have a *secret* room and
tell the gang what to do. To have all the people fear
when they hear my name and not know my real name.
I would also like to baffle the police so that they never
would catch me or any member of my gang. And have
a gang with all brave guys that would die for me. Do
anything I told them to do and no dirty double-crossing
in my gang. I would take the double-crosser and take
him for a ride and shoot him, with a penny in his hand
to show that he was a dirty stool-pigeon."

It is only fair to surmise that this gifted but unfortunate boy, who so obviously manifests the instincts of
genius, would doubtless have arrived even without the
stimulus of "copper and robber" plays or gangster films.
Still, these clearly provided scope for his imagination
and fed his day-dreams with unending material.

4

While there is no law as to how a young spectator will
react to a gangster picture or a crook and crime picture,
a good deal depends upon the neighborhood and the

social environment. As has been pointed out, delinquency is no new thing and some environments are too heavily weighted against their young denizens. Boys and girls living in a so-called delinquency area, however, will no more all derive incentives to crime from the movies than all those living in stable communities will be infallibly pure and honest. Still, by and large, it was found that the difference in the neighborhood experiences will affect the young spectator's interpretation of the motion pictures. Thus, in a certain community where the rate of delinquency is low, a high-school boy of fifteen writes,

"I have often wished that there were no crooks. I like to see crime movies, but I never sympathize with the criminal." Another cries out, "These crime pictures portraying the thief as a man who is good and just and only trying to support his aged mother! The writers ought to be shot for such stuff."

In a tough Chicago neighborhood, on the other hand, with a high delinquency rate, boys tell a somewhat different story.

"I never stole anything till I got to dis neighborhood," says an Italian boy of fourteen. "It was after I moved to dis neighborhood dat I began to like crook pictures. Den I started stealing stuff at de market and taking tings." Another tells how he and his friends followed and discussed gangster pictures, seeking for suggestions helpful in making money easily. They organized a gang and embarked upon a series of petty robberies.

That the milieu or environment has a bearing upon the affinities for certain types of films is further illustrated by some figures worked out by Professor Blumer and Mr. Hauser. In the high rate delinquency areas, for example, eleven per cent of schoolboys examined rank gangster pictures first in order of their preference; yet only four per cent of the boys in the low delinquency areas express a similar preference. The boys in the truant and problem behavior school run exactly with the high delinquency product in their choice of gangster pictures—eleven per cent.

Now, does that merely indicate that boys in high delinquency areas, boys, that is, in troublesome neighborhoods, are keener for stirring adventure than are the boys in a "good" neighborhood? "Is this merely an effect of background?" That was a phase that interested Blumer and Hauser and they made some inquiries. They found that, whereas twenty per cent of the boys in a so-called high delinquency area indicated airplane pictures as their first choice, forty-seven per cent of the boys in a "good" neighborhood preferred airplane to all other pictures. Which would suggest that it is not merely adventure, but delinquent adventure that is the attraction to the devotees of gangster and crime pictures.

And precisely as the boys in the high delinquency regions prefer crime pictures, so the girls in the same neighborhood prefer love and sex pictures. Between the girls of a high delinquency area and those of the low there is a marked difference in this respect—as 32 is to 24. This may be due to a difference in ages—although all girls like love pictures many times more than do the boys.

The various samplings of boys studied by Blumer and Hauser were asked this question:

"Which of the following kinds of life do the movies

usually show in an interesting way—college life, home life, life of the criminal, wealthy or rich life, honest life, hard work, fighting, having a good time?"

Forty-five per cent of the truant and behavior problem boys indicated that to their view the screen showed most interestingly the life of the criminal. In the low rate delinquency area about half that number expressed a similar view.

With straws like this to show the direction of the wind, the question occurs to the present writer, even though none of the investigators touches upon it: Does not the exhibition of gangster pictures in the so-called high delinquency neighborhoods amount to the diffusion of poison? To the influence of bad environment and social disorganization is added a supply of material to feed susceptibility to crime and delinquency. A smouldering flame is fed and encouraged. Always undesirable, in virtually every case and neighborhood, the criminal or gangster picture in congested areas and high delinquency regions tends to combat and annihilate all the major influences for good which society has been at such pains and expense to provide. Here and there a reader, though one hopes there will not be many of him, may say, "The American public is getting what it wants." To the writer such a principle appears pernicious and all the more dangerous in a democracy. The Indian on the reservation is likewise getting what he wants when someone criminally sells him whiskey.

Entertainment like gangster and crook pictures in such neighborhoods appears as nothing less than an *agent provacatuer*, a treacherous and costly enemy let loose at the public expense.

CHAPTER XII

MOVIE-MADE CRIMINALS

POSSIBLY it is a source of pride to us that as a nation we do nothing by halves. If we have the greatest booms, we also have the most appalling depressions. If we manufacture a product, we standardize it, produce it by the traveling-belt system and put it out in millions. Likewise, when we produce criminals, we standardize the product, produce it on a national scale and in unprecedented numbers. Dr. E. H. Sutherland in his "Criminology" shows that between say, 1914 and 1922 burglaries and attempts against members of the American Bankers' Association have increased out of all proportion to the growth of our population. In 1914 the figures per 100,000 members was 19.1; in 1922 it had risen to 97.5. Similarly, holdups in 1914 were 4.8 per 100,000; in 1922 they were 41.3. The writer knows of no other country showing such increases of crime. According to the evidence, as shown in the foregoing chapter and as will appear in this one, the movies, with their nation-wide public of 77,000,000, with their large output of pictures presenting crime scenes though only one element, play a significant part in showing techniques, methods and means of committing crimes.

When careful investigators find that seventeen per

cent of a group of 139 delinquent boys of fifteen or younger indicate that movies have influenced them to do something wrong, the evidence is significant. It may be true that some overstate and that they like to blame their crime upon external influence. But after noting the care of the investigators in getting their material, I must conclude that, as part of a large picture, their data are substantially correct. Where there is so much smoke a certain amount of fire is inevitable. The Blumer-Hauser figure, moreover, is certain to be conservative, since while some boys are braggarts, equal numbers, doubtless, are averse to making such admissions. Yet many autobiographies among all classes of boys, even in good neighborhoods, show that they learned from the movies various forms of delinquency and put them into operation with varying degrees of success.

Like charity, delinquency often begins at home, without any great complexity. "I saw a picture, 'Me, Gangster,'" writes a high-school boy of seventeen. "This gave me a yearning to steal. . . . I went to our register and took out a quarter and went to a show. I did this taking in a sly manner just as in the show."

Numerous minor delinquencies are attributed by boys to the movies—stealing small sums, robbing a chicken coop, a small newsboy or a fruit vendor—little is thought of these acts by the boys or even by their elders. Criminologists, however, are well aware how often this type of early minor delinquency leads to more serious acts and graver forms of crime. Experienced criminals, moreover, join the criminologists in this belief and frequently condemn the movie influence and touch upon it with bitterness as a factor in their own unfortunate careers.

A number of reformatory inmates, lads in their twenties, express themselves very clearly and definitely on that head.

"In my opinion, it is a bad thing for young boys to go to the movies and see pictures showing men stealing," volunteers a boy of twenty-three. "I saw a picture and thought that I could do the same thing." "Pictures of gangsters enabled me to become one of them," succinctly declares another. "Movies have shown me the way of stealing automobiles, the charge for which I am now serving sentence." "I saw how a bad guy in the movies got money and cops could not catch him. . . . When I went to the show I saw the men who needed money. So they got together and stole a car. When I saw how easy it was done I thought I would try it."

These are excerpts from statements written by young criminals in sober mood. They were assured that nothing therein would count against them, in fact, the questionnaire was so contrived that the replies were anonymous. They were convinced they had nothing to gain or lose by the statements. Allowance being made for the criminal's tendency to blame some agency other than himself for his disasters, the evidence is still impressive.

One boy of nineteen serving a sentence for safecracking attributes his unhappy plight largely to a single picture—"Alias Jimmy Valentine." With two other boys of an experimental turn of mind, he attempted to crack a safe according to the Jimmy Valentine pattern. That technique proved beyond him and he was caught. "I couldn't," he adds, "wholly blame the movies for that as the two boys I was with enticed me as much as the movies. I think my desire to have a good time and good clothes," he adds, "were the chief factors in my getting in trouble." But this very desire in itself he almost unconsciously derives from the movies:

"Naturally movies were the cause of my failure because I would see clothes and luxury in pictures and would try to have the same or as near the same as those on the screen. . . . So in order to have all these I had to have money, and that is why I tried to break open the safe."

In his struggle with his dilemma this unfortunate lad manages to present a fairly clear statement of cause and effect. He emerges, in fact, as a movie-made criminal. He was apprehended and is serving his time.

Similarly, in the Thrasher and Cressey study the following case is reported: "A very tall fellow of about nineteen years, a high-school boy, an only child, interested in radio broadcasting and building sets, saw 'Raffles' in 'The Gentleman Burglar' in the movies. With a younger friend of sixteen, he decided that he could try to do that. He made cards with a 'Hand' sign from a rubber stamp on them and printed 'Compliments of Kid Gloves.' He then started a series of robberies of small stores nearby." The police, foiled at first, traced the boy by means of that "Kid Gloves" card which made its appearance at a football game, and the amateur "Raffles" was caught and arrested. Many, however, commit crimes and are not apprehended. Confessions bearing upon this point are naturally rare, yet some boys are frank enough to confess. A high-school boy describes how in a spirit of experimental bravado, he and his friend Jack proceeded to copy a screen bandit:

"The bandit hero drilled the door of the house and stole money and valuables. We talked it over; and then armed with a brace and bit went over to a fruit store combined with a meat market and drilled out the lock. It worked fine. I naturally," he adds, "don't consider it proper to rob a fruit store now." If this boy has but succeeded in outgrowing his propensity, he is lucky. In any case, his statement bids for approval, because now he knows what is proper.

A lad of sixteen makes a somewhat similar confession; "From these criminal pictures I got the idea that I wanted to participate in crime, robbing stores preferably. I have robbed money plenty of times but not large amounts, giving some to beggars, to little children and keeping a large amount for myself." Now, possibly this boy is merely giving the pictures as an alibi, or perhaps he was a Robin Hood bandit in his early childhood, and his progress was but in the natural sequence of events. There is nothing like being systematic, and to those who are bright and ambitious there is much that is helpful in the system.

Of delinquents who come to grief by their delinquency, significant numbers trace their plight to the movies. Their own suggestibility was doubtless a factor, too, but as has been said, we are all potential criminals. The movies, in their cases, supplied the necessary stimulus, the spark. A young burglar, twenty-three, inmate of a reformatory, expresses this influence with great simplicity:

"One of the things that caused my downfall was some of the movies I saw which showed me how to jimmy a door or window. The name of one of the pictures I

saw which showed how to break into a place was
'Chinatown,' with Richard Talmadge. It was about a
gang of crooks and how they would break into a place
and take the money, or what jewels were there; in other
words, make easy money. After I saw the picture I got
the feeling that I would like to try it." He did try it.
His urge had been the instilled desire for easy money,
fine clothes and luxuries. He continues,

"Each idea I got about easy money in the movies put
it in my head that I would like to try it as I always
wanted money to be dressed up in good clothes and to
look big. The things they show in the pictures I have
seen show how a fellow would break into a place and
get enough money to buy a car and some good clothes,
and it makes me feel that I wanted to be dressed up
and have a car, too."

How simple it all was! He wanted money to be
dressed up and he wanted to look big. The same old
ideal, so irresistible to many of us, so helpful in making
delinquents, defaulters and criminals. The pictures supplied that boy with stimulus and a technique for jimmying windows and doors. He is an inmate of the reformatory.

Many young criminals describe how they acquired
their impetus and techniques for robbery from the
variety of methods shown on the screen. "I learned
from the movies," as one young reformatory bird puts
it tersely, "the scientific way of pulling jobs. Leave no
fingerprints or telltale marks."

Science is essential to our lives and must be learned
and acquired somehow. This boy depended for his instruction upon the movies. A young burglar, only six-

teen, throws a similar light upon the education of himself and his gang in their trade:

"In breaking in a store we learned from the movies
to use a glass-cutter and master key and one boy had a
jimmy. If the key didn't work we would use the glass-
cutter, and if that didn't work we would use the jimmy.
We would put the jimmy by the lock and force it open."
This all-round training and eclecticism is illustrated by
others who tell circumstantially how they learned the
use of blackjacks, brass knuckles, machine guns and even
bombs. The hold-up, a seemingly simple process, nevertheless has its own techniques and some tell of acquiring
them from the movies. Even how to escape from the
police in a stolen car has to be learned somehow. And
where, after all, is the ideal school?

"The first stick-up I ever saw," is the frank reminis-
cence of a young robber, "was in a movie show and I
seen how it is done and what the crook usually does after
the stick-up." Some young delinquents awaiting trial
were interviewed by Professor Blumer and Dr. Hauser
upon the route they followed to arrive where they found
themselves. Here is part of a conversation with a seventeen-year-old offender charged with burglary:

Question. "How about the movies? Do you think
they had something to do with your difficulty?

Answer. Well, I think that I learned plenty from
them.

Q. What did you learn, would you say?

A. Jimmying a window and things like that. I tried
to open a safe once, but I couldn't do that.

Q. Did you see that in a picture?

A. I saw that in a picture, so I tried it.

Q. What picture did you see that in?

A. Some funny kind with Evelyn Brent."

"I learned something from 'The Doorway to Hell.' It is a gangster picture. It shows how to drown out shots from a gun by backfiring a car." This is one of the numerous techniques learned from the movies, as one ex-convict explains it. There is a large amount of such terse testimony as to the educational source—the movies —for a great many methods and techniques acquired by young criminals. The investigators under Dr. Thrasher found a number, and Drs. Blumer and Hauser found a great many. So many, indeed, that Blumer and Hauser made a sort of little census from their case material and their inventory, while not exhaustive, is illuminating:

How to open a safe by "feel" of dial.

How to enter a store by forcing lock with crowbar and screwdriver.

To cut burglar alarm wires in advance during the day.

How to take door off hinges to force way into apartment.

How to break window noiselessly for forcing way into store or house to be burglarized, by pasting flypaper on window before breaking it.

How to act and what to do in robbery with a gun.

Use of brace and bit to drill lock out for forcing entrance into store.

Use of glass-cutter to cut glass of window away so window-lock can be opened.

Technique of sudden approach and quick getaway in robbery.

How to jimmy a door or window.

Use of a master key for gaining entrance to a house.

Idea of looking for secret panels hiding wall safes in burglarizing houses.

How to open or close a lock with a pair of tweezers.

How to force the door of an automobile with a piece of pipe.

Idea of stealing silverware in burglaries.

Idea of renting an apartment for gang "hangout."

"The scientific way"—leaving no finger-prints.

How to use weapons—pistols, shotguns, machine guns, blackjacks, brass knuckles, bombs.

Eluding police by turning up alley, turning off lights, then speeding in opposite direction.

Gambling with (and cheating) drunken persons.

To pose as a gas inspector for purposes of burglary.

How to drown out shots of guns by backfiring.

How to maim or kill motorcycle policemen by swinging and stopping car suddenly.

How to pick pockets.

How to accomplish jail breaks by using a truck to pull bars from windows or doors.

The use of ether on sleeping occupants of a house being burglarized.

The use of gloves in burglary.

To beware of alarms or plates in front of safes.

The use of an arc-burner, to burn out combinations of safes without noise.

How to sell liquor in "booze racket" by coercion.

Importance of establishing an alibi.

Carrying a machine-gun in a violin case, as found by Professor Thrasher's investigators.

Thirty-two separate and important items of crime

technique! Fagin's school was child's play to this curriculum of crime. Now, while no one would pretend that every one of us seeing these diverse techniques illustrated on the screen would thereby become a criminal, it is nevertheless true that many retain for a long period what they see. The criminally inclined, those with unsteady inhibitions, the delinquent, or what Blumer and Hauser call "marginal individuals" and what criminals often call "punks"—from whom future criminals are recruited—these are the ones who are apt to store away those techniques and ideas, so carefully wrought out before them on the screen with all the finesse of laboratory procedure. There was no technique for testing their credibility, but twenty per cent of the convicts studied affirm that the movies taught them ways and means in theft and robbery.

Mordaunt Hall, motion picture critic of the New York *Times,* reviewing the situation at the year-end of 1932–33, declares that the public is sick of racketeer and gangster pictures. Hollywood, however, believes that there is money in them.

2

The best way, perhaps, of illustrating the rôle of motion pictures in stimulating young drifters toward crime and providing crime techniques is by quoting more or less fully a single case, that of a young negro of twenty-two in a penal institution. The boy recounts that while still at school, a gang of young hoodlums accustomed to robbing small boys of their pocket-money on the fringes of the playground, interested him in their procedure by robbing him. But upon learning that he had older

brothers who might seek reprisals, they not only re
turned his money but cordially invited him to join
them. He began by absenting himself from school in
order to join this gang and soon the movies began to
appear as an influence in his path.

"I had never pulled a job till I saw Lon Chaney in
'The Unholy Three.' I saw how he broke into a store
and robbed the safe and how he picked people's pockets.
When we came out of the show, a couple of the boys
suggested that we try to rob a store the way we had
seen in the picture." The decision was unanimous and
after getting the necessary tools, they succeeded in robbing a clothing store. This venture offered little difficulty and they proceeded to look about for more worlds
to conquer:

"Whenever we saw that a gangster picture was playing at a theatre, we would all go to find out some other
way of robbing places. . . . George Bancroft was playing in 'The Underworld' in a show at —— and ——
Streets. We saw how he went into a store and cut the
burglar alarm wire. Then he came back that night and
broke into the store and got away with a bunch of fur
coats. We thought we would try that trick, so that afternoon we went out to F—— Street and the Elevated to
a haberdasher's store. We went into the store and pre-
tended that we wanted to buy something. While two
of the boys were looking at some articles I cut the wire
that ran down the side of the door. Then after I had
completed my job, the boys told the salesman that they
would be back. That night we went back to the store
to rob it."

Lack of success in that enterprise was due to the fact

that the proprietor must have discovered the damage, and when they returned and attempted entry with a crow-bar the alarm worked. Later, however, another member of the gang showed them how to take off a door by knocking the bolts out of the hinges, a trick he had learned from some other movie. Our hero was steadily progressing in his education. His narrative goes on:

"I saw another picture at —— and —— Streets in which I got an idea how to rob a store. The title of the picture, I think, was 'No Way Out.' I can't recollect the name of the leading character. It was a picture about some thugs robbing a bank. They tried to get in the door but it was adequately locked. They tried the roof but it was well barred with iron bars and screws. Then one of the thugs suggested that they break the lock on the iron bar that runs around the outside, then paste some fly-paper on the window; about ten pieces was what they put on the window. Then they took a hammer and hit around the edge of the fly-paper until the window was broken. When they took the paper down, the pieces of glass came down with the paper and didn't make any noise. Then they went into the bank and looted it and got away safely without anyone seeing or hearing them. About a week after I saw the show a couple of boys and myself tried the trick and it came out successfully."

It is to be noted that those who committed the crime in the picture were "thugs," whereas the narrator's associates were merely "boys." He goes on to tell how he and his friends looted a store by means of that clever technique so successfully learned, and got safely away.

"I have tried that trick on quite a few stores and it has come out successful each time. I have never been caught in an act of robbing a place. I have been locked up a number of times. I was always put in jail when someone would tell on me or the police would pick me up on suspicion. I have gone to the 'Boys' School' for little things such as being bad in school, riding in stolen autos, etc."

Stirred to enterprise by the adroit techniques he had assimilated from the movies, he began to seek for new information bearing upon his vocation. He found what he describes as a gangster book entitled "The Blue Boy," which gave him the idea of using a glass-cutter for removing panes of glass from jewelry shops to facilitate robbery. Though he was almost caught, he managed nevertheless to escape with several hundred dollars' worth of jewelry. After this he entered a new phase of criminal activity. Heretofore he had been an unarmed young thief and petty burglar. Something, however, gave him a new idea.

"I saw another picture a year or two before I came down here [the penitentiary]. If I am not mistaken the name of the picture was 'The Night Streets of Broadway." [He is probably in error as to the title.] I cannot remember the name of the star character. The character was a young man of twenty-five or twenty-four. His people were in a state of destitution; he was out of work; his father was out of work, and his mother was sick. He had a small brother and sister. He had tried hard for a job but to no avail. One day when he was around a poolroom, he heard some boys about his own age talking about a job they had pulled off. Each of them had a large roll of money. That inspired him to try the same racket. He went to a friend of his and borrowed a gun. He went out that night and stuck up a rich couple in their car. He went home and gave some money to his father, and told him he had a job working nights and had drawn on his salary. He went along for a long time robbing people and taking care of his family. One night he went to stick up a taxi driver; he was caught in the act by a policeman. When he went to jail he told the judge why he had committed the crime. The judge was going to give him a light sentence in jail when a rich man stepped up and told the judge that he would give the boy a chance if the judge would place the boy in his charge."

That story, needless to say, ends happily for the young criminal, but as the narrator frankly admits, "I did not pay that part any attention. I wanted to get some money at the time I was looking at the picture. So I went home and stole my father's pistol out of his writing-desk and went down to F—— (Street)."

Together with a friend he proceeds on this new venture—robbery with a gun. Steadily growing in crime, he has steadily continued to get his suggestions and techniques from the motion pictures as a sort of hand-book. The first efforts of these boys, which he describes in detail, were quite successful.

"K—— and I met the next night. We decided that we would work out north. We got off the Elevated at —— and ——. We went east about a block, then we went north a couple of blocks until we got to a gangway. We saw a man coming down the street. We got ready for him and pulled down our caps and put up our coat-collars. I went up behind him and told him to put up his hands and not to make any noise, the same way I had done the first man we stuck up. He told us to take the money and not take his watch. When K—— was going through his pockets, the man coughed. I thought he was trying to make a break for a gun. I almost shot the man. I told him to walk straight ahead and not look back. K—— and I ran through the gangway, then down the alley to the Elevated. We got on the Elevated and went on the back and counted the money. We had four ten-dollar bills, a two-dollar bill, six one-dollar bills and some change. I got off at T—— and I——, and told K—— that I would meet him around the poolroom the next day.

"When I got home I went in my room which I shared with one of my brothers and thought, I had almost wounded a man or killed him. I said to myself, if I had killed a man and got caught, I would have to pay the death penalty or life imprisonment. I thought for a long time. Then I said I would not try that racket any more because I will sometime run up on some fellow who will try to resist and then I would have to save myself by wounding or taking his life. When I told K—— that I wouldn't go with him any more and told him why, he told me that I was yellow. I told him if he had killed a man, I would be in it just as much as he would. He went and got another partner and I quit the racket. He and his partner are now in the Joliet prison for robbery and attempt to kill with a pistol. I am glad that I quit in time. I have one to ten years for larceny, and he has one to life. I know that I will get out and get a discharge a long time before he will."

Professor Blumer and Dr. Hauser do not, naturally, ascribe the delinquency of this young criminal solely to motion pictures. None of the participants in the four-year research, for that matter, ascribe whatever criminality and delinquency they have found entirely to the movies. Other factors contribute in numerous instances to the formation of the criminal life patterns. Their research, however, was concerned with the discovery of the operation of the movies as an element in these patterns and the evidence they have assembled is impressive. Blumer and Hauser who seldom draw conclusions and usually understate them, observe of this particular history of the young negro:

"It is easy to detect in this case the strand of motion picture experience, sometimes of negligible import but sometimes of dominating significance. In providing suggestions to crime, in stimulating a certain amount of boldness and confidence in the execution of new crimes and in providing detailed techniques of crime, motion pictures operated directly on the criminal behavior of this individual. It is interesting and important to see how this boy sums up his own case." They continue to quote from his autobiography:

"I think that the movies are mostly responsible for my criminal career. When I would see a crime picture and notice how crime was carried out, it would make me feel like going out and looking for something to steal. I have always had a desire for luxury and good clothes. When I worked the salary was so small that I couldn't buy what I wanted, and pay the price for good clothes. When I would see crime pictures, I would stay out all night stealing. I have quit six or seven jobs just to steal."

3

The above case, cited at some length, as well as several cases more briefly referred to, or those for which there is here no space, show not only how crime technique may be learned from the motion pictures, but also how in numerous instances the direct suggestions and influence of motion pictures propelled the spectators toward acts of delinquency and crime. So far as concerns indirect influence, the stirring of desires for ease, luxury, easy money as obtainable through criminal or illegitimate enterprise, these cases are still more numerous.

Forty-nine per cent or virtually half of a sample of 110 inmates of a penal institution investigated by Blumer and Hauser testified that movies gave them a desire to carry a gun. And carrying a gun, while not necessarily criminal in itself, very often leads to crime. Twenty-eight per cent of the same sample stated that movies aroused in them the desire to practice stick-ups, or hold-ups. Twenty-one per cent declared that movies taught them how to fool the police, and twelve per cent state on a questionnaire form that when they saw an adventuresome bandit, burglar or gangster picture, they planned how to hold up someone or "to pull a job."

Perhaps the reader will forgive a necessary reiteration when we recall that in his analysis of 115 pictures studied week by week in the theatres, Dr. Dale found that in them 406 crimes were committed and forty-three more attempted; in thirty-five pictures, fifty-four murders took place; in twelve pictures seventeen hold-ups occurred and in thirty-two pictures, fifty-nine instances of assault and battery. It is evident that on the advertising principle which believes in constant repetition as the road to the prospective purchaser's mind, these images and ideas of crime so ceaselessly reiterated on the screen must sooner or later wear paths in young brains in the least susceptible or suggestible. In the old adage, it is the drop of water that hollows the stone. Dr. Thurstone and Miss Peterson have shown that the effects of motion pictures in any direction may be cumulative. In a way, those constantly recurring crime pictures may become for a portion of the spectators not merely a school, but a very university of crime, with a wide range of techniques, suggestions and patterns cunningly executed and vividly presented.

"Ideas and impulses," summarize Blumer and Hauser, "are checked, are held within the mind for a given time, are held, so to speak, to mere incipient activity. In the course of time they may pass away, without leaving any trace; but they may also work in subtle ways in a pattern of life." That in most cases they do pass away is fortunate, or perhaps all those of us who are motion picture addicts would become criminals and delinquents. In many instances, however, as we have seen, not only do they not pass away, but they leave imprints so powerful that a number of the criminal and delinquent attribute their wrong-doing and downfall in a measure to the potency of film suggestion. When once the full force of this truth comes home to the public, it will feel bound to demand a more carefully planned and a more subtly supervised form of entertainment.

CHAPTER XIII

SEX-DELINQUENCY AND CRIME

TRUANCY used to be a simple thing. A boy stayed away from school to go fishing or swimming, and he was a reprehensible person and he was duly punished for it. Girls played truant but seldom and offered few problems. Then appeared various new elements including the movies—and new temptations in the field of conflict with a sense of duty, the acquisition of which plays so large a part in the education of all of us. "It is apparent beyond a slight statistical chance," observe Thrasher and Cressey, "that delinquents and truants tend more often to go excessively to the movies." Having provided our young with an elaborate and expensive school system, we have proceeded to supply them with new temptations to lure them and tempt them from the paths we wish them to follow. Today it is the girls who play truant most frequently, and generally the temptation is strengthened in the movies. Many of them find this lure quite irresistible. A number of those investigated by Blumer and Hauser give an account somewhat like this:

"One reason I went away from school was I enjoyed movies better than school. I got money from my parents for lunch so instead of going to school, I made some excuse and went to the movies." Another, a girl of fourteen, explains her troubles—

"When I was ten years old I fell so much in love with the movies that I begged and begged my mother to give me money for the show, but she wouldn't. She said it would ruin my life if I went to the movies so often. But as she didn't give me any money, I would be a sneak and take the money off the table and go to the movies. . . . I very often quarrelled with my mother. She told me that movies weren't good for me. . . . She said they were filthy and sloppy for girls like me. Of course I didn't mind her." That girl subsequently arrived in the Juvenile Court.

Were these potential delinquents fleeing from one type of education, the education ordered for them by society, and seeking another, a premature, unsanctioned and dangerous education in sex, luxury, unrestraint and carousal? The investigator makes no attempt to answer this question—nor will the writer—but to some girls these things seen on the screen become apparently irresistible. A fifteen-year-old girl, given to running away from home, supplies this frank explanation:

"The movies make me want to have a good time, but what kind of a good time is the question. Well! I like to go with a fellow to a cabaret or to a lively dance. All I crave is excitement. Also, I like to get up and sing a song or two; in other words, I crave popularity and gayety. I like to be in with a noisy crowd so that when we go out we can have 'a hell of a good time.' I got much of this feeling from the picture in which Clara Bow played. I can't recall the name of the play, but it was like this: Her parents didn't approve of her going with this certain crowd, and she liked this crowd very much. She said she wouldn't stop going with this crowd because whenever she went out with them she had 'a hell of a good time.' I am using the correct words she used. I would feel the same way about it if my mother had disapproved of my going; if there was anything wrong with them I wouldn't care, but if there wasn't, I wouldn't break up with that crowd. Another play I saw was Joan Crawford in 'Our Dancing Daughters' and a week afterwards I went to a party; of course I mingled with the drinks as she had done. I also sang the theme song of 'Our Dancing Daughters.' "

"A hell of a good time" may not be delinquency as yet, but that girl leaves little doubt that she is on the royal road. Of 252 delinquent girls fifty-four per cent, more than half, admitted that they had stayed away from school to go to the movies. Over one-third of them had had trouble with their parents over motion picture attendance, and about one-fifth of the total declared that they had run away from home after such difficulties and quarrels.

There are elements in certain of the pictures that set up cravings in some of the delinquent girls which seemingly they cannot combat. So that we get statements like this: "When I saw Ruth Chatterton in 'The Right to Love,' I craved nothing but love and wild party." Forty-nine per cent of the 252 delinquent girls said that the movies imbued them with a desire to live a gay fast life, and nearly as many admitted a craving for wild parties, cabarets and roadhouses as a result of movie inspiration. The "flaming youth" period, in other words, was inflicted ad lib. upon the screen. And the screen turned about and took to mass production of flaming youth.

Wild parties may not necessarily be delinquency, but

forty-one per cent of the delinquent girls admitted that it was the movie-made urge that inclined them to wild parties, cabarets and roadhouses—a course which ultimately landed them "in trouble." They cry out that they wanted the clothes of the movie heroines, the freedom of the movie heroines, the good times and wild parties of the movie heroines. In the result we get confessions like this:

"As I became older I started to go with older boys. I went to the movies on an average of five times in one week. . . . Then I became dissatisfied with home, and my girl friend and I planned to run away." Follows a long story of truancy, staying in men's apartments, the Juvenile Court and an institution for behavior problem girls. "The movies," declares one girl (and there are many like her) "have given me one idea, and that is how much freedom I should have." Another girl, and she only fourteen, announces with a kind of wild despair:

"I thought one day as I was at the show seeing a good picture, if any of the movie stars want to come home late their parents allow them. Why shouldn't mine? So I started coming home at three or six in the morning and soon I landed in the Juvenile Court, which I thought was a very bad place, of course, for a girl of my age to be. I got out within a month. It didn't do me no good. I started over again."

Say that the movies are not alone to blame, yet it is impressive that thirty-eight per cent of girls in a home for delinquents gave this pathetic succession of steps in their careers: Wild parties patterned after what they had seen in the movies, then truancy, then running away

from home. As one girl of seventeen, a sexual delinquent, rather pitifully sketches the process:

"The most responsible thing for getting me in trouble
is these love pictures. When I saw a love picture at
night, and if I had to go home alone, I would try and
flirt with some man on the corner. If it was the right
kind of a bad man he would take me to a dance or a wild
party; at these parties I would meet other men that
would be crazy for fast life. These are the kind of men
that got me in trouble. I went with some boys that
would tell me they would take me to a party or dance
and at the end it would end up in a lonely road or woods.
These are the kind of boys that led my life astray. Some
boys I went with would kick me out of the car and tell
me to walk home if I wouldn't give them what they
wanted. The best thing I like are wild parties. Movies
were the first thing that made me go astray."

2

The urge young people receive from the movies takes
many forms—from the crudest assaults of certain scenes
upon their emotions, affections and appetites, to occasional bursts of generosity and ambition, and to many
more subtle and often comparatively harmless factors
like imitation of dress, deportment and "make-up." The
instilling of the desire for luxury, fine clothes, automobiles and all the accessories of wealth, which so many
boys and girls bring forward, is one of the commonest
of the indirect influences of the movies toward delinquency. Frequent as is this factor among boys and
young men, as shown by the Blumer and Thrasher studies, it is even more pronounced in the case of girls and

young women. Clothes, appearance and a love of ease play a far greater rôle in the day-dreaming and cravings of feminine psychology. "Many of the girls and young women studied," Blumer and Hauser observe, "grow dissatisfied with their own clothes and manner of living, and in their efforts to achieve motion picture standards frequently get into trouble." A sixteen-year-old Negro girl, a sexual delinquent, expresses the entire problem in a few lines:

"In seeing movies you get a desire to have pretty clothes, automobiles and several other things that make one happy. If you have no relatives to get these things for you, usually you get in trouble trying to get them yourself." There is a kind of dreary fatalism about this philosophy which seems to creep into so many present-day young minds, irrespective of consequences and results. Over and over among the many cases studied substantially the same attitude emerges. A typical story— the teller of it is seventeen and a sexual delinquent:

"I would love to have nice clothes and plenty of money and nothing to do but have a good time. When I see movies of that type, it makes me want to get out and go somewhere where things happen. Like the picture, 'Gold-diggers of Broadway.' The girls were nothing but adventuresses and look what great times they had. I always wanted to live with a girl chum. I saw many pictures where two or three girls roomed together. It showed all the fun they had. I decided I would, too. I ran away from home and lived with my girl friend, but she was older than I and had different ideas, and of course she led me and led me in the wrong way."

Different ideas, possibly, yet not so very different.

For needy girls tempted beyond their control to obtain money, ease and luxury, the means sometimes narrow down to one form—exploitation of their sex. Upon this point there is abundance of testimony gathered, of which only a few representative cases can here be cited:

(White, 18, Sexual Delinquent) Some of the (movies) makes me dissatisfied with my own clothes. Most always I get what I want. Anyhow if it is in my power. Where there is a will there's a way. There are too many men in this world not to get what you want. There are plenty that are free and disengaged and want what you have got, which if they come after they can get. . . . They (movies) make me wish I had a car and lots of money and they also make me think how to make money. They tell me how to get it. There are several different ways of getting money; through sex, working, etc. Most always I get mine through sex.

(White, 16, Sexual Delinquent) In regard to ideas, there are two kinds of ideas, good and bad. The bad ideas I get from such pictures are to go out and have a high, rough and tumble life just like some of the rest. Go to a sporting house and make money and travel from one place to another.

(Negro, 17, Sexual Delinquent) When I ran away from home I went to a show nearly every day, sometimes seeing the same show two or three times over. In this way I got to wanting to live the way the actresses lived. And so I used to go and get men to support me for a month or so and then change around and get me another man to live with.

(White, 16, Sexual Delinquent) When I see pictures with people who have snappy clothes, automobiles, etc., it makes me feel that I would like to have the clothes I see on the wearer. Movies of that sort make me feel that I would like to tear the clothes that I have on right off. I often wish I had a good car like some of the actresses have. When I go out from here I am planning on getting a good car that I could go riding around in. I like to see movies where young girls and boys make a lot of money. I can think of over 100 ways of making money in your younger days, especially in the teens and twenties, with a slow or fast life. I think of making money, such as working in factories, doctor's office or any big office; but I can think of more ways in a fast life, which I will not mention, because I've seen it done and have experienced it myself. Therefore I know something about it."

3

One remembers reading often in the newspapers to what an extent female delinquency has increased in recent years. We have heard of bobbed-haired bandits, female participation in kidnappings and hold-ups and many other instances. Chiefly, however, sexual delinquency is still the one great path to our correctional institutions for women. The question we are here concerned with is, To what extent do the movies with their vivid presentation of visual images, play a part in female sex delinquency? Impossible though such measurement may be in any precise fashion there were, nevertheless, a few indications.

Some of these avenues and incitements we have already seen. Easy money, wild parties, the desire for clothes and luxury, these are the common incentives to erring. In a group of delinquent girls in a state training-school, twenty-five per cent of them conveyed that movies in a variety of ways were a direct contributing influence to their delinquency.

Some of the girls frankly declare that a picture like "The Pagan" rouses them to the pitch of jealousy of the heroine, to a desire to be loved like her. "When I see a fellow and girl in a passionate love scene, such as 'The Pagan,' I just have a *hot* feeling going through me and I want to do everything bad. When a girl really loves a fellow and he takes her to his house and makes her stay there with him, she gives in to his wants like in 'The Modern Maidens'." Another more briefly summarizes her reactions, "The movies that excite me and make me fall into my lover's arms is passionate or love plays. They give you just what you are craving for: *Love.*"

These girls are sixteen. Their experiences speak for themselves, but there are delinquent girls of fourteen and even younger who write much in the same tenor. "After I have seen a romantic love scene," writes a fourteen-year old, "I feel as though I couldn't have just one fellow to love me, but I would like about five." In a state training-school for delinquent girls, one hundred and twenty-one out of 252, virtually half, declare that they "felt like having a man make love to them" after they had seen a passionate love picture. In the cases of these girls, as Professor Blumer points out, the distance between feelings of passionate love and sexual behavior is small. As one inmate, sixteen years old, admits with singular lucidity:

"When I was on the outside I went to the movies almost every night, but only about twice in two months to a dance. I don't like dances as well as I do movies. A movie would get me so passionate after it was over that I just had to have relief. You know what I mean."

A contemporary of hers gives an even more graphic description of her thrills and stirrings under the impact of sex movies:

"When I see movies that excite me I always want to go home and do the same things that I saw them do. Pictures where a fellow kisses a girl and holds her a long time is what gets me excited, and I just want to do that myself . . . Passionate love pictures do stir me up. Some and most times I go out from a movie and stay out late with a fellow. Sometimes never think of coming in until two-thirty in the morning. . . . One night I went to a movie with a fellow of mine who drives a very chic little sport roadster. In the movie he sat with his arms around me, and every time the fellow would kiss the girl, he would look at me lovingly and squeeze my hand: after the movie we went to my girl friend's house and got her and her fellow. Then we all went for a moonlight spooning ride and had sexual relations."

"Movies," declares a seventeen-year-old delinquent, "taught me a lot pertaining to men: They have taught me how to kiss, how a girl should appear in the presence of her beau, how I should go about loving a fellow, how to do hot dances, how to court, etc. A fellow is expected to take his girl to the movies, dances, skating parties, etc., and according to modern times he is expected to take her to a place, whatever the circumstances may be, and to make passionate love to her, and she is expected to show him a good time as he shows her."

The case above is of a girl who probably ought never to see any movies, and least of all such movies as those whence she gleaned her principles. Nevertheless, all movies are open wide, alike to moron and philosopher and to all that come between, with all the sanction and seeming approval that a broad and general publicity carries. The results are—the results.

Girls, of course, differ in temperament and physical constitution. All these who are here testifying were in a state institution expiating sexual delinquency. At least twenty-five per cent of them acknowledge engaging in sexual relations after becoming aroused at a movie. That they were possessed of a propensity to sexual experience is entirely likely. Nevertheless it appears quite clear that motion pictures were a direct contributing influence and incitement. Those who admitted it are, as we see from their statements, exceedingly frank—perhaps merely more frank than their reticent sisters. What, for example, could be more open and explicit than this account of a seventeen-year-old girl?

"I like to see men and women fall in love in the movies and go out on parties, etc. I also like to see them kiss, drink, smoke and make love to each other. It makes me get all stirred up in a passionate way. Love pictures, wild west pictures, murder cases are the pictures I like best, because I like to love, myself, and I know others want to do the same. After I see them I go out and make love and go on wild parties and only do worse. Movies teach me how to treat my men and fool them. When I see a wild west picture, especially when I see a cowboy falling in love with a girl and running away with her and when they go out riding with her it makes me want to be out in the West—Colorado—with someone I could live around with and have relations with. When I saw the picture, "All Quite on the Western Front,' I was so thrilled and excited I could hardly realize I was seeing the picture. It seems as though it was myself and the boy I was sitting with. I have always wanted to have the experience and thrill of being held in the arms of some masculine man and being loved . . . Love pictures are my favorites. They teach me how to love and kiss. Oh! How thrilled I am when I see a real passionate movie! I watch every little detail, of how she's dressed, and her make-up, and also her hair. They are my favorite pictures. The most exciting pictures are passionate plays. I get excited most when they are kissing and loving and having experiences I wish I could have. When I see these movies I leave the movies most always immediately and go out to some roadhouse or an apartment with my man and get my wants satisfied. Especially when I get all stirred up and my passion rises. I feel as if I never want my man to leave me, as if I can't live without him. I have a feeling that can't be expressed with words but with actions."

The excerpt is quoted at some length because this delinquent girl, notwithstanding a certain muddle-headedness, is probably not unique—to her sex pictures have brought a new freedom and a new stimulus, as well, perhaps, as some of the muddle-headedness. In a way, she has always existed. But the movies have brought a stream of suggestions and patterns within easy reach of such large numbers of her that they amount to a school, with the addition of public sanction—a sanction expressed by universal attendance and wide-flung ad-

vertising, by bright lights, vivid posters and press advertisements.

In Dr. Charles C. Peters' study of the effect of the
movies on the national mores appear some telling details of movie exploitation. Among some fifteen hundred
adjectives used in describing the pictures were found
some of the following figures: Adjectives appealing to
the baser emotions, 110; adjectives appealing to finer or
ennobling emotions, 23. Superlatives are rampant. The
adjective "great" figures 410 times; "big," 212; "sensa-
tional," 166; "tremendous," 99; "thrilling," 93. Among
cuts and illustrations the figures are still more pointed.
Pictures showing a man and a woman embracing, 275;
religious scenes, 3; marriage scenes, 2. In the Thrasher
and Cressey study, as will be seen, the actual text of
posters and streamers is even more illuminating.

4

Perhaps the most convenient way of illustrating the
strand of movie influence in the tissue of criminal life in
the case of one man, is to cite more or less fully the case
of a youth of twenty-three who has served a sentence
for rape, and in whose conduct and conviction the movies
played a prominent part. The document, quoted by
Blumer and Hauser, was written by the young ex-convict
himself.

"One night we went up to the ——— (a motion picture
theatre) but couldn't get our regular seats. I got one
right near to a girl I went to school with and she was a
keen kid in school and never fooled around much. So I
just sat there and talked with her and watched the picture. Pearl White was playing in a serial at that time,

and she was a pretty clever actress. It was a good show. After the show was over we went outside, and went walking with E——. We walked around for about a half an hour and then went up to her house and sat on her front steps just talking. Gee, I don't know, but I just couldn't figure it out. This kid falling for me; she had looks—decent girl—and everything. I went home that night promising her I would meet her the next night at the show. The next night I did meet her; and gosh! I am acting and sounding goofy now, but I guess I was falling hard. We went home that night, to, without anything happening. I met the bunch on the corner after I left her and I—— (one of.the gang) started to razz me and said she was pretty hot stuff, and tried to fix it for me to walk over around the beach the next night so the bunch would jump her and have relations with her.

"I refused to do this, telling them that she was a good, clean, respectable girl; and I—— laughed and said, 'Boy, she's had plenty of sex relations.' I was a good fighter, but I was mad, and for winning a fight I was second best that night as far as fighting was concerned. But I was hot and didn't give a damn. I picked up a house brick and started to run and threw it at him and hit him in the back of the head, and he fell unconscious."

The boy, obviously in love with the girl, whom he regarded as good, clean and respectable, actually fought in her defence, severed his relations with his gang and continued to go with her to the movies.

"About a week or so after the fight with I——, I met E—— again and we went up to a show. I started to put my arm around her and kiss her and she didn't move. Now I know she was only a 'little bum,' but at that

time I thought she was in love with me. A new life
opened up to me that night. I was all 'bubbles.' I played
around, contented in just kissing and loving her. We
didn't go to shows much then. We wanted to be alone;
and this went on for a couple of nights or so. I would
meet her at about six-thirty or seven and bum around
until eleven or twelve o'clock.

"We went to a show Sunday afternoon down at T——,
and it was a raw picture—'Adults only'—and we got in.
The part of the picture that aroused me and her, too, I
guess, was when the boy was loving up the girl on a
couch and she leaned back and he got over her and was
kissing and loving her. E—— had a hold of my hand,
and her hand was all wet with sweat, and she said, 'Jim,
that is the way I would like to have you love me.' I
looked at her and she looked into my eyes and looked
as if she was going to faint. We did not wait for all the
show, but left.

"After we got outside, she acted different. I was stirred
up in the show but cooled off after we walked a block or
so. It was about five P.M. when we got over to E——'s
house, and I told her I would meet her after supper. I
went home and had supper. Then I went over there
and whistled for E——. She came to the door and told
me to come up. I was never in her house before and I
went up. Her mother had gone to visit somebody and
no one was home. We went in the front room and sat
down; and after we sat down and kissed a while she
wanted to be loved like that girl in the picture, and I
done exactly that.

"I got all stirred up, but, at first, couldn't ask her to
go the limit. I didn't have the nerve, I guess. She

was aroused, too, and showed it plenty. Finally after fooling around for about a half hour like this, we had sexual relations."

It is not meant to suggest here that their movie-going was the sole factor in their relationship, but it is significant, observe Professor Blumer and Hauser, "that the motion pictures aroused sex passion in both of them and suggested techniques of love-making," which helped to change a typically adolescent love affair into one of illicit sex relations.

The narrator goes on to recount how he secured a position with a reputable business organization and became a successful salesman. In the office he met a young girl of sixteen who attracted him very much and they began to "keep company." She introduced him to her mother and his attitude is plain from his remark, "Boy, I'd have married her right then and there if she'd asked me." Up to this point he is clearly in love with the girl in a socially acceptable manner. But that condition changed. He continues:

"Sunday afternoon I made up my mind I was going to have relations with her if I had to force it. How to get her aroused was the next thing. I read the picture part of the paper, and Elinor Glyn's 'Three Weeks' was playing. I took B——, and that picture was the 'hit.' It was really sizzling in parts. B—— got 'it'; and you know if you ever wanted to have relations with a girl, all you got to do is to take her to one of those plays. They give her the idea. She gets aroused, and the next is up to you. B—— was aroused. I know that because I made many preliminary advances to her during the show, and she liked it. After the show we went to

—— and had chop suey. Next we went to —— (an isolated section of the city) and stopped.

"Well, she petted and became aroused again. I was sure from her reactions and the nature of my advances to which she did not object that she was ready for anything, but when I tried it she screamed and started to cry. I tried to use force, but she resisted. I let her go and tried to patch things up, but she wouldn't talk. I drove her home.

"The next morning when I showed up for work, the girl, her family, my bosses and a policeman met me."

He was sentenced to three years for attempted rape. This story is of interest in that it shows not only the aphrodisiac effects of certain pictures, but illustrates also their conscious use by some men for stimulating and arousing passions and desire in girls.

One youth under sentence for robbery tells how his associates and himself would go to a sex picture as a prelude before adjourning to a house of prostitution, and another, serving a sentence for burglary, makes this frank statement:

"I would go to a sex picture but I always have a girl with me. Whenever I would see the lover on the screen making love to the heroine, I would put one arm around my girl (we always sat in the back of the theatre so that nobody would be around us) and do the same. If she became aroused, and if it happened to be during the early part of the afternoon, and not many people within the show, we would go the limit there in the theatre."

Later, in considering the Thrasher-Cressey survey of a congested area in a big city, it will be seen that in certain types of movie theatres, the conduct of this youth is quite common. As the late Dr. R. L. Whitley, one of the New York University investigators, observes: "A variety of sexual practices are observed by the boy ordinarily in the movie house and occasionally he engages in various forms of sex-activity in the house himself." The youth quoted by Drs. Blumer and Hauser concluded his remarks:

"Later on I got invited to parties and did we have hot times? We'd begin by discussing the different sex pictures we had seen and the manner by which the hero made love to the girl. It would finally end up with a girl in each boy's lap, kissing and playing with each other; and finally each boy would take his girl."

"After leaving a sex picture," recalls a young convict, "I would go back to the neighborhood and start talking to the gang about the picture and my subsequent reaction to it. We would all get together and discuss various means of getting a girl to come down to our hang-out (which was situated in an old abandoned quarry) and then hold a 'tête a tête' with her." He goes on to describe their success in enticing a girl and raping her in these quarters.

The accounts of these various young criminals show a variety of experiences in which passionate love and sex movies played a part, either as consciously used aphrodisiacs or as leading to more serious crimes, such as rape by an individual or a gang.

5

These are samples of some of the amusement supplied to the masses. When forty-three per cent of delinquent girls examined state that movies gave them the itch to make money easily; when fourteen per cent declare they acquired ideas from the movies for making money by 'gold-digging' men; twenty-five per cent, by living with a man and letting him support them; when considerable numbers of young men and boys in penal institutions declare that they used movies as a sexual excitant—then it means that a load is added, the burden of which they are unable to bear; that there is probably something socially wrong, something subversive of the best interests of society in the way a substantial number of present-day movies are made, written, conceived. To those delinquent girls, a few of whose pathetic cases have been presented here, the movies clearly emerge as a school. No less than seventy-two per cent of them admit having improved their attractiveness by imitating the movies. But what is more important, nearly forty per cent admit that they were moved to invite men to make love to them after seeing passionate sex pictures. For them the movies constitute an education along the left-hand or primrose path of life, to the wreckage of their own lives and to the detriment and cost of society.

The road to delinquency, in a few words, is heavily dotted with movie addicts, and obviously, it needs no crusaders or preachers or reformers to come to this conclusion.

CHAPTER XIV

DETERRENT AND CORRECTIONAL

AMONG all the many cases presented by Drs. Blumer and Hauser in their monograph, the writer can find only a single one in which the chastening effect of seeing a picture of crime-punishment had a provably tangible effect. A youth of eighteen in the reformatory contributed this pathetic statement:

"Well, the last picture I saw before I was sent over the road was 'The Big House.' After I have seen that picture I wanted to go straight. It made me get cold feet whenever I thought of pulling a job; but the next day I gave myself up to the police for some jobs that I had done a month before I had seen 'The Big House.' If I should of seen 'The Big House' before I did the crime I wouldn't be where I am now. I felt as though I wanted to be a gangster but after I seen of how quick they get caught and sent to jail, I soon gave up all hope of being a gangster and I would always think that the criminal got too much punishment. Such pictures as 'The Big House' should not be shown."

Confused, illiterate and pitiful as the above confession appears, it possesses a singular merit and interest; a young criminal, after seeing a motion picture of crime and punishment, was moved to give himself up to the police. How rare are such occurrences and how much rarer the stimulus toward them! The more frequent type of "deterrent" confessions are often less convincing. A fifteen-year-old boy tells us, "When I see a picture or a burglar in a picture and he gets his time I don't feel so good because I might get the same if I would commit the crime." Such boys might have been deterred from crime, had no other temptations intervened. "But other times," he adds, "I hardly care anything about it." In any case, this boy is under sentence for robbery in a state training-school. Of two sixteen-year-old girls one announces that "The punishment I see they receive just makes me want to go out and lead a good life," because she feels that nine women out of ten who go wrong "*always* get paid in the end"; and another declares that she "wouldn't like to be like those women that go wrong." Both girls are inmates of a state institution for sexual delinquents.

Fifty-six per cent of a sample of male convicts, Blumer and Hauser find, indicate that punishment as shown in the movies did not deter them from crime; forty-nine of the same lot declare that the punishment given to the criminal in the movies is likely to stop them from committing crime. Twenty-six per cent state that such punishment shown in the movies made them at one time or another hesitate about committing a crime. The glamour and the technique of crime, in other words, as well as their own tendencies, vastly outweighed the deterrent effect. In view of the contents of movies, as found by Dr. Dale, 406 crimes committed and forty-three attempted in 115 pictures, averaging almost four crimes committed or attempted per picture, the force of iteration is too great, evidently not to produce definite effects upon unformed, susceptible and unrestrained minds—be the deterrents what they may.

"We have," state Blumer and Hauser, "no instance in our materials where an individual was completely deterred from a delinquent or criminal career through the influence of motion pictures." Possibly such cases exist. Large percentages of grade-school boys and girls declare that punishment of bad men in the movies stops them from doing "bad things." An ex-convict who had served time for robbery puts it—he is thirty-four years old and mature enough to reflect:—

"Movies I don't think could make one go straight. Sad pictures sometimes make me think a good deal, but after you get back out on the street you have other things to think about. This world goes too fast and one doesn't get enough time to think. He acts, does things, and thinks afterwards. Everything is done on the spur of the moment. A couple of nights ago I was on my way home fully intentioned to go to bed; on the way I passed a joint, went in and got drunk. There you are, proof of what I say. People don't think about anything; they do it and answer questions afterwards. Check yourself and you will find what I say is true."

Too true in our present conditions. And one great object of those who are working for better motion pictures, particularly for the young, is that the movies, in the midst of this chaos, should not supply that additional shove down the slope of Avernus, descent to which is so fatally easy.

Two boys of sixteen and seventeen respectively, charged with robbery and burglary, were asked whether any pictures ever made them want "to be good." One said that Al Jolson's "Sonny Boy" and "Say It with Song" had this effect upon him. "But," he added, "after I got out of the show I forgot all about it." The youthful burglar of seventeen declared that "The Singing Fool," also an Al Jolson picture, had exercised a similar beneficent influence upon him.

"How long," he was asked, "did you feel that way?"

"Till next Sunday," was the answer.

"When did you see the picture?"

"That was about on a Tuesday."

Now, as Professor Thurstone and Miss Peterson have shown, mental attitudes may be changed by a single picture, and the effects may persist for a long time. Why then are deterrent effects so brief? The only explanation the writer can suggest is that too few of the right kind of pictures are shown; the life of today, particularly in certain areas, is too confusing, and the rare good picture fails in the struggle against all else that fills the young lives.

Sometimes they become accustomed to the punishment shown on the screen and ignore it, centering their attention on ideas of "how to pull a job." Or, living as many of them do in delinquent areas, they find that pictures are not true to life as they know it; or that punishment is presented with insufficient realism. A youth of seventeen held on a burglary charge, speaking of movie prison scenes, explains that "they don't really show what he (the prisoner) has to suffer. It shows they play baseball and what they have to eat and things like that." One ex-convict has worked it out that, "the moral of all criminal pictures is, that the wrong-doer gets caught, which is only true in about nine per cent of true-life crime." Some are merely callous, as this girl, a sexual delinquent explains:

"When I see pictures about women who 'go wrong' it only makes me wish I was in their place . . . because I do know what thrill and pleasures they get about going wrong."

Other considerations, such as a feeling they cannot outwit the law, a feeling of sympathy for the criminal, of resentment toward the machinery of the law and punishment, all these tend to make deterrent effects of pictures too faint, or, for some, to nullify them altogether.

The young criminals and delinquents of the Blumer-Hauser inquiry are, in short, in a different category from the children used in the Thurstone-Peterson experiments. As slates, their minds are smeared over with quite another type of life in a delinquent area, with antisocial patterns of living, supplemented by a long record of indulgence in movie-going; these tend to overlay and largely to efface the rare good effects of the infrequent wholesome movie. It would be surprising if their already exercised passions and desires had left them as susceptible as the less experienced children to effects contrary to their case-hardened states. They too, are affected by the right kind of pictures, as the evidence tends to show, and as appears scientifically quite certain.

Their environment, however, as well as their long continued and promiscuous movie-going with no selection other than their own tastes and proclivities has virtually immunized them to the good and sensitized them to the others.

2

What might be described as the catharsis theory, the Greek idea that the pity and terror of a dramatic spectacle will act upon the audience as a purge of evil passions and emotions, forms one of the defences of the present-day motion picture, and in especial of the picture with the violent type of action in it, which, as we have seen, is so numerous, though not as numerous as the love and sex film.

The first and readiest answers to this defence is that children have no need of catharsis and that, in any case, the present-day movie is a considerable distance removed in quality and nobility from the Greek tragedies. Their audience, moreover, was not 77,000,000 a week, nor did it include 11,000,000 aged thirteen and younger. However, we are not here concerned with academic theories but rather with facts based upon a mass of substantial evidence.

Do motion pictures act as a deterrent influence against bad or unsocial actions, evil conduct and crime? That is the question to which we are seeking an answer. It has been frequently asserted by representatives of motion picture producers that not only are films consciously planned to illustrate the eventual ill-fate of the wrong-doer but that by stressing this phase, movies actually discourage evil conduct and crime. To what extent they have the effect of suggesting and stimulating wrong-doing we have already seen. But we have also seen, in a previous chapter, that such pictures as "Beau Geste," "Over the Hill," "The Old Nest" and even "Ben Hur" moved certain young people to various degrees of tenderness, kindness, family affection, and sense of duty, or even to religious emotion.

Now, if there are pictures which, in combination with their function of entertainment, can also stir the spectator to emotions toward good, that effect is of great importance and those pictures should receive all the credit they deserve.

In a sample of 875 grade-school boys and girls, almost seventy per cent expressed the opinion that motion pictures at different times make them do "good things," and fifty-three per cent in a truant and behavior problem school expressed a similar conviction. Even allowing for "credibility discount" these percentages are impressive. When asked what type of picture moved them to this goodness, about twenty-four per cent replied that religious and moral pictures produced this effect; only about six per cent of the boys declared that gangster and crime pictures brought them this beneficent influence. It would appear, then, that it is easy to overemphasize the deterrent effects of motion pictures.

Evidence sought in a state training-school for delinquent girls produced these results: Seventy per cent of a sample of 252 delinquent girls declared that movies had at times made them "want to be real good." When asked to specify the type of picture that so actuated them, forty-five per cent indicated that moral, religious or sentimental pictures produced this effect; twenty-five per cent conveyed that they felt chastened by crime and gangster pictures which showed the ill-fate of women who go wrong. Here again it becomes apparent that the nicely calculated structure of punishment and retribution in crime pictures, as avowedly planned by producers, at least according to the testimony of those sample groups, is far from being as successful as the religious, moral and sentimental pictures in inciting the desire "to be good."

Granting, however, that the desire "to be good" is actually aroused by certain pictures, how long does it last? This matter of the duration of such influences interested Blumer and Hauser and they made some inquiry into the subject. The statement of their findings based upon the children's memories, in these particulars, is as follows:

Of the fifty-four truant and behavior problem boys who responded to the question, fifty-five per cent answered that the movies made them stay good for less than one day; twenty-eight per cent, from one day to a week; twenty per cent, from one week to a month; thirteen per cent, from one month to a year, and four per cent for over a year. Thus, eighty-three per cent of the truant and behavior problem boys indicated that although some pictures they had seen made them want to be "real good," they remained good as a result of the picture for a period of less than one month. Of 191 boys in the three areas combined (high delinquency, medium and low-rate delinquency) who answered the question, sixty-eight per cent conveyed that movies made them stay good for a period of less than one month. Similarly, of 138 girls in these areas who answered the question, fifty-five per cent, though moved toward goodness by certain pictures, indicated that they remained good for a period of less than one month, thirty-one per cent of them not exceeding a week.

Among the delinquents it is not much different. Of

191 delinquent girls, sixteen per cent declared they stayed good for about a day and fifty-four per cent for a period of one month or less. Among the males fifty-one per cent acknowledged that they had seen movies at times which made them want to be 'real good' and go straight.

"Basing our remarks," observe Blumer and Hauser, "merely on these *questionnaire responses,* it seems that although some pictures make boys and girls, delinquents and non-delinquents, want to be 'real good,' the immediate effect is on the whole temporary, of longer duration among girls than boys, and among non-delinquent boys than among delinquent boys."

In other words, the deterrent effects of motion pictures, be they what they may, seem short-lived. Now, Professor Thurstone and Miss Peterson might possibly have found by their technique that the good effects persisted longer; May and Shuttleworth found few persistent effects; and it is true that Drs. Blumer and Hauser did not enquire how long the bad effects persisted. Before passing from this subject, however, some specific ways in which motion pictures are said to act as deterrents of crime and misconduct are touched upon in the Blumer-Hauser study and should be mentioned, especially in view of the fact that the number of cases they discovered were so few. Here is a sample instance:

A young inmate of the reformatory declares: "I have never had the idea of being a gangster, because of the pictures I have seen where they took a gangster for a ride. That put a scare in me because I value my life."

Similarly a sixteen-year-old girl, a sexual delinquent, absolves the movies from blame for her misbehavior:

"It was when I'd see passionate plays, I'd go home and then resolve to behave. The girls always became diseased, and then if they had a child it was blind or deformed. Those plays always seemed to teach me a lesson. . . . When I see pictures of women going wrong I think that I'll behave because I wouldn't want a terrible disease, and if I had a child I wouldn't want it to be blind or deformed. I certainly do think that such pictures are true to life."

So that though the forty-four per cent of young male inmates in a reformatory declare that, judging by the movies, the risks and dangers of being a gangster are too great, they are all serving time for a variety of crimes. Likewise, if fifty per cent of over 250 delinquent girls state that movies taught them that the woman always pays the price for a good time, still one cannot lose sight of the fact that most of them are detained on grounds of sexual delinquency. One is always grateful for any constructive influence, but it is just as well to remember that forty-five per cent of these girls seem to have forgotten those fruits of enlightenment when they were with men. What does deter for long from wrong-doing? We do not know. Many forces in life, we hope, act as deterrents. That fear of punishment, and of the ill-fate that overtakes offenders acts at times as a deterrent of crime is not to be doubted. Blumer and Hauser find that "the portrayal of long periods of incarceration and the monotonous routine life of penal institutions and of punishment by death sentence makes its imprint on the minds of both delinquent and non-delinquent observers." Among the cases cited by Blumer in illustration of this fact, here is

one of a youth of twenty-four under sentence for burglary:

"A picture I consider very interesting and inspiring
to the criminal in the line of his profession is 'London
After Midnight.' This picture has a cast of daring gangsters and murderers. I took a great liking to this picture as it was very exciting. This picture kept the law
on the go, as there were daring crimes throughout.
Like every other crook picture, the criminal is caught
and punished. . . . The movies always have the crooks
brought to justice at the end of their underworld pictures. I am for more of this sort . . . [Dr. Dale finds
otherwise—in the case of sixty-two major crimes in forty
pictures analyzed, only nineteen per cent of the criminals
were legally punished, their punishment either implied
or actually carried out. An additional thirty-nine per cent
were punished, but by extra-legal forces, and twenty-four
per cent went wholly unpunished. The remaining seventeen per cent were all arrested, but twelve per cent
of these either escaped or were released, and the others
were simply held, no punishment being implied.] The
above explains what I have gotten out of movies and so
I think I will include this information also. An exciting
picture gives me many thrills throughout its showing.
I hardly think it causes me to do daring things, although
I bear in mind the ways they show ways of getting easy
money, committing murder, etc., and finally of how the
law takes a hand in the crime. Several times before I
would start to commit a crime, I would often think of
the penalty I would have to pay if I were caught. This
thought has come to me again and again, and I'm sure
it has saved me from committing many crimes. 'The

Drag Net,' 'Ladies of the Mob,' and 'You Can't Win' are great pictures for a fellow to learn vital lessons from." The lad is serving time for burglary.

3

An inquiry concerning motion pictures in prisons and reformatories, though not originally included in the Payne Fund survey, was undertaken in order to verify a statement in *The Motion Picture,* (the journal of the Hays organization) for January, 1930, to the effect that "Penologists proclaim the motion picture as a definite aid not only in providing needed recreation but in directing the thoughts of prisoners towards the futility of continued lives of crime." The investigators were asked to check the facts particularly with regard to this statement.

The showing of motion pictures in penal institutions, both for amusement and for what reformatory value there may be in them, has greatly gained in popularity during recent years. The 1929 Handbook of *American Prisons and Reformatories* shows that in nearly eighty per cent of the institutions studied pictures are shown. In eighty-five per cent out of 109 institutions nearly 91,000 prisoners out of a total of 114,248 have the opportunity to enjoy motion pictures during their period of imprisonment. The facilities were being increased and by now an even larger number of prisoners will have access to motion pictures.

The question, so far as it concerns us here is, have motion pictures any reformatory value in penal institutions? The only way possible to answer it is by appealing for information to both prisoners and institution heads. This inquiry, made by Blumer and Hauser, though not exhaustive, was fairly thorough.

First of all, institution heads to the number of about twenty per cent of those who answered complained of the difficulty of obtaining good or suitable pictures, owing to the fact that "good pictures were scarce." Taking the ratings of the magazine *Educational Screen,* widely used as a guide by teachers, parents and those responsible for guiding children and adolescents, it was found that of the pictures seen in penal institutions, where most of the inmates are young, nearly forty per cent of the films would fall under the ratings "questionable" or "not advised" for the age groups of fifteen to twenty, to which much of the reformatory population belongs. Even for intelligent adults, one out of every four pictures shown in penitentiaries and reformatories is either of questionable value or objectionable. The writer would suppose that for inmates of penal institutions such pictures may be positively deleterious.

That the movies, however, have a needed recreational value for prisoners, a sort of equivalent for contact with the outside world, a break in the monotony of institutional existence, there can be no doubt. Very naturally prisoners desire them. Ninety-five per cent of the girls and young women and sixty-seven per cent of the boys and young men indicate a demand for films. Of the wardens and superintendents seventy-four per cent conveyed that they believe in the recreational value of motion pictures in institutions. It is a detail that girls prefer love pictures and the boys comedies.

When, however, the investigators endeavored to establish the comparative appeal of motion pictures, a surprise was in store for them. So far from ranking the movies first, the girls gave outdoor athletics, training for a job and band concerts as activities they preferred to motion pictures. Similarly, for the male inmates outdoor athletics, training for a job, outdoor work and band concerts definitely out-ranked the movie in preference. These, of course, are averages. A certain number of both classes, twelve per cent of the girls and five per cent of the men gave first choice to the movies.

Loss of privilege to attend the movies is frequently used by institution heads as a means of maintaining discipline, infraction of the rules being punishable by deprivation of the privilege. Yet only seventeen per cent of institutional heads rank the movies first as a factor in maintaining discipline. Seventy-two per cent rank outdoor athletics as first, second or third. Besides, by stirring up sex impulses and arousing the girls, especially, so many of whom are sexual delinquents, the movies in penal and reformatory institutions may actually create disciplinary problems. Fully seventy-five per cent of the girls and sixty-eight per cent of the male delinquents and criminals confess to being sexually stirred by the movies. Some of the cases of autoeroticism and homosexual practices caused by this stirring up of sex impulses in prisoners are cited by the investigators but for good reason we shall detail none of them here. Many inmates complain of being overcome by melancholy after such films.

Such problems, as Drs. Blumer and Hauser point out, were prevalent in institutions before the introduction of motion pictures. "Nevertheless," they add, "motion pictures may serve as an agency in inciting some to sex passion and so contribute to what is regarded in institutions as sex misconduct." An important point, however, is this: do motion pictures play a part in instilling in the minds of criminals and delinquents a desire to reform?

In view of the Thurstone-Peterson findings that a picture may leave some effect upon the mind, it would follow that movies depicting scenes of warm, interesting, colorful life outside the institution, scenes of intimate home life, scenes showing that "crime does not pay," portrayal of success through honest effort and struggle —all these must of necessity make some impression upon the minds of the inmates who see them. Blumer and Hauser, discovered a considerable number of delinquents who testified to profiting from such wholesome effects. The words of some of these inmates have a heart-breaking quality about them.

"The feeling that I have when I see crime pictures," says one young robber, "makes me think of the things that I did and want another chance to make good." "Some of the movies," declares a young Negro convict, "make me think of the outside and the times I have had when I was out in the free world. Also the great mistake I've made in life. And if I have the chance to make good, how I would try hard to stay out of this and all the rest of the institutions." Another now sees clearly that his hope after liberation lies in earning enough money to open a shoe-shining parlor, and a girl of seventeen, a sexual delinquent, admits that "*some* of the movies here have made me see some of the mistakes I have made." She adds:

"The more important things I have learned from the

movies is how I can be good and yet have a good time."
Which is indeed important. Boys and men in a reformatory were asked:

"Do the movies make you feel like going straight?"

Girls in a state training-school were similarly asked:

"Do the movies make you feel like keeping out of
trouble?"

Eighty-four per cent of the girls and young women
and sixty-one per cent of the boys and young men indicated that motion pictures they see in institutions,
make them feel like keeping out of trouble and going
straight. According to these figures, the reformatory
value of motion pictures should be substantial and the
movies should be one of the important reforming
agencies of the delinquent population in our criminal
institutions and reformatories. What, however, are the
facts?

Rather astonishing. This influence in relation to other
constructive forces is not great. Only two per cent of
the reformatory inmates, when asked to rank in order
the reforming values of a group of activities, gave the
movies first place. Even among the delinquent girls
only three per cent ranked the movies first. With unexpected but not wholly surprising firmness, sixty-two
per cent of the males ranked training for a job first,
second or third in importance toward helping them to
go straight after their release. Of the delinquent girls,
no less than seventy-two per cent, about three-fourths,
likewise ranked training for a job first, second or
third for its importance in keeping them out of trouble
in the outside world. They do not want to give up
movies, quite naturally. Pictures provide some variety

in a monotonous life. But, also, as we have seen, pictures have in some degree, they believe, contributed to their tragedies. As a factor in reformation, therefore, they rank the movies very low.

The heads of penal institutions, when questioned, were quite in accord with their charges. Twenty-nine per cent of them agree that motion pictures play some part as a factor in reformation. In no case, however, did any of them assign first rank to the movies. Sixty-two per cent of them ranked school work first, second or third, and overlapping as some of the percentages do, fifty per cent assigned these places to vocational training. Athletics, shop work and chapel service were ranked far above the movies in value. When asked pointblank if any prisoners had been led by the pictures shown in institutions to give up lives of crime, seventy-seven per cent answered "no," and twenty-two per cent left the question blank. In the case of only one prisoner was there an affirmative answer. That prisoner after liberation went to work with a film company. In this case, Blumer and Hauser drily remark, "the motion picture influence was rather indirect."

Indeed, movies, as clearly emerges, though naturally desired as entertainment by those immured in prisons and reformatories, often arouse feelings of bitterness in them, and the conviction that they are not receiving "a square deal." People on the screen, they feel, "get away with" so much, whereas they, the convicts, were caught and suffered penalties. A girl of seventeen, a sexual delinquent, speaks her mind:

"When I see pictures that show where a girl gets away with a lot, it makes me feet bitter." "When I see

movies," asserts another, "like 'Modern Maidens,' where
young boys and girls are kissing, lying down on sofas,
telling each other how much they really love, I don't
think I am getting a fair deal." Pictures portraying
wealth, comfort, luxury, often arouse the bitterest resentment. As one young burglar puts it:

"Well, pictures in a way make me resent society.
Why? Because I am not out there while they are. I
never did have or get a square deal as yet. Because I
hate them, hate them. None other but the society pictures." It was found that thirty-nine per cent of the
young women and thirty-seven per cent of the boys and
men were embittered towards society in varying degrees by the motion pictures they had seen in institutions.

Briefly, for purposes of entertainment, the movies in
prisons and institutions are a definite help. As a deterrent to delinquency and crime, or for purposes of
reformation, the effects of the movies appear unimportant. And, as we have seen earlier in this chapter,
even outside of institutions the deterrent effects of
pictures, generally speaking, seem to be of brief duration.

CHAPTER XV

MOVIES IN A CROWDED SECTION

"THE street, the sidewalks swarm with people, push-carts stand along the curb; their proprietors hawk their wares to all passers-by. In the store windows bordering on the street is a bizarre assortment of dry-goods, cheeses, condiments and liquors, and from open doors issue a host of smells even more provocative. People elbow each other for passage along the sidewalk, while others pause to bargain loudly with the pushcart ped-dlers. The shrill notes of a hurdy-gurdy are heard down the street, and from somewhere overhead in the solid block of six-floor tenements comes the strident noise of a radio out of control. A street-car clangs its way along among the pushcart peddlers and their customers, and a moment later an elevated train roars by overhead. The traffic lights change and from another direction a heavy truck drags along, scattering the dust of the street in its wake. The boys in the street at their game of ball give way before it, but in the ensuing traffic are able in some way to continue their play. Through a nice judg-ment of distance and a dexterity in traffic born of long experience they continue their game—even though at the risk of life and limb. Such is the street world to which many of the under-privileged boys of a large city are exposed."

This is the setting as described by Thrasher and Cressey of the motion picture research in a congested area of New York City.[1] A number of large cities in America have areas somewhat similar to this one, though not in all respects alike. Even as New York communities go, it is among the most cosmopolitan. Its inhabitants, although predominantly Italians, include Porto Ricans, Negroes, Russians, Jews, Filipinos, Finns, Poles, Czecho-Slovaks, Yugo-Slavs, Turks, Irish, Lithuanians, Germans, Austrians, Rumanians, Greeks, South Americans, Scandinavians, Syrians, Armenians, a few Dutch and French and a tiny fragment of the older American stock left over in the wake of its own migration. It is neither a League of Nations nor a melting-pot. Or, if it is a melting-pot, there is hardly any knowing what will emerge from it as a final product. Certain parts of this section are what is called high-delinquency areas. Many youthful gunmen have had their origin here during recent years, and some of the most notorious of them have become known throughout the country.

Murder, kidnapping, organized violence, hold-ups, burglary, racketeering and bootlegging are but a part of the list of crimes these young graduates have engaged in since their emergence from this area. Several

[1] This chapter and other references in the volume to the New York University study have been based upon a tentative and preliminary report prepared by Mr. Paul G. Cressey, Associate Director of the New York University investigation. His completed and final report was not available at the time to be used in the preparation of this book.

of the most successful of underworld chieftains who now live in splendor have come from this locality. Poverty is common here, overcrowding is the rule, and unemployment a constant condition for large portions of the bread-winners. The average wage per week of adult males in this section *when employed* was reported to be but $26.96 a week. Its infant mortality is high; in point of juvenile delinquency, in greater New York, this section is second only to Negro Harlem.

Among its twenty or more nationalities or races, the largest proportion of the community population is of Italian stock, with over seventy per cent. Twenty-three per cent of the remainder come from such countries as Russia, Poland, Austria, Hungary and Germany. About forty-six per cent of the community is foreign-born, and only four per cent native born of native-born parents. In other words, it is largely a first generation immigrant settlement. Playgrounds are scarce and play life fills the teeming streets. The public school system is the chief Americanizing influence in the community. It is a community very little organized in the sense of neighborliness and neighborly responsibility, and the gang, the hangout, the poolroom, or the "private social club" and the taxi dance-hall are the ordinary methods of social cohesion. Speakeasies and bootlegging establishments abound, but the great and established source of entertainment is the motion picture and the movie theatre.

There are fifteen motion picture houses in the community, ranging from a large, somewhat luxurious one, built fifteen years ago, to several dilapidated store compartments which have been converted into cheap movie houses. These the boys with a certain folk precision in nomenclature label as "dumps." Generally speaking, they do not go to them if they can help it, but the low price is a lure and to see a picture for a dime will take one even to a dump.

All varieties of films are shown in the region with the exception of what the researchers label as "intellectual pictures." For these the score is zero. Comedy and adventure are fairly represented, but the largest number of pictures shown, over sixty per cent, group themselves under the headings—*mystery, romantic love, crime* and *sexual impropriety*. Stridently advertised and loudly "ballyhooed" are these pictures, not only by "trailers," posters, local newspapers and all the usual means, but by such lobby displays as the use of stilettos, a hangman's noose, or a replica of an electric chair. A lurid drinking scene painted over a large expanse of beaverboard showing young girls in suggestive poses may be used to indicate that the photoplay is of a sexy nature. Various as is the motion picture diet, the proprietors of film houses in this region agree that gangland pictures draw the greatest number of young people. Sex pictures are a second choice and advertisements are not wanting to indicate that the picture is immoral, so that the natural tendency is to see it early—before the "cops" come along and close up the theatre. A poll among the proprietors as to the photoplays which in recent years have proved to be of the greatest box-office value reveals the following titles as outstanding: "Little Caesar," "Underworld," "Taxi," "All Quiet on the Western Front," "Alias Jimmy Valentine," "Cimmaron," "Skippy" and "Up for Murder." The catchlines and the il-

lustrated posters used are seductive, the patterns alluring. Here only a few are listed:

"Gang War. Beware Gang War—is Sweeping the
Nation—the story of the greatest Underworld War ever
told!"

"What does a Travelling Man do after he kisses his
wife goodby?"

"One Wife against Six Blondes."

"She stopped at Nothing! The Shockingly real
Drama of a Modern Woman!"

"Married Just Enough to 'make her Interesting! It's
New! It's Original! It's Different! It starts with a bang
as Madame loses her dress!' It leaps into high as her
lover hires a sin-thetic wife! It reaches an amazing
height amid the love gondolas of Venice! It's peppery
in Paris. It's intimate in Italy! Which all means that
it's Hot-Cha in the good old U. S. A.! Snappy as a
French magazine!"

Advertising tips (available to exhibitors in a given
chain) often carry suggestions which are played up,
particularly in areas like this:

"DO YOU FEAR SEX? You learn about the riddle
of sex on our screen Tuesday, Wednesday and Thursday,
April 5th, 6th and 7th." Or this other advice to theatre
proprietors:

"Get over the hot-love flavor of this thrill-romance
and you will be heading in the right direction for the
big grosses. And with Lupe Velez to sell as the principal exponent of this peppery brand of the sex-business,
your campaign should be a pleasure!

"There are ample scenes of Lupe, whose high position as a queen of scorching love is well known to all

movie fans. The love poses with Melvyn Douglas whose handsome and arresting masculinity was made apparent in Gloria Swanson's "Tonight or Never."

The investigators believe that while this type of advertising doubtless stimulates certain sexual and morbid interest, it is also a factor contributing to sexual precocity. They know whereof they speak because they have cases on record of such positive mischievous and unwholesome stimulation.

2

Judging by some of the attendance records obtained by the investigators, the motion picture theatres in this community should be highly successful. As one of them, the late Dr. R. L. Whitley, observes: "Second only to the time spent in the home, in the school, and on the street is the time the boy spends at the movie. Among 1356 boys examined on this subject, 627 declared that they go to the movies once a week, 455 twice a week, 137 three times a week and 57, four or more times each week. In other words, eighty per cent of them go to the movies once a week or oftener. On an average, all these boys of various groups see over eighty-three programmes a year."

It becomes obvious that the investigators are quite correct in their assumption that the motion picture theatre is of proved educational importance to the community with an immense influence either for weal or woe. Add to this the facts we have already learned from the investigations of Drs. Holaday, Thurstone and Peters of the significant impression made upon young minds by the movies, and also the fact that the stimuli in the motion picture theatre are much more intense than any in the school, charged as they are with emotion, and it becomes apparent that, with the street and other unsupervised recreational activities, the movies play a tremendous part in the lives of these young people in a congested area.

It may be surprising to some of us to discover that in this region, according to the preliminary evidence, it is more frequently the brighter and intellectually superior boys who go to the movies excessively rather than the very dull. (It must be borne in mind that the intellectually superior may 'in some cases also be retarded in school.) Adolescent boys, however, growing up in homes in which old-world patterns of life still dominate feel they are becoming Americanized and picking up American ways by means of the motion picture. The educational significance of motion pictures, therefore, in a region like this is not open to question. And since, as we have seen, more than sixty-one per cent of the pictures offered in this area belong to the love, sex and crime trinity, the trend of the education these youngsters receive becomes self-evident. And some of the scholastic conditions that may be expected under such circumstances appear in due course.

For instance, of those who go to the movies four times a week or more, fifty-eight per cent or more are found to be retarded in their school work. Of those who go three times a week forty-two per cent are so retarded. The largest percentage of those who appear among the accelerated pupils in school is from the group that goes less than once a week. In view of the findings of Drs. Renshaw and Ruckmick concerning sleep disturbance and the emotional strain of movie attendance upon the young, it is a question whether children go to the movies because they are retarded or whether the retardation is the result of the movies.

Of the delinquents and truants more than twenty-two per cent attend the movies three times a week or oftener; of the non-delinquents 13.8 per cent attend the movies as often. Whether the greater frequency of movie attendance is due to the fact that they are delinquents, or whether they are delinquents because they go to the movies excessively, it is naturally difficult to say. The chances are that both are true, namely, that delinquency may be caused by excessive movie going, and also that the thrills and excitement of the movies appeal more to the delinquents and truants as a release from irksome controls. A test made by these investigators shows that there is a persistent tendency toward higher emotional instability on the part of those who attend the motion pictures most frequently.

"These boys," declares the Thrasher study, "who in this community attend the movies most frequently are clearly individuals of intelligence above the average of the community, but who for reasons other than intelligence are very often retarded in school, are often truants and delinquents and, as far as the data reveal, are somewhat higher in emotional instability. . . . Their attendance is no doubt in part a reflection of certain school and social maladjustments and it is quite probable that in individual instances excessive motion picture attendance creates emotional conditions and attitudes which in turn contribute to more movie attendance."

For much of the social interest of the boy in this

region centers about the motion picture theater. Special contacts, special activities, and certain dark practices are made possible or facilitated by the dimly lighted movie house. Mothers can leave their children there knowing that they will stay until called for, as illustrated by the statement of the theater nurse in an earlier chapter. In rare instances a local criminal gang, whose members are known to the proprietor or attendants, may visit the motion picture in a body as a means of establishing an alibi. At times, during the cold months of winter, whole families may come and remain the entire day in order to save the expense of heating their rooms. "A complete inventory of the activities in the local theaters in this community," concludes the report, "would have to include everything from the 'spotting' and 'planting' of victims for gangland bullets to clandestine sexual activity in the darkened movie house—and even to childbirth."

3

In a projected book by the late Dr. R. L. Whitley he presents some of the uses of the cheaper grade of motion picture theaters of the region in this manner:

"In a number of cases the motion picture house is much more important in relation to delinquency than is the material shown on the screen. The motion picture house is generally dimly lighted. Ordinarily there are some sections of the house where few people are sitting. The house in general is one of the most convenient spots in the community, for these reasons, in which boys may engage in a variety of sexual practices; especially during daylight, there are few spots in the community

where boys may engage in sexual practices with girls
without being apprehended and punished. Occasionally
the boy is able to find a vacant or a secluded spot in the
park, but ordinarily he confines his sexual activities
outside the movie house to the night. As a consequence,
a variety of sexual practices are observed by the boy
ordinarily in the movie house, and occasionally he engages in various forms of sex activity in the house itself."
Dr. Whitley cites a number of illustrative cases which
cannot for a variety of reasons be quoted here. The
following, however, is one of the cases:

" 'In the pictures you see guys necking. The ———
Theatre is a dirty place. All the girls are cursing and
the guys holler, 'Hey, any chance?' After the show
is over they have a good time upstairs. They are drunk
nearly every night up there. These ushers are always
drunk.' The boy saw a man handling a girl intimately.
He saw 'guys fooling around' with girls in a number
of ways."

Cases are adduced in which the movie house of this
area is used as a place of assignation. As a means of
making acquaintanceships, the "pick-up" of the local
movie house is known by most young people and
utilized by many. So common an institution is it that
the local theater proprietors and managers accept it as
a part of the situation. As one of them explained it to
the investigator:

"In most cases they (girls) either come for the express purpose of petting, in which case they do not
disturb anyone, or else, if they come unattended, they
are willing enough to receive attention from a stranger."
He said, "The type of girls who come to the movies,

in most cases, do not say no, and we don't bother with these cases in which both are willing."

Being unsupervised, in short, the motion picture theater in this region has in some cases noted made easy contacts for younger boys with older and more mature criminals. The researchers did not undertake to study this particular phase of the situation, and yet a number of cases spontaneously appeared showing several instances in which initial contacts were made with criminal or more hardened characters. There is a case on record in this research in which two high-school boys who became acquainted under these auspices subsequently engaged in a series of crimes which finally ended in the murder of one of their victim. The prestige of the criminal and gangster both on and off the screen in the community is curiously illustrated in a footnote to this study by the investigators. It is indicated that in certain cases the local theaters have asked notorious local gangsters to help in quelling by intimidation the boisterous conduct of some in the children's section of the theater. In cases where this has occurred, of course, it has enhanced the gangster's prestige in the eyes of the boys and on occasion has served to bring the youngsters to the attention of the local "big Shots." "And we have one or two instances on record," Mr. Cressey informs the writer, "in which a boy without a criminal record was interested in a delinquent career by other delinquents with whom he chanced to see a gangster picture." Fired by enthusiasm, in other words the boy laid aside his inhibitions and proceeded then and there to indulge in delinquent acts.

In a way a neighborhood like this is a sort of lab-

oratory where the conclusions by investigators in all
the previous studies of the survey are illustrated in the
chaotic jumble of life as it runs and whirls and eddies
along, for good or ill. The findings of Blumer, for
instance, as regards the fixing of criminal and delinquent
patterns in the lives of his subjects are no less visible
here. One boy tells how in his childhood he had a
deep prejudice against Chinese, Mexicans and Indians
as they were usually all "bad men." "I recall," he says,
"that whenever my father would take me to Chinatown,
I would be afraid we would be kidnapped. If I saw an
Indian in one of the side-shows, I would be afraid he
would pull out a tomahawk and scalp me." Another,
born in New York City who had never been beyond the
limits of the metropolitan district, when asked whether
the "West" was as shown in the movies, replied, "Naw,
I went way out to Irvington and it's the same out there."
Irvington is not more than twenty miles from New
York. Notwithstanding the overlaying of sophistication,
certain stereotyped impressions remain, such as that the
college professor is always a caricature of a man, that the
cowboy is always wicked, and that the sole measure of
success in American life is the monetary one. Much that
is learned in this school of the movies abides for a long
time, and perhaps forever.

It is in the same manner that crime and gangster
pictures, murder, mystery and detective films, all seem
to contribute to instruction in crime for those so inclined. Many of the crime techniques listed by Blumer
are listed by these boys as having been learned from the
movies. One must, for instance, wear gloves when carrying a revolver or committing a crime to avoid finger-

prints, and a machine gun may be concealed in a violin case in order to avoid suspicion. An investigator tells of going to a photoplay called "Union Depot" with a boy of the neighborhood. One of the scenes in the film shows Douglas Fairbanks, Jr., opening a violin case. When the lid was thrown back, packages of paper money appeared in full view. The entire audience gasped but the boy, "Zip" did not move.

"What's the matter?" asked the investigator, "doesn't that money bother you?"

"Naw, I expected a machine gun," answered the boy.

"Why the machine gun?" asked the investigator.

"Tell me any picture that ain't got a machine gun in it. They all got typewriters (machine guns) in them."

"Who's your favorite actor?" the investigator asked of a boy.

"Jim Cagney." His answer shot out virtually as the question ended.

"You like the way he acts?"

"I eat it. You get some ideas from his actin'. You learn how to pull off a job, how he bumps off a guy, an' a lotta tings."

A little girl as young as nine years of age, arrested for purse-snatching and shoplifting, when asked where she learned her particular way of doing things, declared that she learned it in the movies, and a stenographic report of the examination leaves no doubt in the matter. Similarly, in some cases of felonious assault by delinquent boys in this research, three cases involving serious stabbings were found upon examination to trace back to movie patterns. One of these young criminals, a superior boy in the high-school, tells of having seen a picture in which one of the characters of the play stabbed a person, jumping at him from behind and striking in a manner quite similar to that used by this boy in his own offence. He denied having learned his particular kind of stabbing from the picture and yet he very circumstantially described the act in the picture as resembling his own. Certainly while the children in delinquent areas are young these film patterns are very real to them. As they grow older, their sophistication rises at least to the extent of discrediting cinema preachments or moral lessons. As one boy put it:

"Sure, I like Little Caesar and Jim Cagney, but dat's de boloney dey give you in de pitchers. Dey always died or got canned. Day ain't true. Looka Joe Citro, Pedro Salami an' Tony Vendatta. Looka de ol' man."

The names he mentioned were those of "big shots," or gangsters, in his own neighborhood who seemed to thrive unpunished, and his own father now legitimately employed, once owned a café and a string of brothels and, indeed, was himself something of a big shot. This boy prefers pictures "dat show a lotta action wid gangsters, bootleggers and hi-jackers." "I ain't goin' get in Dutch wid de law cause I'm goin' to get protection before I do anything. An' I ain't havin' any broads aroun' while dere's work to do. You can't trust 'em and dey get you in trouble. If it wan't for a broad, dey never would a got Little Caeser."

He dresses Cagney style. Soft green hat, tight-fitting suit, puffed shoulder coat and leather heeled shoes. His education is complete.

While data are lacking to establish statistically the

extent of movie imitation among the delinquents in this area, the foregoing and following cases clearly illustrate how the process works and our intimate knowledge of social life in the district strongly suggests the probability of widespread imitation.

4

It is best perhaps to narrow down the reader's attention to a single case possibly unusual, certainly curious, which shows how the idea of movie imitation developed in the minds of certain youths in this urban area.

Dr. Thrasher's survey finds that the imitation of behavior patterns from the motion pictures forms a powerful factor in the general education of these lads. In a single group of twenty boys in their teens, thirteen declared that they preferred gangster pictures to all others and ten of the twenty were observed to imitate Cagney in dress and mannerisms on the ground that he was "tougher" (on the screen) than Edward G. Robinson. They absorbed even the language of the films in which their heroes appear. Phrases like "You can dish it out but you can't take it," from Robinson's dialogue in "Little Caeser" regularly entered into their speech. Almost all of those in this group used Cagney's friendly "One, two" punch to the rib, chin and shoulder. They imitated his little jig, his big Cagney swagger. They smiled like Cagney and even wore spearhead shirts like Cagney.

The photoplay of "Little Caeser" seemed to have swept certain groups of boys of the region like a cyclone, leaving a host of consequences.

Ernie Rico, aged twenty-three, told his friends after

witnessing the photoplay, "Call me 'Little Caesar'," "Gee, I'd like to be a guy like that!" A short time after that he was found in a dying condition on the street near his home. He had been stabbed twice, once near the heart and once near the abdomen, in an altercation which was found later to have resulted from an argument over a division of profits from hauling a truckload of bootleg beer. Inquiry after his funeral revealed that he had served as a taxi driver and used to attend motion pictures casually until he chanced to attend the film of "Little Caesar." He came back from the theater very enthusiastic, announcing that "it was a great picture," and insisted that his father should see it. The report continues:

"His father further states that in the next two days his son attended two other showings of this film, each time coming home with a renewed enthusiasm for the picture. The father said that following his son's renewed efforts to tell of this photoplay, he became angry and ordered his son to refrain from any more comments regarding it. The father reported also that shortly after seeing the picture his son became associated with a group of petty robbers and bootleggers with whom he had been acquainted, but with whom he had never had, to his knowledge, any regular associations." Newspaper accounts and the reports of the father and mother indicated that the boy made frequent references to "Little Caesar," and insisted upon being called "Little Caesar."

In another case a Jewish boy, only fourteen years old, after seeing the film, "Little Caesar" began to assume the chief rôle of that film immediately thereafter among his playmates. Presently he began a career of shoplifting

and purse-snatching and, on one occasion, while stealing a pocketbook through an open window of a tenement
house near his home, he was joined by a newcomer in
the community, a boy two years older, who demanded a
part of the profits as compensation for silence. From
this chance meeting resulted an association in crime
which ultimately ended disastrously. This older boy,
and other playmates of the lad who was possessed by
"Little Caesar," told of the transformation which went
on in his behavior in the weeks immediately following
the witnessing of the photoplay. David (that was his
name) went around among his playmates telling them
they should not call him David, but "Little Caeser the
2nd," threatening to "give them the works" if they did
not do so. On one occasion he is reported to have beaten
severely a little girl who teasingly refused to call him
"Little Caeser." Later his activities ended in an attempted holdup of a small shopkeeper by the use of a
borrowed revolver. In the excitement of the hold-up
the boy pulled the trigger and the shopkeeper was
killed.

A third case was that of a young man of twenty-one,
who went by the name of Tony Colombo until the day
he witnessed the picture of "Little Caeser" with Edward
G. Robinson. After seeing the picture he ordered his
friends to call him thenceforth "Little Caesar." Edward
G. Robinson, who acts the leading part in the film, is
short, stocky, square-shouldered, square-faced and of
dark complexion. In his portrayal of the character he
registers the emotional tension of the gangster by means
of an alert and ready posture, roving eyes, deepened
facial lines, an aggressive, braggadocio manner in ad-

dressing his henchmen, and a continuous movement of his cigar from side to side in his mouth. Tony's general appearance after seeing the picture changed radically. He began to wear the tailor-made clothing of his older brother who was doing time at Sing Sing, and to wear spats. Tony's facial expressions were markedly altered. Square-faced and swarthy in complexion, of the same stocky build as Edward G. Robinson, he accentuated some of the lines of his face, assumed a deeper, more commanding tone, his scowl became more "menacing" and his thick lips acquired a cynical curl. From cigarettes he shifted over to cigars, and made a point of rolling them from one corner of his mouth to the other like his hero in the photoplay. The investigators' report goes on:

" 'Little Caeser' was quite conscious of this change in his manner and appearance. He frequently made reference to his sartorial effects, his girl, his threats toward his enemies, and his 'toughness.' Frequently he asks concerning his resemblance to Edward G. Robinson, and his appearance of being 'tough.' 'Do I look like Edward G. Robinson?,' he asks with the evident desire to be answered in the affirmative. 'Since you're hanging around me they think I'm leading you wrong, cause I'm marked 'lousy' around there.' And then regarding his dress, 'Don't dis suit look de nuts?' 'Like dis hat? It's a John B. Stetson.' He looks forward to the day when he can buy hundred dollar suits for himself, apparently with the feeling that by so doing he will be able to demonstrate that he is, after all, 'making good.' 'Wait'll I get on my feet,' he boasts, 'I'll have de laugh on dese guys when I start sportin' some real genuine hundred dollar suits, wid a big car and a flashy blonde by my side.'

"Toward his henchmen he assumes a dictatorial yet individualistic attitude. Even on minor matters he asserts his authority. 'Dis joint is gettin' too damned dirty. I don't want any more cigarette butts on de floor. Dat goes for everybody. If somebody don't like de idea let 'em start trowin' butts on de floor and there'll be some busted skulls.' He constantly threatens any who would question his authority. 'Little Caeser' in the picture said that he was leading his outfit, but the local 'Little Caeser' goes him one better and says, 'I'll put a bullet in his skull if he don't stop messin' around wid me.' And again the struggle for independent glory. 'Dey t'ink I'm livin' on my brudder's rep [in Sing Sing]. But I can prove I ain't a phoney, cause I'm willin' to fight dem wid guns, hands, knives, anyting.' And even toward his own henchmen he assumes an attitude of indifference. 'Wait'll I make de dough. Dese guys are phoney. Soon as I make de dough I'm packing in (quitting) dese guys.'

"Toward the police, Tony affects the typical attitude of gangland. Like 'Little Caeser' in the picture who hated cops, Tony constantly refers to 'dem grafty moochers, de bulls. I'll show dem.' Like 'Little Caeser' in the photoplay, Tony doesn't think women should be mixed up in his activities. Yet toward his 'frail' (girl), who is reputed to be a 'nice girl,' he is supremely vain, in his own way. While threatening violence toward anyone who would even dare to speak disrespectfully to her or about her, he assumes a proprietary attitude himself toward her which permits him to speak in the most disrespectful way about her, or to her in the presence of others. 'Where's my broad? She's late. I'll put a load of dynamite under her.'

"Like 'Little Caeser' Tony also conceived of himself as starting poor, without a chance, making the most of his opportunities. After seeing the photoplay, Tony also was ambitious. He undertook a new form of activity for him—something which he was not known to have participated in before, 'muscling in' upon other rackets, in a very similar manner to what was shown in the photoplay, 'Little Caeser.' 'Now watch me get started; I'll be a boss someday soon,' he confided to a friend. An acquaintance of Tony, with the nickname 'Cal,' had opened a 'joint' in a three-room apartment on the ground floor of an old tenement house.

"He had three tables, seven or eight chairs, a dog called Fido, a nickle slot machine, a dozen decks of cards, a bed, a coal stove, a cupboard that served as a candy store and cigarette counter, table utensils stolen from a local 'coffee pot,' a phonograph, an alarm clock, prophylactic tubes, contraceptives and suppositories, a rubber syringe for venereal treatments and many other household comforts.

"Cal's racket consisted of allowing the boys to play cards or shoot dice while he took a cut on the winnings. The 'mob' played whenever it had 'de dough,' which was almost every evening.

"One day 'Little Caeser the Second' walked into Cal's joint and called him aside.

"'Listen, Cal, I know you're makin' velvet. How about me gettin' in on it?'

"'I ain't makin' a helluva lot.'"

" 'Dat's what you say but I've been told different. From now on you an' me are partners. You put up a sawbuck ($10) for me an' when I get it I'll make good. If you don't like the proposition lemme know an' I'll put dis place on de Fritz. I'm broke and I'm desperate, so you better t'ink it over fast.'

"Cal, knowing that 'Little Caeser the Second' was likely to put the 'joint' on the 'crimp' with the aid of his tough bunch, decided to go into a partnership with him, after all. Tony was still Pete Colombo's kid brother and Pete Colombo was a pal of Joe Citro, who was the community's biggest racketeer."

These "Little Caeser" sequels may be an extreme picturization of many lesser cases. We know that many children seeing gangster and crime pictures do not become gangsters and criminals. But we have had evidence by both the Blumer and the Thrasher surveys that significant numbers are adversely affected, whether or not they become delinquents. In certain areas, it has been seen, those types of pictures, never salutary, are more harmful than in others. Certainly, as Dr. Thrasher puts it, "in a crowded section stimuli and patterns of this character would be more dangerous than in any other section of the population, particularly since there is great lack of restraint, inhibition and emotional stability in such a section." The children are here in actual contact with the underworld. Criminal careers sprout and blossom here and here, so often, they bear their fruit.

Much of the problem of the motion picture bearings upon delinquency, it would seem, lies in their effects within a section of this type, from which no large American city is free. That the unfortunate influences of certain species of pictures are not confined to such regions we have had ample evidence. But that these so-called interstitial areas are peculiarly susceptible to what is evil in them, the Thrasher-Cressey survey makes equally clear. If, therefore, as appears, the movies act as a system of education for large portions of the population, then we must not delay in taking the necessary measures to treat them as a system of education.

CHAPTER XVI

SUMMARY AND CONCLUSION

To summarize a book of this kind, in some degree already a summary of a vast mass of material is, as the reader will apprehend, no easy matter.

By selecting certain salient portions of an immense body of research, included in a score of monographs, the writer has endeavored to present, how briefly soever, the chief results obtained by a group of highly trained investigators in the matter of motion picture influence, physical, mental and moral, mainly upon children and young people. These closing paragraphs, therefore, are but the recapitulation of a summary.

Motion pictures, scarcely a generation old in our experience, have proved themselves to be one of those necessary inventions of mankind whose absence or deletion from our civilization is by now virtually unthinkable. At their best they carry a high potential of value and quality in entertainment, in instruction, in desirable effects upon mental attitudes and ideals, second, perhaps, to no medium now known to us. That at their worst they carry the opposite possibilities follows as a natural corollary.

All these things are true because of the vast numbers of the population the pictures are able to reach. Estimates which run as high as 115,000,000 spectators making up the weekly audience, have been pared down by the conservative calculations of Dr. Dale's research to 77,-000,000. Even so careful a body of investigators as those who produced "Recent Social Trends" estimates the figure to be (in 1930) "about 100,000,000 admissions to motion picture performances weekly in the United States." The Dale figure of 77,000,000, we see, therefore, may be a considerable under-estimate.

But even so, it is tremendous. It means a population larger than Germany's, a population as large as those of Britain and France combined, all movie-goers! And if all this be true, the motion picture becomes to us of immense national and social importance. The chief part of our interest, however, lies in the fact that 28,000,-000 of this movie audience is composed of minors, children and adolescents under twenty-one years of age; and that of these 11,000,000 are aged thirteen and younger. The total enrollment in American schools and institutions of higher education as estimated in "Recent Social Trends," is approximately 29,500,000. Allowing for the fact that movies are inaccessible in certain rural areas, the two populations almost coincide; the movie population of minors includes virtually the children of the entire nation, and they average a movie a week or fifty-two a year.

Now, even in a recapitulation it is useless, indeed, impossible, to repeat all the striking facts that emerge in this volume. On the other hand, even the briefest recapitulation must present, or at least hint at, some of them.

It must be said at the outset that many influences play upon the experiences of children—the home, the school, the community—and it is impossible to state that one influence is more powerful than another. Yet it is entirely practical and useful to estimate the credits and debits of one agency without claiming that it is more or less powerful than another.

Always remembering that certain excellent pictures are from time to time produced, as witness "The Covered Wagon," "Ben Hur," "Grass," "Abraham Lincoln," "Arrowsmith," and many others, Dr. Dale found, upon examination of 1500 feature pictures, that the average is heavily weighted with sex and crime pictures. An analysis of a smaller sampling of pictures shows a predominance of undesirable, often tawdry "goals" in life, and with a population of characters to match the goals. By this over-loading, moreover, life as presented upon the screen is too often inevitably distorted, so that the young and especially children, so far from being helped to the formation of a true picture of life, often derive its opposite.

We need not necessarily look upon our children in the light of young-eyed cherubim to realize that the visual impressions of the screen, as viewed by their eyes, register with especial cogency and force upon their minds. The very youngest children carry away at least fifty-two per cent of what their parents would carry away from any given picture, and the average for all children used in the samples studied by Drs. Holaday and Stoddard is seventy per cent retention—which is a very large percentage! Curiously, too, this percentage of retention seems to grow with time and after the lapse of a month many children actually remember more than the day after seeing the picture.

Stoddard and Holaday's guess is "that pictures play a considerably larger part in the child's imagination than do books," and Drs. Blumer and Hauser found that most children are movie-minded in that their imagery, in drawings, essays, compositions, often takes the shape of movie characters and scenes. All the way, too, from the second grade to the second year of high-school, the children tested seem to retain best such items as sports, *crime, acts of violence,* general action and titles.

2

In the matter of physical effects of pictures upon children and adolescents, one of the most important studied is the effect upon their sleep. By their cleverly devised apparatus, the hypnograph, Drs. Renshaw, Miller and Marquis were able to obtain actual measurements of the sleep disturbance that follows upon seeing a movie.

The sleep pattern of every child is a highly individual affair, depending upon various factors, such as age, sex and mental "set." By no means all react alike to the same stimulus. After two and a half years of research, however, covering 6,650 child nights of sleep, the investigators found that, *on the average,* boys after seeing a movie showed an increase of about twenty-six per cent in their motility over the amount peculiar to them in normal sleep, and girls about fourteen per cent. That even where their motility decreased, the decrease was also due to the same cause: that is the movie had acted as a depressor, owing to fatigue. The effects, though diminishing, were found to persist as long as four or five nights.

The frequently marked reactions of children to certain scenes in most pictures, but notably to scenes in pictures of horror and fright, at least in part explain the effects measured upon children's sleep. Drs. Ruckmick and Dysinger, by means of a psycho-galvanometer, found that in the case of ordinary danger pictures the intensity of emotional reaction of adolescents is twice as great as that of adults, and that of young children, aged six to eleven, three times that of adults. At times the reaction is still greater though at times, too, in the case of adolescents, it is zero. Adolescents were most affected by erotic or suggestive scenes. The pulse and heart action were found to increase considerably, some times to double the normal rate. Nervous and emotionally unstable children, naturally, are more affected than others. Ninety-three per cent of 458 high-school children answered that at some times they had been frightened by the movies.

That does not say that children don't like being frightened. In a class of forty-four, thirty-eight declared that they liked being frightened. Whether that is good for them is another question.

The "adult discount," secured through the presence of an older person to explain to the child, particularly in pictures of horror, fright or violent action, that "this is only a picture," appears to be virtually a necessity. Otherwise it may lead to what Professor Blumer calls "emotional possession." The child does not see the outcome of the picture, or the moral, in terms of the adult mind. Rather does it see them in terms of isolated scenes.

"An exciting robbery, an ecstatic love scene, the behavior of a drunkard and the like," observe Ruckmick and Dysinger, "cannot be toned down by the moral situation at the end of the picture"—hence the importance of the "adult discount."

Professor Thurstone and Miss Peterson found in experiments with carefully selected pictures that children's mental attitudes can be effectively changed by viewing those pictures. They found that a pro-Chinese picture makes the children more pro-Chinese; an anti-Negro picture makes them anti-Negro. They found these effects to persist for a long time, in one case as long as nineteen months. Their conclusion is that "the effect of the motion picture on social attitudes probably persists for a much longer time."

With a less sensitive technique May and Shuttleworth, in attempting to find differences between "movie" and "non-movie" children discovered, to begin with, so few children who had never attended the movies that their non-movie group consisted mainly of children who went infrequently to the movies, and the other group of those who attended two, three, or four times a week. In their tests for attitude they found no differences of significant import. In other tests, however, they found that movie children averaged lower in deportment records and in school work; are rated lower by their teachers, are less coöperative, less self-controlled, more deceptive and less emotionally stable. Their classmates, though naming them more frequently as "best friends," rate them lower than "non-movie" children in the "Guess Who" test.

Dr. Peters in enquiring how far current motion pictures square with the national mores examined a number of groups including not young children, but adolescents and adults of varied interests, forming virtually a cross-section of the nation. In a total of 142 feature pictures studied he found, for instance, 726 scenes of aggressiveness in love-making that were rated by all groups as below the national standard of mores.

In such scenes, however, as portrayed "democratic practices," treatment of subordinates, employees, or treatment based upon racial discrimination, and also in the matter of treatment of children by parents, he found the movie scenes meeting with approval.

3

Imitation is to such an extent natural to children that we can scarcely conceive of non-imitative children. It forms a large part of their education. Movies, because of their concreteness, their visual vividness, now supplemented by the auditory channel, present numerous patterns for imitation. Dr. Blumer found imitation of the movies wide-spread among the young, not only in such harmless matters as dress and beautification, but in such other particulars as love-technique, flirtation, kissing, caressing, "vamping," "necking." Some of these things enter into the day-dreams of adolescents, which as Dr. Blumer puts it, "may stimulate impulses and whet appetites." In this way movies tend to become a school of conduct for children and adolescents.

They imitate movies, their mental imagery is shaped by movies, their very conduct is affected by them. This, as some of the students quoted by Blumer declare, makes "adjustment to life . . . more difficult." Fifty per cent of the high-school students examined by Blumer indicated that their ideas of sexual love came from the movies. By presenting, often, "the extremes as though they were the norm," the movies tend to bewilder the young, to make them rebellious against necessary restraints, to confuse them in their process of being educated. Indeed, Thrasher and Cressey, as a result of their study of youth of immigrant stock, regard the movies as an institution of informal education which serves these young people in a large variety of ways, but which remains socially uncontrolled.

Sometimes certain pictures have a socially desirable effect. Cases are recorded where pictures like "Ben Hur" and "The King of Kings" turned young minds to religious aspiration, and pictures like "Beau Geste" and "Over the Hill," to a closer family affection. Some have been swayed toward ambitions for study, a collegiate training, or foreign travel. The screen, in short, is an open book, a school, a system of education, amounting often to a molder of the characters of the young.

In the matter of delinquency patterns both Blumer and Thrasher find not only that many young people sympathize with the criminal in motion pictures, but many, too, imitate mannerisms and ways of conduct. The presentation of a life of ease, "the creation of a desire for riches," observe Blumer and Hauser, "may dispose many, and lead some, to criminal behavior." Many young criminals declared that they were in this manner led to criminal conduct, and that particularly in certain high-rate delinquency environments did crime pictures produce this effect. It is in such areas that crook and gangster and sex pictures are most dangerous.

A number of adolescent and youthful criminals give circumstantial accounts of their path to, and arrival at, criminality, and, rightly or wrongly, but very positively, they blame the movies for their downfall. In cases cited by both Blumer and Thrasher, they tell of learning their criminal techniques from certain of the movies; Blumer's list alone includes thirty-one different techniques culled from autobiographic accounts of delinquents—all movie-acquired. Thrasher both parallels some and adds to these from the New York research—altogether a considerable curriculum in crime.

Similarly, large percentages of girl inmates in an institution for sex delinquents rightly or wrongly attribute to the movies a leading place in stimulating cravings for an easy life, for luxury, for cabarets, road-houses and wild parties, for having men make love to them and, ultimately, for their particular delinquency. Male delinquents, likewise, testify to using certain types of movies as excitants for arousing and stimulating the passions of girls. The Thrasher survey of a congested area contains similar evidence. As a mass form of entertainment this obviously has social consequences highly undesirable.

Motion pictures, however, at times can and do, according to the evidence, have an effect of deterring young people from crime, misconduct or delinquency. Many persons of both sexes adduce such deterrent effects. The influence, however, is brief, owing perhaps to the small number of pictures capable of producing these effects and to the antisocial habits of delinquent areas, and Professor Blumer was able to find no single instance "where an individual was completely deterred from a delinquent or criminal career through the influence of motion pictures"—though possibly such cases exist.

Religious and moral pictures are frequently cited by school-children as moving them to "do good things" and even in a state training school for delinquent girls seventy per cent of the girls declared that religious and sentimental movies had at times made them "want to be real good." The impulse in nearly all these cases, however, was found to be of exceedingly brief duration.

In an examination including both prisoners and wardens of prisons, though large percentages agreed that movies are much desired for entertainment in these institutions, the reformatory value of movies was given but small importance, such activities as outdoor athletics, training for a job, and even band concerts outranking the movies as preferred activities.

And yet, in a broad and comprehensive study of a congested area in New York, Thrasher and Cressey found that in such a section, both a high-delinquency area and a region where most of the youth is of foreign-born parentage, the movie enters into innumerable patterns of their lives and constitutes, in effect, an institution of informal education, socially uncontrolled and wholly unsupervised, Dr. Wesley C. Mitchell, however, without reference to any specific area, summarized the matter in a few words when he said: "Motion pictures are one of the most powerful influences in the 'making of mind' at the present time. They affect great masses of people and they affect these masses during the impressionable years of childhood and youth." And to what is evil in motion pictures interstitial areas are peculiarly susceptible. Yet, as Dr. Charters in his introductory essay to the studies so reasonably puts it:

"Exclusion of children from all theaters is clearly not

the solution. It cannot be done, because the children would crash the gate to see the thrilling scenes. Nothing like this has happened in the world of drama before. In general, the adult drama cannot be understood by the children. In the theaters they cannot comprehend the legitimate drama. But the movie is within their comprehension and they clamor to attend." All of which brings us back to the words of Dr. Charters in his introduction to the present volume:

"I agree with the author in the fundamental position that the motion picture is powerful to an unexpected degree in affecting the information, attitudes, emotional experiences and conduct patterns of children; that the content of current commercial motion pictures constitutes a valid basis for apprehension about their influence upon children; and that the commercial movies present a critical and complicated situation in which deep interest, keen intelligence and sincere coöperation of producers, parents and public are needed to discover how to use motion pictures to the best advantage in the development of children."

The aim of all the studies upon which the present book is based, as well as of the book itself, is to bring us face to face with the facts—and they are grave. Once in possession of the facts, the public, it is hoped, will find the remedies; for, after all, it is the public that is most vitally concerned. It is a social problem which touches everyone of us, "a critical and complicated situation," and by concerted thought and effort we must, imperatively, solve it.

The Motion Picture Research Council, originally instrumental in causing these studies to be made, will watch the expressions and comments of the public with keen vigilance and, by a careful scrutiny of these against the background of the materials of the research, will doubtless formulate its own conclusions and even, possibly, propose remedies.

At all events, the first great step has been taken and now, largely, the facts are known.

INDEX

"Abraham Lincoln," 2, 53, 275.
"Adult discount," 101, 109, 114, 118, 120.
Aggressiveness in . love-making, 136.
"Alias Jimmy Valentine," as crime pattern, 198.
Attitudes. *See* Social attitudes.
Audience, movie, 12.

Bakshy, Alexander, 36.
Beaton, Welford, 49.
"Beau Geste," 33.
"Ben Hur," 32.
"Big House," the, 233.
"Big Shot," 188.
"Birth of a Nation," 126, 127, 176.
Blumer, Dr. Herbert, 6, 99, 105, 107, 108, 110, 112, 113, 116, 123, 134, 141, 149, 155, 158, 159, 161, 166, 168, 169, 170, 173, 174, 176, 177, 181, 184, 186, 187, 189, 190, 197, 202, 211, 213, 214, 219, 226, 229, 231, 233, 234, 235, 237, 242, 246, 249, 262, 271, 276, 278, 280.
British Film Commission, 139, 140.
Burgess, Prof. Ernest .W., 5.
Butler, Dr. Nicholas Murray, 5.

Catharsis theory, 238.
Chaplin, Charlie, 42.
Characters, movie, 39; attractive, 39; dress of, 44; idealism of, 52; goals of, 46; marriage of, 48; morals of, 50; occupations of, 43.

Charters, Dr. W. W., 4, 282, 283.
Children, rate of movie attendance, 15; a movie a week, 16; time spent in theatre, 19; companionship, 21; duration of performance, 24; movie retention, 62; restlessness, 76; growth of, 77; sleep loss after movies, 82; unstable children, 84; fatigue, 84, 87; sleep loss, 86; sleep hygiene, 89; emotional disturbance, 92; measure of, 94, 95; intensity of emotion, 97, 106; effects according to age, 100; absence of criticism, 101; heart beat, 101; over-stimulation, 103; "shell-shock," 103; frightened, 112; guidance, 118; hygiene, 120; treatment of, 138.
Columbus, Ohio, field of investigation, 16.
Confusion and mental adjustment, 163.
Congested areas, 256.
Content of movies, 29.
"Covered Wagon," 1, 31.
Cressey, Paul G., 22, 134, 147, 187, 199, 214, 230, 252, 261, 272, 282.
Crime, in motion pictures, 34, 38; gangsters and racketeers, 36; crime percentages, 37–38; made attractive, 39; punishment of, 40; crime pictures, 119, 128, 143, 180, 183, 188, 190, 192, 193, 195, 198, 200, 202–204, 205, 211, 212, 213, 214, 234, 263.
Crime increase, 196.

Crime techniques, 202–205, 211, 262.
Criminals, preponderance of, 41.
Criminology of the screen, 40.
Critical condition, presented by movies, 283.
Culture and movies, 159–161, 163.
Cumulative effects, 130.

Dale Dr. Edgar, 10, 15, 17, 18, 21, 25, 29, 30, 34, 35, 36, 37, 38, 40, 41, 43, 46, 47, 48, 50, 51, 52, 117, 121, 137, 139, 141, 147, 149, 150, 172, 181, 186, 188, 212, 234, 243, 274, 275.
"Danger" pictures, 97.
Day-dreaming, 152, 153, 155, 172.
Delinquency and movies, 180, 181, 193, 197, 211, 212, 214, 229.
Delinquency areas, 194, 195, 237, 240, 252.
"Democratic practices," 138.
Desirable effects, 31, 170, 282.
"Dr. Jekyll and Mr. Hyde," 99, 110, 112.
Dysinger, Dr. Wendell, 7, 95, 99, 100, 102, 105, 107, 110, 277.

"Emotional possession," 113, 116.
Erotic scenes, 100.

Fatigue effects, 84.
Female delinquency. See Girls, delinquent.
"Frankenstein," 99.
"Fu Manchu," 102.

Gambling, 128.
Gangster pictures, 190, 192, 195, 205, 263, 265.
Girls, delinquent, 214, 220, 221, 222, 232, 234, 237, 239, 241, 248.
Good movies, 170.

"Gorilla," 110.
"Guess Who test," 131, 132, 278.

Hall, Mordaunt, 205.
Harmful effects, 27, passim.
Hauser, Dr. Philip M., 107, 108, 113, 134, 181, 184, 186, 187, 190, 197, 202, 211, 213, 214, 219, 226, 229, 231, 233, 234, 235, 237, 242, 246, 249, 276.
Hays, Will, 17, 34, 121, 130, 244.
Hibben, Dr. John Grier, 4.
Holaday, Dr. P. W., 6, 9, 55, 57, 59, 60, 61, 66, 67, 68, 83, 97, 139, 141, 160, 162, 257, 275, 276.
Hollywood, output, 29, 205.
Hollywood Spectator, 49.
Holmes, Dean, 2.
Homan, Dr. T. P., 101, 102; experiment with heartbeat, 102.
Horror pictures, 105, 108, 109, 110, 111, 119, 120, 162.
Hypnograph, 72, 74.

Imitation, 142, 144, 147, 151, 156, 164, 165, 166.
International Educational Cinematographic Institute of Rome, 93.

James, William, 35.

Legislation, 67.
Lewis, Dr. Park, 93.
"Little Caesar," 254, 264, 265 et seq.
"Lost World," 99, 110, 115.
"Love, Sex, and Crime," 29, 35.
Love technique, 148, 154, 166.

Marquis, Dr. Dorothy P., 70, 71, 74, 88, 89, 97, 103, 276.
Marriage in the movies, 46.
May, Dr. Mark A., 7, 123, 131, 132, 133, 139, 278.
Miller, Dr. Vernon L., 70, 71, 74, 88, 89, 97, 103, 276.
Mitchell, Alice Miller, 54.

Mitchell, Dr. Wesley L., 282.
Mores and movies, 135, 139, 158, 165.
Motion Picture Producers and Distributors of America, 17, 121.
Motion Pictures Research Council, 4, 283.
Movie advertising, 255.
Movie characters. *See* Characters.
Movie theatres, 231, 254, 259; gangsters in, 261; practices in, 260..
Movies, audiences of, 12, propaganda value, 7; harmful effects, 27; contents of, 29; analysis, 29; desirable, 31; educational influence, 33; world of, 44; marriage, 46; ideals, 48; retention study, 55; correct knowledge in, 57; incorrect, 58; movies *vs.* books, 60; children's retention, 62; and sleep, 69; excitement of, 78; effects on sleep, 80, 82; selection, 84; equivalent to soporific drug, 88; "danger" pictures, 97; erotic and suggestive scenes, 100; effect on adults, 101; emotional content, 103; horror pictures, 105; hygienic effects, 110; emotional possession, 113; sentimental, 116; salutary effects, 117; hygiene, 120; cumulative effects of, 130; duration of, 130; direct influence, 133; mores, 135; and conduct, 141; imitation of, 144; and education, 146; vividness, 156; molding quality, 159; imagery of, 159; confusion-breeding, 163; rebellion, 167; conduct, 170; desirable effects of, 170; ambitions stirred, 173; and ideals, 178; wealth and luxury patterns, 184; and crime, 204–213, 226; deterrent effects, 236, 250; recreational value in prisons, 245; attendance in congested areas, 256; emotional conditions, 258; religious and moral, 282; critical situation, 283.
Movies, as educational system, 157, 159, 167, 179.

Newspaper Enterprise Association, 50.
"Non-movie children," 123, 131.

Occupations of screen characters, 43.
Ohio State Bureau of Juvenile Research, 73.
"Old Nest," the, 33.
"Our Dancing Daughters," 176, 216.
"Over the Hill," 33.

Payne Fund, 4.
Peters, Dr. Charles C., 8, 39, 134, 137, 138, 139, 226, 257, 278.
Peterson, Miss Ruth, 7, 122, 123, 131, 160, 161, 213, 237, 247, 257, 278.
Peterson, Dr. Frederick, 94, 103, 110, 111.
"Phantom of the Opera," 91, 99, 110.
Prisons, movies in, 244.
Propaganda, 122, 124.
Psycho-galvanometer, 94, 95; technique, 96.
"Purilia," 47, 150.

R., Mrs., trained nurse, experiences with movies, 90.
Rebellion against home, 167.
"Recent Social Trends," 3, 274.
Reformatories, movies in, 244.
Religious and sentimental pictures, 170–171.
Renshaw, Dr. Samuel, 8, 70, 71, 74, 84, 88, 89, 93, 97, 103, 107, 110, 257, 276.
Rice, Elmer, 47.

Rice, Stuart A., 3, 4.
Ruckmick, Dr. Christian A., 7, 95, 99, 100, 101, 102, 105, 107, 110, 118, 257, 277.

Screen images, 177.
Sentimental pictures, 116.
Sex delinquency, 214, 220, 222, 224, 226, 232.
Sex pictures, 53, 119, 230, 231.
"Shell-shock," 104, 110.
Short, W. H., 4.
Shuttleworth, Dr. Frank K., 7, 123, 131, 132, 133, 278.
"Singing Fool," "Beau Geste," "Over the Hill," "Coquette," "The Old Nest," effects of, 116–117.
Sleep, and movies, 69, restlessness, 75; motility, 76, 80.
Social attitudes, 124, et seq., 133.
"Son of the Gods," 124, 127.
Stefansson, Dr. V., 33.
Stoddard, Dr. George D., 6, 9, 55, 59, 60, 61, 66, 67, 68, 83, 139, 160, 275, 276.

Sutherland, Dr. E. H., 196.
Sympathy for criminals, 181.

Thrasher, Dr. Frederic M., 6, 18, 22, 106, 110, 118, 123, 134, 146, 147, 187, 199, 214, 230, 252, 258, 265, 271, 272, 281, 282.
Thurstone, Dr. L. L., 7, 122, 123, 131, 133, 134, 139, 141, 160, 161, 162, 177, 213, 237, 247, 257, 278.
Tigert, Dr. John T., 1.
Truants, 258.

"Unmarked Slates," 121, 130, 180.

Visual fatigue, 93.
Visual flicker, 93.
Vulgarity, 51.

Wealth and luxury patterns, 184.
Wells, H. G., 42.
Whitley, Dr. R. L., 110, 231, 256, 259, 260.
Willey, Malcolm M., 3, 4.